Linguistic Fieldwork

Linguistic Fieldwork

A Practical Guide

Claire Bowern
Rice University

First published in 2008 by
PALGRAVE MACMILLAN
Houndmills, Basingstoke, Hampshire RG21 6XS and
175 Fifth Avenue, New York, N.Y. 10010
Companies and representatives throughout the world.

PALGRAVE MACMILLAN is the global academic imprint of the Palgrave Macmillan division of St. Martin's Press, LLC and of Palgrave Macmillan Ltd. Macmillan® is a registered trademark in the United States, United Kingdom and other countries. Palgrave is a registered trademark in the European Union and other countries.

ISBN-13: 978–0–230–54537–3 hardback
ISBN-10: 0–230–54537–8 hardback
ISBN-13: 978–0–230–54538–0 paperback
ISBN-10: 0–230–54538–6 paperback

This book is printed on paper suitable for recycling and made from fully managed and sustained forest sources. Logging, pulping and manufacturing processes are expected to conform to the environmental regulations of the country of origin.

A catalogue record for this book is available from the British Library.

A catalog record for this book is available from the Library of Congress.

10 9 8 7 6 5 4 3 2 1
17 16 15 14 13 12 11 10 09 08

Printed and bound in Great Britain by
CPI Antony Rowe, Chippenham and Eastbourne

For my parents

Contents

Acknowledgements

I owe a huge debt to the Aboriginal people I've done fieldwork with in Australia; in Western Queensland, the Kimberley region, and Arnhem Land. Special thanks go to Bessie Ejai, Margaret Nyuŋunyuŋu and Rayba Nyaŋbal for discussions on what they think about linguists working on their languages and feedback about ways researchers could do things better.

Several groups of students have been experimented on with this textbook: my field methods class at Rice University in 2005/2006; Masayoshi Shibatani's field methods class at Rice in 2006/2007; and the Fall 2005 classes at the University of Minnesota under Marianne Milligan, and at the University of California at Berkeley under Andrew Garrett. Many thanks for the comments which greatly improved the book. Thanks also to Barry Alpher, Robert Englebretson, Colleen Hattersley, William Hawkins and Jane Simpson, who provided very detailed comments on parts or all of the manuscript. Q. Pheevr and Yoram Meroz did stirling work with index proofing. Many students, especially Linda Lanz, Josh Levin, Michelle Morrison and Vica Papp, gave feedback that has resulted in a clearer and more interesting book. Thanks also to the people who've taught me about fieldwork in classes, by collaboration and by example: Sasha Aikhenvald, Gedda Aklif, Barry Alpher, Bob Dixon, Ken Hale, Luise Hercus, Harold Koch, David Nash and Jane Simpson, although I suspect that they won't all agree with all the advice in this book. Thanks are also due to Rice University for the award of a Humanities Faculty Writing Stipend for Summer 2005.

1
Introduction

1.1 About this book

This book describes methods for doing fieldwork on language. It grew out of a need for a text which would be useful both to new fieldworkers in linguistics and linguistic anthropology and to students in field methods classes. Although elicitation strategies and data processing are the focus of a field methods class, in the field there are many more skills needed than just data collection, and it may well be that linguistics is the least of the fieldworker's worries. Therefore here I cover not only linguistic data recording, but also grant-writing procedures, ethics and living in the field.

What does fieldwork involve? What is the relationship between the data that we collect, the theory that shapes our research questions and guides our data collection, and the speakers of the languages we are working with? What biases do we introduce by collecting data in a particular way? How do we go from the 'raw' data to a research paper? And what are the rights and responsibilities of the linguist and the consultant in the process? These questions form the core of what fieldwork entails and the framework for this book.

Some may feel that I concentrate too much on archiving, metadata and ethics to the exclusion of what have been traditionally thought of as 'core' fieldwork – that is, elicitation and working out the features of the language under study. I disagree. We do not have the luxury of working in a discipline with limitless funding, and students do not acquire extensive ethical training by osmosis alone. Ethical practice is just as much a part of fieldwork as finding out about the language, and organizing data is just as much a part of fieldwork as analysing it and writing up the results. It is impossible to do the one well without also taking care of the other. We cannot afford to think of these topics as non-core.

When using this book for a field methods class, the early classroom chapters will be of most use at the beginning of the course, for example when discussing recording devices and preparing for the first elicitation session. But the ethics sections should also be read early on, as notions of informed consent and the appropriate treatment of consultants are very important in ethical fieldwork. Chapter 13 should be read early on if you are going to the field; I've included it towards the end of the book because in most field methods classes students do not look at previously recorded materials on the language, but if you are going to the field you will want to prepare as thoroughly as possible.

1.2   What is 'the field' and what is 'fieldwork'?

1.2.1   First principles

Our discipline's stereotype of the fieldworker seems to be some rugged individual who spends large amounts of time working with speakers of 'exotic' languages spoken in remote areas. The fieldworker lives a life of deprivation and austerity, comforted and nourished by weird insects and by the satisfaction that they are preserving a knowledge system for humanity. Rubbish. Fieldwork (not just linguistic fieldwork) is about collecting data in its natural environment. It's not about how tough the linguist is. When biologists go to the 'field', they go to observe the behaviour of the species they are studying in its natural environment rather than in cages in the lab. When archaeologists go to the 'field', they are going to where the bones and ruins are, as opposed to studying something that's already been dug up. And likewise, when linguists go to the field, they too are going to study the natural environment for their object of study – that is, they go to study a language in the place where it is spoken, by the people who usually speak it.

Of course, it's not quite that easy. Linguists don't just 'dig up' the grammar of a language to put it in a grammar book. We work with real people, and become part of the data collection process ourselves (cf. Hyman 2001).

1.2.2   What do fieldworkers do?

Fieldwork is not just about linguistic data. A fieldworker wears many hats. One hat *does* involve data collection – that is, there are established techniques for obtaining linguistic data (which are discussed in this book). The fieldworker doesn't only collect data as it falls from the sky, though. There is more to data gathering than just asking questions. Decisions need to be made as to what to record, what to collect, and what to write down. Then data must be interpreted. How do you know that your data answers your original research questions? Is a sentence ungrammatical for the reason you think it is? How will you decide between the three possible hypotheses that explain a particular data point? This is where your previous linguistic training comes in.

You also need some way to organize your data effectively. Unless you have a photographic memory and can do corpus searches in your head, you will need some method of categorizing, coding and storing the information you collect – that is, you'll need a database hat.

Another hat the fieldworker wears is that of administrator and community liaison officer. Community-linguist interaction issues tend to consume a large proportion of a fieldworker's energy. You will need to organize ways to pay your consultants for their time, you will need housing and food at the field site, you will need to administer your grant monies and keep appropriate records. Furthermore, you will need to arrange appropriate dissemination of your research results within your field community. Fieldworkers are also sound engineers and film directors. You will be making audio (and maybe video) recordings of your consultants, and you need to be able to operate your recording equipment effectively.

Fieldwork involves not just getting the data, but getting it ethically, without violating local customs. Fieldworkers need an ethics hat too – the process of going to a community to work on a previously undescribed language has non-linguistic implications. Could harm result from your working on the language? Does the community approve the writing of their language? Do speakers mind being recorded? Perhaps you are working with the last few fluent speakers of a language; do you have an obligation to provide teaching materials, learner's guides and dictionaries, even if they might not be used and younger members of the community are not interested?

Fieldworkers have an anthropological hat (or pith helmet?) as well. It's impossible to do fieldwork of any length without also (consciously or unconsciously) observing human interaction and cultural practices. Learning about the culture of the speakers whose language you are studying is vital, not only as a key to the language but also as a key to better fieldwork. For example, you are unlikely to get good data in a field session involving both men and women if the culture has strong prohibitions against men and women interacting!

Fieldworkers have their own hats too. They need to be aware of their own behaviour in the field and how it reflects on them and their culture. They are also required to fit in with a new society and learn a new language, while retaining contact with their other lives as academics. Fieldworkers don't leave behind their own identities and culture when they go to the field. This is why there is much more to linguistic fieldwork than just turning up to record someone!

Fieldwork is not done in a vacuum. While it is good practice to rely only on your elicitation in a field methods class, in the field you need as much information about the language and culture as you can find. Make the most of available resources so you are not duplicating the efforts of others. There is further discussion of this in Chapter 13. Many fieldworkers also have an epigrapher's hat too.

1.2.3   Why do linguists do fieldwork?

Many linguists do fieldwork in the first place because of the personal satisfaction they get from it; from the intellectual satisfaction of working out original complex problems, to use the language to research culture, to help gain political recognition for a traditionally oppressed community, or perhaps at a more personal level to make some old people very happy that their language will be recorded for future generations. Perhaps they go to the field because there is no other way to get the data they need. Any particular person's motivation to do fieldwork is probably a combination of motives. Whatever the reason, it's important that there be one (or more than one) – doing fieldwork you feel you have to is a bad reason. On the other hand, perhaps in the field you will discover reasons that you didn't know about before you went.

Fieldwork (and associated language description) feeds into many different areas of linguistics. On the one hand there is the descriptive element of field research – adding to what we know about the languages of the world. Recently (cf. Himmelmann 1998) there has been a movement to treat the documentation of languages as a subfield of linguistics in its own right. Then there's what we do with the documentation, such as producing reference grammars, dictionaries and other descriptive materials. Then there's what we do with those grammars, such as typology, theory, etc. Fieldworkers also conduct more specialized research in areas such as semantics, discourse, phonetics, phonology, syntax or morphology. Then there are all the ways that language research feeds into cultural theory, anthropology and the study of language in society. Fieldworkers have specializations in all these areas.

1.2.4 Fieldwork and experimentation

There is more than one way of viewing the practice of fieldwork.[1] One is as a type of experimentation; the linguist conducts 'experiments' on language consultants to obtain data. The questions asked by the linguist form the sole means of data gathering and shape the form the record of the language will take. Abbi's (2001) manual of linguistic fieldwork focuses on this type of fieldwork, as does Bouquiaux and Thomas (1992).

Focusing on this view of field linguistics allows us to treat linguistics on a par with other experimental disciplines. For example, when psychologists do research, they design the experiment first, recruit the 'subjects' and run the tests, without the subjects necessarily knowing why the experiment is being conducted or having a say in its design. The experimenter has sole control over the data flow. Traditional ethnographic and linguistic fieldwork also follows this model, where the researcher goes to the field, makes their observations and conducts their experiments, and then leaves to write up the results.

There is, however, an alternative view, where the work is a collaborative effort between the linguist and the language speaker(s). Speakers have a much greater say in what gets recorded, what materials are produced, and what happens to the materials afterwards. The linguist in this situation is, in fact, a 'consultant' to the community – the 'community' has a problem to be solved and they bring in a person with expert knowledge.

This second type of fieldwork has more uncertainty and takes some of the power away from the linguist. If the community don't like the idea of you making spectrograms, there is not a lot to be done about it – or if you go ahead and make them anyway, you run the risk of placing future research in jeopardy. The second view binds you to several ethical systems: your university's (and your own culture's) and the system of the community in which you're working. The two will not always be in agreement (see §11.6). This type of fieldwork requires the negotiation (and renegotiation) of both the processes of fieldwork and the outcomes. Some argue against this view, saying that 'the bottle of sulphuric acid does not have a say in the type of research a chemist does' (Cameron et al 1992:14–15). The simple answer to this is that the chemist is not doing research involving a sentient being who has a vested interest in both the process and the outcomes of the research. Put simply, language scientists do not have *carte blanche* to conduct research on whatever and whoever they want, without regard to the wishes and wellbeing of their research participants and respect for the history of interaction between that community and science.

Much of the resentment caused by linguists/anthropologists in the field is probably the result of the community expecting a 'consultant' who will help them (i.e., a 'Type II' researcher) and the linguist expecting to be a 'Type I' researcher or experimenter. A wholesale pursuit of the linguist's aims at the expense of any community input will simply continue to promote mistrust of researchers. Academics are used to putting their research first, above other commitments, but not everyone shares the same set of priorities. Furthermore, many people do not know what linguists really do; the general public assumes that 'a linguist' is just someone who speaks lots of languages (or someone who will tell other people how to speak correctly), and they might be disappointed that what linguists actually do isn't what they thought it was. Such views can be surprisingly difficult to dislodge.

Community negotiation does not imply that the data collection has to be less rigorous or that you cannot negotiate appropriate permissions for doing the type of research you want or need to do. It may take time to get started, and you may need to do some extra work, but there is no reason that you should not be able to do the academic work you want to.[2] Some fieldwork is bound to be 'experimental' in nature in that you have set up a project which aims to confirm or disprove a particular hypothesis in a way that is replicable. To do that you may need to record a particular number of people or extract information in a particular way. There is no reason to suppose that this is not possible with community consultation as well.[3] Of course, this discussion supposes that the community will be interested in such a collaboration. It may be that the community are happy that the linguist wishes to work on (or learn) the language and do not wish to shape the products of the research.

1.2.5   Field research and impartiality

It is part of the scientific method that the linguist/researcher is not personally involved in the experiment in a way that might influence the outcome. Part of the scientific method is removing potentially confounding variables (including experimenter-induced bias) in order to isolate the most probable cause of a particular effect. In most types of linguistic fieldwork, however, there is no such thing as a double-blind experiment. The researcher is actively involved in guiding the results of the fieldwork. The fieldworker responds to data as it is collected, reshaping hypotheses and working out the next set of questions to ask. The fieldworker has a vested interest in getting the data in the first place; they may or may not also have an interest in getting a certain answer to a particular question.

Furthermore, the linguist will usually be personally involved in some way in the community. Fieldwork involves working closely with people and a better personal relationship between the linguist and the consultants will result in better data collection. Close collaborations produce better work. In some areas the linguist is adopted into the community, given a place in the kinship system and by being entrusted with linguistic knowledge is expected to make a commitment to that language and to the people who speak it. The linguist may also be involved in the non-linguistic lives of their consultants.

Even if you do your best to remain 'detached' and impartial and uninvolved in the research, your consultants probably aren't going to do the same. They are going to shape their responses based on their relationship to you; for example, how well they think you're going to understand what they tell you, or what they think you want to hear, or in some cases, what they think you don't want to hear. They might have an emotional or political stake in the outcome of the research (just as you do). They might have misunderstood the question you asked, or drawn a different interpretation from what you intended. So, completely 'impartial' fieldwork is impossible. But you can be aware of some of the potential biases and minimize them.

1.2.6   A definition of fieldwork

So, after all that, what is 'fieldwork'? My definition is rather broad. It involves the collection of accurate data in an ethical manner. It involves producing a result which both the community and the linguist approve of. That is, the 'community' (the people who are affected by your being there collecting data) should know why you're there, what you're doing, and they should be comfortable with the methodology and the outcome. You should also be satisfied with the arrangements. The third component involves the linguist interacting with a community of speakers at some level. That is, fieldwork involves doing research in a place where the language is spoken, not finding a speaker at your university and eliciting data from them (see also Hyman 2001:16–22).

There are several underspecified concepts in my definition. The first is the 'community'. Minimally, the community is the group of people who are affected by your data collection; they are the people to whom you are responsible. For some languages, this *community* may simply be the people you are working with. In other areas it may also include their families; it may even include most (or all) of the people who own or speak the language. In general, the more endangered the language and the smaller the group, the greater the proportion of the community you will need to consult.

The second ill-defined concept is the 'language'. No language is without variation and even languages with few speakers may be very diverse (cf. Dorian 1994). Therefore which variety or varieties of the language you describe will also be important, and may require negotiation. One variety might be more prestigious than another, or lects might differ greatly depending on the age, class or gender of its speakers. Jeff Good (pers. comm.) has introduced the term 'doculect' to refer to the variety of the 'language' that ends up in the documentation.

Thirdly, 'approving of the outcome' might mean quite different things in different communities at different times. It might mean that the 'community' has no stipulations regarding your research. Or it might mean they want copies of the results, such as an offprint of articles or a copy of your PhD Dissertation. Alternatively, they may want to be active participants in the process of deciding what the final products of your research are. Producing final products that everyone is happy with is important; making a good impression can have positive results for other linguists in neighbouring communities, and negative impressions can hamper the research of others and reduce the possibilities for your own fieldwork in future. People are also more likely to help you if they have a genuine stake in the outcome.

Part of how we define fieldwork also depends on what methods are used. In this book I discuss a model which balances elicitation (i.e., asking questions *about* the language) with data collection by other methods, including free conversation, narrative recording and interviewing. There are other types of linguistic fieldwork. Some fieldworkers don't use a contact language and work in the fieldwork language from the beginning. Others gather most (if not all) of their data through elicitation. Some people stay in the same village for 20 years, while others visit one a week and survey an entire region.

There is some disagreement in the field about the extent to which quasi-ethnographic fieldwork on previously undescribed languages is similar to, for example, sociolinguistic interviewing, the acquisition of discourse data and 'qualitative studies' in anthropology. There are more similarities than people sometimes think. Whether you are working on variation in Quebecois syntax or writing the first description of Xish, you will need to be conscious of ethics and the way your data collection methods influence the results of your research. You will need to be familiar with your equipment (which is likely to be similar) and you will need to be aware of how your place in the community influences your data. Moreover, the differences in field sites in various parts of the world probably dwarf the differences between intra-linguistic methods. Fieldworkers have a lot to lose by defining their activities too narrowly and there is a lot to learn from other data-rich linguistic fields (although, for a different view, see Crowley 2007:ix).

1.2.7 Fieldwork and language learning

Learning a language is a little different from analysing a language in order to write about it. One can attain functional fluency in a language without ever consciously mastering the morphology and syntax, and likewise one can have an excellent understanding of the workings of a language without being able to make use of that knowledge to put a sentence together in real time.

Spending time learning your field language to speak it might seem like a waste of time. After all, linguists spend a great deal of time telling people that linguistics is not the same as language learning. Shouldn't you be working on your paper/article/dissertation, rather than memorizing vocabulary? However, for fieldwork there are numerous advantages to being fluent in the language you are studying. One is that in order to write a grammar of a language you have to construct sophisticated theories about how the language works, and in order for you to make yourself understood in the language you have to put those hypotheses into practice. I've also discovered many things about the languages I've worked on through the mistakes I've made while talking, and through making guesses that turned out to be right!

Speaking the language increases your control over the data. You will have a larger vocabulary, a better idea about social factors of language use, and therefore a better conception of why particular sentences might be infelicitous. You will develop intuitions about the language which you can then test. Hale (2001:81–2), along with several other authors in Newman and Ratlif (2001), makes the point that becoming fluent in the field language produces a richer and more accurate description. Hale's way of putting it is 'do whatever you can in order to learn the language.' Being a 'language learner' can be a community role, as Nagy (2000) points out; she was often introduced to new potential consultants as 'the American who wants to learn Faetar'. Being a language learner can be a role in the field community that others can relate to and help with.

Finally, quite apart from the personal satisfaction that comes from learning to speak another language well, knowing the language is very useful for the non-linguistic aspects of fieldwork. In some parts of the world it's polite to talk to other people in 'their' language, especially when you are a guest in their country. I found an excellent Bardi teacher this way. She had heard that someone was learning Bardi, but she didn't believe it. No one has learnt Bardi as a first or second language for 50 years. So, she came up to me in the community shop one day and started testing me. I was able to respond, and we soon became friends. We worked together a lot after that. Another example of why learning the language is important involves less happy circumstances. In 2004 my main Bardi teacher had a stroke and I called her in hospital. We were speaking Bardi because she couldn't communicate in English.[4]

1.3   The term 'informant'

There are various opinions as to what to call the person who is teaching you their language. Some are happy with the term 'informant'. Others feel that this term carries unnecessary overtones of 'police informer' and moreover downplays the role and importance of the language teacher. Fieldwork is not like library research; you cannot go and simply 'look up' the answer in the brain of a speaker of the language.

In this book I am using the term 'consultant(s)'. This term has the connotation of an expert who is consulted for specialized information about a particular topic. In some areas, consultant has negative connotations (it's equivalent to 'highly paid blow-in'). Others (e.g., Hinton 2002) use 'teacher'; another term is 'language helper' (although to be honest I find this a bit patronizing). 'Research participant' is another useful neutral term.

1.4   Fieldwork and 'Theory'

For every view of the field, there are also opinions on the place of fieldwork in linguistics and its relationship to other branches of the field. Opinions appear to cluster around a dichotomy between theoretical (or theory-oriented) and empirical research. This division is not at all confined to linguistics; it's a point also made in Barnard's (2000) history of anthropology, and one finds it too in 'pure' versus 'applied' disciplines such as mathematics and physics.

For various reasons, the theoretical/empirical (fieldworker) divide in linguistics is also broadly correlated with the formalism/functionalism divide these days. There are many formalist fieldworkers (as well as functionalist theoreticians). The most famous formalist fieldworker was probably the late Ken Hale, from MIT, but Sapir, Boas and Bloomfield were also 'theoreticians' in their time as well as documenters of Native American languages.

We also find a rather unhelpful set of comments from prominent fieldworkers along the lines of, 'the data speak for themselves, theory is useless, spend enough time with the data and you will come up with the right answer'. Abbi (2001:3), for example, writes that 'theory binds the fieldworker's hands', and Dixon (1997) draws a firm line between the armchair formalists and the field linguists. There seems to be a competing feeling that linguistic fieldwork is like library research and requires no special training. My view is much closer to Rice (2001). The theory/data divide is at best unhelpful and at worst dangerous. In short, it prevents empirical people from asking the best questions of their data, and it encourages theory people to model what they like without adequate testing.

The most common argument is articulated in Abbi (2001:3) – theory 'binds one's hands' and that the only way to write an unbiased description is to be theory-neutral. This argument is specious. 'Theory' is inherent in research. As soon as anyone uses a metalanguage for natural language description, they are making choices, categorizing and labelling their data. That is, describing linguistic behaviour cannot be done without forming hypotheses about how the language works. A phoneme is a theoretical construct, as is a lexical category. There's no such thing as a theory-neutral or atheoretical linguistic description.

The next argument concerns a quotation from Sherlock Holmes (i.e., *A Scandal in Bohemia*) – 'it is a capital mistake, Watson, to theorize before one has data.' That is, like Holmes, proponents of this argument dislike purely theory-internal motivations for analyses or assumptions based on very little evidence. However, Holmes makes several comments about method and evidence. For example, he states (in the *Hound of the Baskervilles*, ch. 6), that Watson's task is just to observe and not to draw conclusions; Holmes claims that Watson won't be able to make any sense of what he sees because he has no theory to structure the facts on. That is, trying to model reality in the absence of data is not very likely to produce a good model, but a framework is needed to interpret observations. Elsewhere (in the *Silver Blaze Story*) Holmes talks about constructing a theory on the initial data and being ready to alter it as necessary, as more facts come to light. This is, I would argue, the sense in which 'theory' is most relevant to fieldwork.

Rather than 'tying one's hands', 'theory' provides ideas on where to look for data and what to test. Using a coherent theoretical framework of any sort will allow you to make testable predictions. Here is an example from my own fieldwork. I did my PhD on the verb morphology of the northern Australian language Bardi (Bowern 2004) and in working on the syntax I spent a lot of time reading about non-configurational polysynthesis and the expected behaviour of such languages. I used the Morphological Visibility Criterion in Mohawk (Baker 1996) to formulate tests for the equivalent behaviour in Bardi syntax. In designing tests for these predictions for Bardi, I had to think a lot about the principles of Bardi syntax, what would be a good test, what a meaningful answer to my questions would be and why certain sentences might be ungrammatical. The predictions were not borne out for Bardi, but I never would have asked those questions if I hadn't read Baker (1996). As a result we know a great deal more about the fine workings of many parts of Bardi syntax than we would have otherwise done. Evans's (2003) grammar of Bininj Gun-wok arose under similar circumstances: through testing various theoretical predictions and through gaps in other descriptions. Don't let 'theory-neutral' be a euphemism for 'superficial'.

We also need more theory-oriented research on so-called less familiar languages. Whether we are looking for a flexible architecture for grammatical description or for the set of universal categories expressed by human languages, most of our models are heavily oriented towards certain types of well-described languages with large numbers of speakers. Do your part to change that!

Finally, it's obvious from the previous paragraphs that 'theory' and 'description' are not (or should not be) mutually exclusive. Fieldwork is about discovery and asking questions. But you need to know what questions to ask. What you ask will be guided by what you want or expect to find, and this is determined to a large extent by your training, your experience and the theory you work in. Be aware of that, and use it to your advantage. You don't need to subscribe to the tenets of a particular theory or model of language in order to use it – the important thing is to recognize how your model leads you to ask certain types of questions. Working within a theory (as we all do) does not preclude open-mindedness, as Mithun (2001) and Rice (2001) make very clear.

1.5   Fieldwork and identity

Various researchers have discussed the metamorphosis that fieldworkers undergo when in the field, and the possible crises of identity that result. Abbi (2001:2–3), for example, says that a fieldworker should 'almost forget his/her identity', and good fieldwork involves keeping only '"ONE" [sic] aim in mind; that is, to forget everything except data collection and analysis'. The anthropological literature tends towards a somewhat similar view; Evans-Pritchard (1973:2–3) discusses the suspension of the fieldworker's identity, the subordination of identity, and the potential damage that temporary or permanent loss of identity can cause. Macaulay (2005) makes a similar point.

This is probably related to the status of fieldwork in linguistics. There is a theme in cultural anthropology (and to a certain extent in linguistics too) on fieldwork being one of the *sacra* of the discipline. That is, there is a perception that doing fieldwork is part of the identity of being a linguist of a certain type, and thus there is pressure to conform to a set of identity tropes. One is the rugged Indiana Jones-like character. Another (equally, if more objectionable) trope is the linguist as saviour of a culture. This one is particularly favoured by journalists writing on endangered languages.

Fieldwork involves a peculiar displacement: the fieldworker is displaced from their own community and culture, and is sent to think analytically about another social and linguistic system. They suspend participation in the norms of their own culture, and are yet not a wholesale participant in the other. Standing against the loss of identity that results from displacement to a new culture is the new identity that the fieldworker constructs (and has constructed for them) by participation in their field site.

I suspect that both of those ideas are wrong. That is, a good fieldworker doesn't fully lose their identity, and a good fieldworker doesn't remain unchanged by their experiences. A successful fieldworker can compartmentalize – partition, as it were – identities, ideas, and social practices. It may, at times, be necessary to consider views that are mutually contradictory. Some fieldworkers find this disorienting, while others enjoy the illusion of multiple lives.

Macaulay (2005) notes that fieldworkers tend to romanticize their field experiences. That is, we say that it's not a *real* field site unless it has no electricity or running water and the intrepid linguist runs across at least three deadly species a day before their breakfast of witchetty grubs and hand-slaughtered crocodile. It's certainly true that field linguists at conferences tend to swap stories about the gruesome things they've had to eat and the near-death experiences they've had (and a friend of mine has a section on his CV for field diseases). That sort of site is not for everyone. Not everyone enjoys living without an espresso machine, air conditioning and familiar foods, and there's no rule of fieldwork that says that you have to be Indiana Jones in order to be a real linguist or fieldworker.[5] Going to live among speakers of another language, with a different culture, is going to be disruptive to you, to put it mildly. You might not be able to get your favourite foods, and depending on where you go you might not be able to rely on electricity, or a decent supply of fresh food, or you might not be able to remain vegetarian or keep kosher. Fieldwork is not something to be undertaken at a whim. It is emotionally intense, and can be physically dangerous. Depending on where you go, you may need to be prepared for the possibility of a serious illness or accident. Some linguists find it very unsettling and would never do fieldwork if there was any other way of getting the data they need. However, fieldwork is also intellectually exciting and the chance for many unique experiences as a guest in another culture.

1.6   Summary and further reading

1.6.1   Summary

Several ideas about fieldwork inform this book. First is that the documentation of a language and linguistic description/analysis are not mutually exclusive (cf. Himmelmann 1996) and cannot be done independently. Secondly, an adequate description of a language will need to utilize a variety of methods, including (but not limited to) elicitation. A comprehensive description and documentation of a language will benefit from creativity and variety and well as depth in a particular type of data collection.

A further theme is the building of trust between the linguist and their language consultants. I do not subscribe to the idea that linguistic work is purely experimentation and that research participants in documentary/descriptive linguistic fieldwork have no say in the research process. They are stakeholders as much as the linguist is, particularly if the language is endangered. Finally, I stress an interdisciplinary approach, even in cases where the data gathering might be targeted at a specific area. The greater your general awareness of techniques and pitfalls, the better your fieldwork will be.

1.6.2   Further reading

Links to web sites and updated suggestions for further reading will be given on the web site which accompanies this book. The URL is http://www.ruf.rice.edu/~bowern/fieldwork/

- **Experimentation:** Cameron et al. (1992) and Kibrik (1977). See also Rieschild (2003), Stebbins (2003) and Wilkins (1992).
- **Ethnography/anthropological fieldwork:** Agar (1996), Bernard (2006), Ellen (1984: ch. 3), Fife (2005). See also Clifford and Marcus (1986) and Duranti (2001).
- **Fieldwork in sociolinguistics:** Coupland and Jaworski (1997: Part II), Feagin (2004), Johnstone (2000), Milroy (1980, 1987).
- **Language documentation:** Himmelmann (1996, 1998), Woodbury (2003).
- **Other field methods books:** Abbi (2001), Bouquiaux and Thomas (2001), Crowley (2007), Everett (forthcoming), Newman and Ratliff (2001), Vaux and Cooper (1999). Earlier works: Craig (1979), Hale (1965), Kibrik (1977), Nida (1947) and Samarin (1967).
- **Role of theory:** Green and Morgan (1996), Singleton and Straits (2005: ch. 10).

2
Technology in the Field

2.1 Why make recordings?

If you are going to the trouble of travelling a long way to ask someone about their language, you want to have some way of recording their answers. You might want the recordings later on so that you can check your transcriptions. Perhaps the narratives you've recorded will be used for a talking book, or maybe you transcribed your recordings with one aim in mind and later will wish to go back to them for other data. Transcriptions are a pale shadow compared to the original audio and video.

Among the first language documentation records we have are clay tablet primers in Sumerian cuneiform, from about 3000 BCE. Clay has certain advantages as a medium for preservation of materials. Once fired it's quite durable. If the scribe makes a mistake, the error can be easily erased. As a writing system cuneiform is suitable for several languages. But the tablets are cumbersome to carry around. They don't give us any audio information, and once the clay is fired the record can't be changed.

These days we have considerably more sophisticated ways of preserving language materials than clay tablets. We still want durable materials, so that all our work (and the work of our consultants) will be useful to others in the future. We want to store materials in a medium that others will be able to read, and we want to be able to access our data easily. Obsolescence and durability are a real problem in modern recording technology. Bird and Simons (2003:557–8), for example, make the point that the more recent and advanced the technology, the quicker the time to obsolescence. We could decode Linear B and Sumerian, but could we 'decode' the information on 5¼' floppy disks the same way? Certainly not.

Here is another example. The first sound recordings were made just over 100 years ago and were made on wax cylinders. The speaker would speak into an 'amplifier' (similar to an ear trumpet) and the sound vibrations would trigger the movement of a stylus, which would scratch a path into the wax. The cylinders could later be replayed. Only a few places in the world can now play these cylinders, and in many cases they have been damaged and are unplayable. The wax can also grow mouldy, and scratches on the surface distort the sound. The recordings are also of not very high quality.

Nowadays we have digital audio recorders, CD recorders, minidiscs, mp3 (and mp4) recorders, and so on. But these too will quickly become obsolescent. This section will date quickly, so I will discuss some general points about what desirable equipment is.

2.2   Choosing recording equipment[1]

2.2.1   Technology specifications

I strongly recommend using a digital recorder. They are similar in price to high-quality analogue recorders and the recording quality is much better. Digital audio is also much easier to use – you can edit the files easily, make spectrograms, link text and sound, and create useful materials without redigitizing.

There's some terminology you need to know to choose the best recorder. Most of this information can be found on the back of the box or in the instructions (or online from the manufacturers' web sites). Assistants in general electronics shops almost never know what these terms mean. Specialist audio shops, other fieldworkers and academics in other disciplines who use recorders (especially musicologists and archivists) are excellent sources of information.

The **pitch** of sound is measured in Hertz. Humans can hear frequencies between about 20 and 20,000 Hz. Recording quality can be measured in several ways, including fidelity to the input and the relative loudness of the input you wish to record versus background noise.

The **frequency response** is the set of frequencies that the device can faithfully record (or that headphones/speakers can play back). The ideal recording device will record frequencies and play them back at the same loudness that they were recorded at in the first place. No system is absolutely faithful to the input, although a good microphone and recorder will come quite close. There is some distortion at the top and bottom of the sound spectrum. The frequency response should be as good as possible; a good quality machine will record within frequencies between 80 and 11,000 Hz with an error of 2 dB or less (Ladefoged 2003:18).

The **signal-to-noise ratio** is the difference between the signal that you are recording and the 'noise' (background noise, machine noise, and so on). The higher this number the better. The signal to noise ratio is stated in decibels (dB). There is a discussion of this and how to test for it in Ladefoged (2003:18–20).

For a digital recorder, you will need to choose the sampling rate, bit depth and file format. The **sampling rate** is how many frequencies the recorder takes a 'sample' of each second. The more samples, the more information is recorded, and the larger the file is. The sampling rate is double the number of Hertz; therefore to record sounds up to 8000 Hz, you would need a sampling rate of 16,000 Hz. A sampling rate of 44,100 Hz has become the *de facto* standard for digital field recording and archiving, although when you work on your files you may find that downsampling your recordings produces files which are easier to work with. Many linguists use files downsampled to 22,050 Hz. **Bit depth** refers to the amount of information in the sample; 16-bit and 24-bit depths are the most common at time of writing. Opinions vary greatly as to whether the extra information on a 24-bit recording justifies the increase in file size.

You should be careful of the format that your audio file is in. Just like text documents can be in different formats (Word (DOC), Acrobat (PDF), Rich Text format (RTF) and so on), there are many different formats for the way that sound is encoded digitally. Waveform audio format (.wav) is a very common digital audio format, as is MP3. One of the reasons mp3 players can record for so many hours is that they compress the signal as they record it. The compression algorithm is proprietary, however, which means that we don't know exactly what they do to the signal! That's why MP3 is called a **lossy** format: information is lost in the recording. You should record using a lossless format (such as wav) wherever possible.

2.2.2   Factors to consider

Whatever your field situation (and this goes for classroom recording as well) there are certain requirements for audio and video recording devices.

First of all, your recorder needs to be **portable** and **robust**. There is no point having a recorder that will break easily: you need to be able to get it to your site and use it. Dust, heat, cold, humidity and vibrations all do terrible things to electronic equipment. You need something robust to keep your equipment in too; good protective bags or boxes are worth the investment. You should also have backup equipment.

Secondly, you should not have to rely on mains electricity. Your field site might not have electricity at all, or the supply might be unreliable. Even if there is mains electricity if it comes from generators the current can be variable and a surge can damage the machine, and 'brown outs' (current fluctuation) can cause data corruption. Devices that need mains electricity are also inherently less portable than those which use batteries. Recording while running the unit plugged into a wall outlet (on mains power) causes an electrical hum from the line in some devices.

Units also vary in their power efficiency. Different tasks also use up different amounts of power: recording is more battery intensive than play-back, for example. Furthermore, there is an annoying lack of standardization in batteries and equipment chargers. Video and audio recorders often have their own specific batteries, which require their own chargers, each at slightly different voltages. This can add considerably to the weight and bulkiness of your baggage.

You need to be able to get your data off your recorder easily. Analogue tapes are easy to play back in small portions, but they have to be digitized in real time. You should be able to make backup or archive recordings of your tapes. You will want to make working copies so you can store the originals in a safe place, and you don't want to tie up your machine for hours while you do it. You should also record in a format that lets you easily make copies for community members, especially if you are doing a salvage project. You don't want to be using all your battery and work time making copies.

Some recorders are easier to use than others. You'll need one that shows the recording levels, so you can make sure you are not clipping the recording, or that the recording is loud enough.[2] One that has a battery level monitor is also highly recommended. Displays that are impossible to read in bright sunlight are not very helpful. You should always be able to tell if the pause button is on, if sound is coming into the unit and if the unit is recording.

You also need to have a backup device in case something goes wrong with your main recorder. All sorts of things can cause equipment malfunctions. Modern electronics are designed not to last very long (because companies want you to have to upgrade constantly) so many brands are not very durable. Sophisticated recording devices (unlike wax cylinder recorders) can't be fixed by non-specialists. Make sure that you can mix and match equipment; for example, your backup microphone should be usable with both your primary and your backup machine.

It goes without saying that your recording device should produce good quality recordings. (Naturally, the quality of the recording will also depend on your site and where you can work.) If your recordings will be the primary record of the language, you'll want to make it as data-rich as possible. Even if not, you will make things easier for yourself by having clear recordings that are easier to transcribe. Recording quality is a function of many things. The quality of the recording unit is important, but so is the microphone, the cables that are used to transfer the data between machines, the number of times the signal is copied, as well as any ambient noise, the room and the placement of the recorder.

There is a trade-off between portability, quality, price and durability, and there is no equipment which is ideal on all of these points. Get the best equipment you can afford. A summary of types of recording devices is available on the book web site.

2.2.3 Audio recording devices[3]

Recording devices are either **analogue** or **digital**. The most common analogue device is a cassette tape recorder. Digital devices include mp3 recorders, compact flash recorders, DAT tapes, CD recorders and hard drive recorders. They vary greatly in cost (the most expensive machines are 20 times the price of the cheapest ones), in quality, and in appropriateness for field recordings.

The best recorder will be different, depending on what you can afford, and what the purpose of your work is. However, in all cases I recommend a digital recorder which can record in a lossless format. You can always archive your files in this format and make working copies using mp3 or a compressed file type (e.g., if you want to put many hours of recordings on the web). A summary of types of equipment, along with their pros and cons, and estimated prices, is given on the web site for this book. The summary given here highlights the most important considerations for different types of fieldwork. It's important to remember, though, that even the best recorder won't compensate for a badly placed microphone, a clipped recording or intrusive background noise. Furthermore, bear in mind that you may not just be making recordings for yourself, and that your data may be potentially useful to others later on, and your choice of recording equipment may limit the future usability of your data. For example, you might not care whether the files are mp3s or a lossless format, but a phonetician will not be able to use mp3 files.

Type of research	Most important feature(s)
Acoustic phonetics	Lossless digital recording at a minimum of 22,100 Hz uncompressed audio. High-quality condenser head-mounted or lavalier microphone
'General' fieldwork aiming to produce a description and documentation	Highest quality recorder you can afford, with lossless recording, durable, and several high-fidelity microphones
Sociolinguistic variation, discourse, conversation analysis	Portability and unobtrusiveness (+considerations for phonetic research if studying phonetic variation); omnidirectional microphones if recording more than one person
Syntax, morphology, oral history	Lossless recording might seem less important, but bear in mind that your data may be useful to others later on, in which case they might have higher requirements

2.2.4 Microphones

Even if your recording device is excellent, your recordings will be bad if you have a low-quality microphone. Microphones can be mono or stereo. Mono microphones record a single channel, whereas stereo microphones record two 'streams' or channels. Stereo microphones will give more sound depth and are useful when you have several speakers. I recommend a stereo recording even if you are working only with one speaker.

Microphones are classified according to the technology they use to relay the sound to the recorder. **Condenser microphones** have better fidelity to the input sound but they require their own power supply, they are quite fragile and can be susceptible to changes in humidity.[4] **Dynamic microphones** produce a worse quality recording but they are much more durable and they do not require their own power source.

Another distinction is between **low-impedance** and **high-impedance** microphones. Low-impedance microphones more accurately reproduce the sound being recorded, but they are more expensive and more fragile. Some types of recording device work with both types of microphones, whereas others require either one or the other to make adequate recordings.

The other most common variance is the shape of the target recording area. A shotgun microphone is one that only records a narrow area of sound directly in front of the microphone. They are highly directional and are better in areas of ambient noise. They don't record from any further away though. They also need to be placed quite carefully. A cardioid microphone records a 'heart-shaped' area. It is maximally sensitive in front of the microphone head but also records at an angle, so they are more forgiving if the speaker is not directly in front of the microphone. The third common shape of recording area is 'omnidirectional' – that is, the microphone records from all angles. 'Business' microphones tend to be omnidirectional. These are excellent if you have a group of people – you can put the microphone in the middle of the group. They also pick up a lot of background noise. Some microphones have variable settings for recording areas; for example, a narrow setting and a wide setting. These are very useful if you record both single speakers and groups of people.

Lapel (or lavalier) and head-mounted microphones are also used. These are good if you are just recording one speaker. They produce very good recordings of the person wearing them and eliminate much background noise. I don't use these type of microphones in the field because they are more difficult to forget about and they counteract my aim of producing a non-threatening recording environment (i.e., one that is a general conversation that happens to be recorded). Also, I never know how many people are going to turn up to the session and how many people are going to speak. Having a microphone that can be passed around is more useful in such situations. Moreover, using lapel microphones presupposes that the speaker is wearing clothes that the microphone can be clipped to without touching anything, such as a collared shirt. In some cultures it might be inappropriate for a male researcher to touch a female consultant (or vice versa) to clip on the microphone. In that case either use a microphone with a stand or demonstrate on yourself and have the consultant clip the microphone on themselves.

Many of the higher end microphones require pre-amps and their own power supply. As always, there is a trade-off between quality and portability. You will get the best recordings in a sound booth or radio station, and in some cases you might be able to use this for part of the time.

2.2.5 Headphones

It is worth spending some money on headphones; after all, transcription in a foreign language is hard enough already without using bad-quality equipment. The two most important considerations are the quality and fidelity of sound reproduction and how comfortable the headphones are to wear.

Pick headphones with a good frequency response and low levels of distortion. There are different kinds of headphones, including buds and over-ear. The over-ear models can be open or sealed. The open ones provide more ventilation, and are lighter, but they let more noise in (and out). Bud earphones are smaller and very portable, but the quality is often not as good. Some of the over-ear models are quite heavy; this can cause neck discomfort if worn for long periods. There are also models designed to sit in your ear canal, which are often excellent.

If you are working in a tropical/humid climate and wearing earphones for long periods, watch out for ear infections. Bud earplugs and in-ear models can be problematic. Wipe off the earphone casing with alcohol (or something else sterile) from time to time and don't wear the earphones for long periods.

Noise cancelling headphones are also a possibility, but I don't recommend them for fieldwork. Many brands of noise cancelling headphones reduce background noise, but the actual quality of the sound is not very good. Secondly, some other 'noise cancelling' headphones just create a seal between your ear and the outside world (i.e., they don't filter out external sound electronically, they try and keep it away from your ears in the first place). If you're going to spend large amounts of time with these things in your ear, you run the risk of ear infections.

You will also want backup headphones and a small pair of external speakers (or a way of playing back recordings to a group of people). If your laptop speakers are good they will probably suffice.

2.2.6 Cables

Make sure you have all the necessary cables to connect your equipment. This includes not only power cables but also ways of connecting equipment together. You will need USB cables (and a compact flash reader is useful if you're using a flash recorder). Your headphones will need to be able to be plugged into your computer, recorder and any other audio devices (e.g., your video recorder). Your microphone will have its own cables and it's helpful to be able to plug it into your computer (so that your computer can be used as a backup recorder). Bring a spare USB cable. Make sure the cables are labelled; video and audio RCA cables look almost identical, and using the wrong one will stuff up your recording. Make sure your microphone and headphones have the right jacks for the equipment (and get an adapter if not).

A very useful item to have is a splitter. It's used for plugging in two headphones or microphones into a single input. You want one with a male on one end and two female inputs on the other – you can also have one with a female input on one side and two on the other, and use an adapter.

2.2.7   Video equipment

There are many advantages to making video recordings for linguistic data. People use gesture and facial expressions to get their meaning across as well as speech. Some spoken languages have auxiliary sign languages too, and if you are studying a signed language, video will be your recording medium. By only recording the audio channel of communication we are not recording the whole picture of a language. If your aim is a comprehensive documentation of the language, no visual recordings would be a big gap. If you are recording narratives which go with cultural practices such as weaving or dyeing, having the visual demonstration is often vital to understanding what is going on. For example, I have a text recorded in Yan-nhaŋu about weaving pandanus into baskets. The text roughly translates as:

(1) Now...you take these ones, not a lot, just a few, about this many, and you take them and put them here. Now, take these three, and put them here and here in this order, one, two three...

This description, although completely accurate, is not something we could use to reconstruct weaving techniques 50 years in the future if we didn't have video to go with it. There is only so much that still photography can capture.

It's good to have people on video when recording narratives, because there's often a lot of extralinguistic information in facial and hand gestures which you won't get on tape. For example, some deixis markers are always accompanied by a gesture (e.g., the Kuku Yalanji example in Patz 2002:67). The consultant's gestures may be vital to decoding the narrative (as in my example above); some words may always be accompanied by gestures; or some narrative types may have gestures/actions associated with them. Storytelling may be accompanied by sketches on the ground.

As with audio recording, you have a choice between analogue and digital recording technology. I highly recommend digital recording from the start. Archival formats are subject to ongoing discussion and video formats are in a state of flux too. Once the files are on your computer you can use software to convert the files to different formats, but this requires huge amounts of hard drive space and may result in the loss of information. Mpeg is one common format. If using video, it's especially important to plan workflow (see §4.1.2) and backup, since the files are so large.

Many digital stills cameras also have video functions. The quality is usually not very good – they have a small number of frames per second – but they are good in emergencies. Some have limits on the length of video (e.g., three minutes) while others are limited by space on the storage media.

The audio recording on just about all videos is of quite low quality, so whatever type of recorder you decide to use for visual recording you will want a separate audio recorder too (or an external microphone which you can plug into the video camera). There are various computer programs which will let you synchronize audio and video recordings (see this book's web site for details). Transferring them to computer needs to be done in real time, so make sure you budget enough time to do this.

Finally, remember that your consultants might be uncomfortable about being videoed and it might detract from the quality of material. For example, one of my consultants never used gestures while being videoed. There may be cultural reasons why someone might not want to be videoed. It is worth explaining some of the benefits of having a linguistic record on video, but if your consultants are unhappy about it, leave it; it is a trade-off between better quality data that is less rich and data that might have more modal information but might be acquired at the cost of community friendships or at the expense of the linguistic data.

2.3   Computers

Over the last few years laptops have become much easier to take to the field. It is now possible to set up solar power just about anywhere, and there are sufficiently light-weight and durable models that there is no reason why you should need to be without one if you want to take one.

There are small, light-weight ultraportable computers that are useful in the field (although bear in mind some of these don't have built-in CD/DVD burners or drives, you'll need to bring ways to back-up your data too). If your field site doesn't have electricity, you can use solar cells attached to car batteries. If you have generator power, take several batteries and charge them (using a high-quality surge protector) at off-peak times. In the communities I've worked in this was the middle of the afternoon and about 5am.

Buy the best computer you can, and try to buy one with features which will make the unit more able to withstand hard use. Size and weight are also important. Ultra-portable laptops are very useful for fieldwork, although the screen area is quite small. Make sure that the unit has enough battery capacity for your needs (e.g., that you can install an extra battery, or that the laptop can take long-life batteries), and that it has enough USB ports for all your equipment. Hard drive size and processor speed are also important considerations if you are editing sound and video.

Bugs dying in your equipment are a problem in some places. The light of the screen attracts them. You can minimize this by having a blank screen saver set to come on quickly, and by not sitting with the screen facing a window (sitting with your back as close to a wall as possible seems to work quite well). Have good dust- and heat-proof protective bags for all your equipment. You should also use silica gel packs to dry out your equipment. Put them in the bag with the laptop.

Another possibility if you don't want to take a computer is a PDA. If you just want to type your notes for later interlinearization, this can be effective. There are also database programs for Palm and PocketPC operating systems which can be used for vocabulary collection. You can also buy portable printers for them. Advantages include portability, long battery life, the possibility of adding a full-sized keyboard, but disadvantages include the very small screen size and limited program functionality. Taking a PDA instead of a computer implies that you have a way of duplicating and transcribing your recordings that doesn't involve a laptop.

If you cannot bring your own computer, it may be possible to work through a local school or university, especially if you are doing language revitalization work with them. If none of this is possible, it's still possible to do a lot of work by hand, as in the 'old days' (Crowley 2007 is a book that assumes you won't have much access to technology).

2.4   Pen and paper

Don't rely absolutely on electronic equipment no matter where you are. Your laptop battery might run out at a crucial moment, or you might be out with friends talking casually, where pulling out your laptop would spoil the moment, or you might be on a boat and so on.

Consider not only what is most convenient for you, but what is most convenient for your consultants. Old people without much experience with computers might be put off by them. They might already find the recording equipment overwhelming without having another piece of equipment to be put off by. If they have cataracts, reading the screen might be uncomfortable or difficult.

Laptop screens are hard to read in bright sunlight. They put up a screen between you and the person sitting opposite you, which might create an unfriendly dynamic in elicitation.[5] It can be hard for someone to look over your shoulder when typing, whereas it's easier when you're writing. You may want someone to see what you're writing so they can correct errors (e.g., Dimmendaal 2001). And computers have fans that make noise, whereas pencils and paper do not contribute to background noise unless you shuffle them. Paper notebooks can be used as extra wind shields if you are recording outside and as microphone stands. If the paper gets dirty you can brush it off, but if you get dirt in your computer it can stop working completely! It's easier to draw diagrams and small illustrations on a notebook. You can rip out a corner of a page to write a phone number on, and you don't have to stop working if the power goes off.

Handwriting is much slower and retranscribing onto computer wastes time. On the other hand, it forces you to go through your notes in detail soon after you make them, which has great advantages. You see what information you have, and you get a chance to go over what you don't understand (and can use this to think about further questions).

2.5 Recording practicalities

Once you have your recording device(s), you need to use them to get the best recordings you can.

2.5.1 Looking after equipment and media

There should be two watchwords for equipment and media: *clean* and *dry*. Make sure your equipment is clean, as are your storage containers. Clean out the equipment with compressed air from time to time. Have head/lens cleaners for your recording devices, know how to use them, and use them regularly.

Humidity does terrible things to electronic equipment, so if you are working in a very humid environment be careful about this. Damp conditions promote mould too. This can be ameliorated (although not entirely prevented) by storing your equipment in airtight bags with

Silica gel packets. Dry out the gel periodically (in a very low oven, for example). Make sure the place you keep your equipment and blank media is cool. I keep a lot of stuff in the fridge on fieldwork. It's cool, dust-free, bug-free and when things are in airtight bags they aren't exposed to humidity. Make sure that things return to room temperature before using them though. (I don't keep my equipment in the fridge because of the large temperature difference between inside the fridge and out.) The same applies to working in very cold areas, in reverse; problems arise when bringing your equipment in from the cold dry air outside to warm and humid inside air.

Audio equipment is fragile and expensive, so look after it. Be careful not to drop it and don't keep it loose in a bag with lots of other things. Be careful with the recorded media, too. You should always store blank and recorded media separately, and they should be kept in an airtight and lightproof container with desiccant. Ultraviolet light can affect CDs and DVDs, and storing any type of media in humid conditions runs the risk of mould growth.

2.5.2   Audio recording tips

Recording conditions are almost never perfect. There will always be something that could be improved. Make the best of what you have and seize the opportunities you are given. Don't worry if it takes a while to get a really quiet session. On one trip, I had to wait for over a month before I could get a place quiet enough to record a word list illustrating phonemic contrasts.

Good microphone placement is important. A stand microphone should be about 8 to 12 inches (20–30cm) away from the speaker's mouth. You should use a microphone stand wherever possible. If you do not have to hold the microphone, your hands will be free for notetaking and so on. If you have to hold the microphone, keep it steady, move as little as possible, and if you have a stereo microphone, be careful of keeping the balance constant (i.e., make sure the microphone does not move from side to side). It will make you feel sea-sick when you listen to the recordings.

Be constantly aware of background noise. This requires a bit of practice, as we are used to training ourselves to concentrate and tune out background noise. Constant background noise from generators, air conditioners, traffic, wind or rain may not bother you while you are making the recordings, but they will hinder clear playback and analysis. They make it hard to hear. Audio recordings have no depth so it is much more difficult for your ear to differentiate the close speech signal from the background noise.

If you're working outside, chances are that sooner or later you will have flies and other insects landing on or crawling over your microphone. You can prevent this by putting insect repellent on the popshield. You will also need to have some way of shielding the microphone from the wind. A strategically placed notebook is better than nothing in an emergency, and a thick sock over the popshield also works. Making sure that the consultant's body shields the microphone from the wind will improve the recording.

Recording inside also has its problems. Large empty rooms produce echoic recordings; fridges, air conditioners, and other whitegoods produce background noise which it is easy to ignore while recording, but which will often mar the tape and make transcription and spectrographic analysis difficult. On the other hand, turning off the fans, air conditioners/heaters and fridge might also produce discomfort. If it's too hot for you and your consultants to concentrate, you won't get very good data even if there is little ambient noise. Finding somewhere quiet to record is the most common problem that fieldworkers have.

Turn off mobile (cell) phones if you're in an area where you have them. They are annoying and there's some evidence that they can send out pings that can interfere with recording. You may want to unplug your land line during elicitation sessions to prevent the phone ringing in the middle of something important.

It is a good idea to monitor the recordings while you are recording. That way you can easily adjust the levels if the signal is being clipped. There are situations where you will not want to do this (or where it will be impractical). It creates a different dynamic from one where you are not wearing headphones,[6] as it is much harder for the consultant to ignore the fact that they are being recorded. Finally, never use the voice activation feature on your recording device, it causes you to miss the first half-second or so of the recording.

2.5.3 Producing good videos[7]

If at all possible, use a tripod when making video recordings. It leaves your hand free to do other things, and the picture will be stable. If you can't use a tripod for some reason, try to steady the recorder on something solid. If nothing is available, as a last resort steady yourself against something (e.g., a tree) and rest your elbow on your hip/waist. Sitting and resting the camera on your knee also produces fairly stable pictures.

Make sure that the battery is charged before each session and that you have a charged spare. Power consumption on most models is high. Leaving the unit in 'pause' mode for long periods uses up battery power, so turn off the machine if you are not recording for a while. Batteries also do not perform optimally in very hot or cold conditions, so take this into account. In Northern Australia in the dry season (in temperatures of about 33°C/90°F) I never got more than 90 minutes from a video battery, and usually less.

Most video recorders have automatic settings for focus and brightness adjustment. Try not to have too bright a background; it makes the people in the foreground come out very dark and can obscure their facial expressions. Your consultant's clothes may also cause the brightness adjustment to obscure features. Never point the camera directly at the sun – it will damage the lens. If you are filming a lot in bright conditions, consider buying a UV filter. The angle of the camera is important and the wrong angle can cause reflections and streaks in the picture.

Resist the temptation to use the zoom a lot, because it's very distracting when watching the video. When you move the camera to pan around the room/area for a shot, make sure you move the camera slowly. What looks fine to you as you move the camera can be a dizzy blur when watched on the screen (and if you move the camera too much you can make your audience sea-sick). It's better to set the camera up and leave it. Do not use long-play mode on a video. It results in data being recorded at a higher compression rate (or in the case of DV tapes, fewer frames per second are recorded).

2.5.4   Putting consultants at ease

If you are working with people who have never been recorded before, it is worth explaining a bit about what will happen and how the recording works. It's also worth reminding them to speak normally. There's a tendency for people new to recording to shout into a microphone (to make sure the microphone picks up the sound), or to mumble because of shyness.

Some people are quite happy being recorded, whereas others can be quite nervous about it. For some people it is a really big thing to put their language on tape for the first time, or even to speak it in front of someone not from the community. Your work might go more smoothly if you begin by not recording anything, by just getting the consultant used to the sorts of questions that linguists ask, or just by having a chat and a cup of tea. Others may want to rehearse what they are going to say first, before they put it on tape. Don't worry about this – it's important that you give your consultant time to gain confidence. After all, you want them to come back for the next session! It is worth mentioning that it doesn't matter if a mistake is made on tape, they can just say the word or sentence again and you will use the correct version.

Always have a way of playing back what you've recorded. You might want to do a short test, with you speaking into the microphone, then playing it back so that your consultants see how it works. Always be prepared to demonstrate things on yourself.

It's also good to have a way for people to know that the tape is on and that they are being recorded, especially if you control the recorder. For example, you could turn the microphone on its side when the recorder is off, or move it away from the person, so they know that if the microphone is in front of them, they are probably being recorded.

2.6 Checklist for equipment setup

2.6.1 At the start

Get into the habit of setting up your equipment and checking it before every recording session:

1. Make sure you have batteries in the unit and that they have enough charge for your session and some extra. That is, know how long your batteries last in your recording device, and know how long the current set have been used for. If in doubt, change them. Partially used batteries can be used for transcription or given away. Always have spares with you.
2. Listen for background noise. Is there anything you can do something about? (e.g., turn off fridge,[8] phone, washing machine, etc.). If there's noise you can't do anything about (e.g., birds, passing traffic), can you do anything to minimize it?
3. Is your microphone connected to the recording unit? (Don't laugh, it's happened...) Is it plugged in the microphone jack (and not the headphone plug)?
4. If your microphone has its own power switch, is it on? Does it need its own battery?
5. Is there blank recording media in the unit?
6. If you are recording one person, are they sitting about 8 inches away from the microphone? If you're recording a group of people, is the microphone situated where it will pick up the best number of people at the best quality?

7. Do you have your elicitation materials, and so on, in easy reach so you can write without shuffling papers too much?
8. Is the video tripod secure? Are the batteries charged? Is there blank media in the recorder? Are the people to be filmed in the viewfinder? Can you operate the video with a remote and still check the recording from where you're seated? Is the noise from the motor on the video likely to affect the recording quality?
9. Start recording. Check the levels on the machine to make sure you aren't clipping the signal. The signal should be as loud as possible without clipping.
10. Make sure that the pause button is not on!

2.6.2   At the end of a session

Have a routine for packing up at the end of a session too:

1. Make sure that the recording unit and auxiliary devices (such as microphones) are turned off, so as not to waste battery power or damage the units.
2. Disconnect the microphones from the unit. Stress on the microphone jacks can cause them to torque and come loose, which results in hiss on the recordings and makes the unit unusable.
3. Don't leave anything behind. The best way to avoid doing this is to pack things up in the same order each time and to have a place for everything (or a mental checklist).
4. Have a place for recorded media which you will need to do audition sheets for, and keep them separate from blank media.
5. Transfer digital recordings to your computer and back up the recording as soon as possible. If you are using flash cards, wipe the card after you have made sure that the recording is transferred and backed up, so the card is ready to go for your next session.
6. Have a quick check to see if anything is dirty; if so clean it as soon as possible.
7. Recharge batteries if necessary.

2.7   Summary and further reading

2.7.1   Summary

Technology is really useful, make the most of it. Learn how to use your equipment. Know what it does, how it works, and what its limitations are. Vaux and Cooper (1999:182) say 'many linguists are technophobes, and there is nothing wrong with that'. I disagree. Not making videos because you are not keen on learning new technology is distinctly unimpressive. After all, we are very unkind at conference talks when the presenter argues from raw averages because they didn't know which statistical test to use. Technophobia is curable. Get help from techno-junkie friends and colleagues. Musicologists and sound archivists can often give advice on equipment, software and recording practicalities.

Don't be overawed by technology, though. It won't solve all your problems. Recordings with music in the background will still be bad whether or not they were made with a $50 cassette recorder or a $3000 Nagra solid state compact flash machine. However, a recording with some background noise is better than no recording at all. Conditions will never be perfect; make the best of what you have at the time.

2.7.2 Further reading

- **Equipment, computing and linguistics**: The *Language Archives Newsletter* provides reviews of equipment, as does *Language Document-ation and Conservation*. See also Ladefoged (2003).
- **Solar power:** see web site.
- **Technology problems:** Bowden and Hajek (2006) and Honeyman (2004).

3
Starting to Work on a Language

Before you go to the field for the first time, there are a lot of preparations to make. You need to find a field site, gather the previous materials on the language, plan your early elicitation sessions, and work out how you're going to find people to work with. You probably also need to apply for human subjects' research approval and take care of the associated paperwork. In a field methods class, all of this is done by the instructor. Usually you are not permitted to look at previous materials, and instead in the class you will rely completely on your own data and judgements. This chapter is rather concerned with what to do when you arrive in the field or when you start your first class. Other chapters in this book describe the different preparations that you need to make before actually starting work.

3.1 What to do at the first session

You should have several aims during the first field sessions. The first is to get a grip on the phonetics and phonology of the language, so that you can transcribe accurately. Otherwise, you will be seriously hampered in all other aspects of your work. Secondly, you should be setting up your fieldworker routine for the rest of trip. It is very difficult to break habits once they've been entrenched. Get into the habit of labelling recordings, transferring digital data to a backup and to your computer hard drive, filling out the metadata sheets and organizing future sessions.

Set the tone for your fieldwork sessions as early as possible. First impressions are quite important. You do not want to bore your consultants, otherwise they might not come back! It gives the consultant an idea of the type of work that you'll be doing with them, and it also sets in motion the type of interaction that the linguist and the consultant will have.

34

3.1.1 Preliminaries

Do not start elicitation with your consultant as soon as you sit down. There are some preliminaries that you need to do first. Get to know each other a little. You'll be spending a great deal of time together. Getting to know each other isn't wasted time.

There are also administrative details to take care of at the first session. For example, you cannot record someone until you have their permission. In order for them to give informed consent, they need to know something about the project and the form that the sessions will take.

Assuming your consultant agrees to be recorded, you then need to set up and test the equipment. You will already be familiar with how to work the recorder, so it should not take a great deal of time to set up, but make sure that the microphone is on and pointing in the right direction, and that there is no interference in the signal from electrical equipment, or too much extraneous noise.

3.1.2 Starting linguistic work

It's a good idea to start with a wordlist and some very short sentences. That will give you information about phonetics and phonology, as well as word boundaries. The accurate transcription of longer utterances will be almost impossible without a firm grasp of the phoneme system and cues to word boundaries. Not only will you be more confident in your transcriptions, but you will be able to process longer streams of speech. When you first begin to work on an unfamiliar language the length of speech string that you can hold in short-term memory is very short; it increases with your familiarity with the sound system, vocabulary items and syntax. Even if you already have some familiarity with the language, starting with a wordlist on the first trip is a good way to check your equipment, to practise transcription, and to give your consultants a relatively easy task.

3.1.3 First wordlists

When getting their first data, some people start with the Swadesh list of basic vocabulary, or a similar list adapted for the region in which the language is spoken. Abbi (2001) gives a list for South Asia, and Sutton and Walsh (1987) is a much longer list for Australia. Basic vocabulary is not the same thing as most frequent vocabulary, though. You'll pick up high-frequency items early on in your fieldwork if you make some attempt to learn the language.

For first elicitation of wordlist items, it's good to start with body parts, natural surroundings or something else that can easily be pointed at. Using concrete terms minimizes the problem of ambiguity of reference, and allows speakers who aren't practised at translating from one language to another to look at the referent and think of the word in their language without having to go through the contact language. Furthermore, if you have any doubt about the fluency of the speaker, body parts are a way to get some information without being overly intimidating. Having a first session with a part-speaker where they cannot answer most of the questions will make things much harder for future sessions. Finally, using body parts as the first elicitation device lets you naturally move on to eliciting possessives, such as 'my hand' and 'your hand'. It lets you get the dual number and plural number easily, if they are marked, too.

Organize your elicitation list by semantic field even when you move beyond the first sessions. Working within a single semantic field at a time helps a lot, particularly with old people or part-speakers where jumping around the semantic space will be quite confusing. It also facilitates thinking of synonyms and near synonyms. Your idea of the contents of a semantic field might not be the same your consultants', however. In that case, working out semantic categorization in the language can be a set of elicitation topics in itself. Sorting wordlists in alphabetical order can make it hard, so if you use a survey list (and I recommend doing this, it saves time in writing, and you can record several speakers on the same list and use it to make comparisons in phonetics later on) code it by semantic field before you go to the field. See the book website for some sample lists.

Here is a list of useful vocabulary that it is good to know very early on in your language description, especially if you want to use the language to talk as much as possible:

- Ways of greetings people
- How to introduce yourself – you'll be doing a lot of that early in the field trip
- Asking about the health of your consultant and their family
- What you should call you consultant(s) and their family
- 'One more time (please)'
- 'What is that?'; 'What is <insert unfamiliar word>'
- 'How do you say X (in the language)?'
- Apologies

Once you've mastered these expressions, the next useful set of phrases to know is how to talk about where you've been and where you're going to, and some common activities that many people in the community do. Note that this already gives you quite a bit of syntax, including a possible allative case, some tense marking, argument structure and more vocabulary. Don't worry if you can't parse the phrases at this point, just learn them. That way you will be able to say something to others about what you are doing.

3.1.4   During the session

Monitor your recorder while you're working. You want to know as soon as possible if the batteries have run out of space, or if the recording is clipping. Therefore, the recorder needs to be where you can see it. It takes practice to remember to watch the recorder while concentrating on your other work.

Keep the recorder running as a note-taker – it's handy for self-monitoring,[1] it saves time, and it can help you in interpreting your notes once you return from the field. But don't use it as an excuse for not taking notes at all. You will elicit better data and ask better questions the more knowledge you have of your data. You can't acquire a good knowledge of the language by leaving the thinking portion of the work until you return home.

Finally, the essence of fieldwork is multi-tasking. One of the skills that you should train yourself in is being able to do several things simultaneously. So, not only are you listening to what your consultant is saying, you are also taking notes and making rough transcriptions, you are keeping an eye on the recorder to make sure it's working, and you might be also keeping an eye on your environment. On one of my field tapes there is an entertaining section where I see a deadly King Brown snake slithering towards us!

3.2   Discovering a phoneme inventory

You've asked your consultant what the word for *head* is in their language, and they've replied. You have a data point! What will you do with it? Write it down and remember it! Your first task in eliciting words is to get enough data to work out the phoneme inventory of the language. Ask for more data, and write it down phonetically (see §3.3).

Approach the phoneme inventory as you would approach a class phonology problem. Make a list of the segments and their environments, watching out for complementary distribution. Number your examples and note which examples are evidence for which segments. Note any minimal pairs in your data. Use a spectrogram program to check the accuracy of your transcription for voicing, etc., and to play and compare segments. This type of work is harder to do than a class phonology problem, because there is always the possibility that you have made a transcription mistake, or that you do not have all the required information represented in your data, but the principle is the same.

Once you've been through all your data carefully, take stock of what you have. Circle the segments you are fairly sure about on a phoneme chart. Write down all of the phones in your data and then circle all the allophones of a single phoneme. Make a note of the environment in which each allophone appears. Now, make a list of everything that you aren't sure about. This could be anything from apparent gaps in the phoneme system to doubts about whether two sounds are both phonemes, or one is an allophonic variant. Note any difficulties you have with transcription: it may be that you're not sure that what you transcribed as a palatal stop is really a stop; it may be an affricate, for example. Make note of variants in your data set.

The next stage is to work out what additional evidence you need to test your hypotheses. This may take the form of inventing minimal pairs to test, trying free variation of sounds, or simply gathering more natural data to add to the number of lexical items you've recorded. Here's an example. If you suspect that [g] and [ɣ] are allophones of the same phoneme, try substituting one for the other and getting the reaction of your consultant. Ladefoged (2003:11) recommends holding up one finger for the first item and two for the second. Asking which of the two items is *better* is preferable to asking 'which is right' as neither may be right.

(2) 'I've got two words, (1) taga and (2) taɣa. Are they the same word or different words?'
(3) 'I've got a word taɣa – is [taxa] also a word?

Make sure that your consultant knows that you want to be corrected. Sometimes people will assume that you're speaking with an accent, or they'll ignore the mistakes out of politeness, or they'll be so amused/pleased at anyone trying to learn the language that they'll ignore the 'errors'.

Another way to elicit similar words and potential minimal pairs is to ask for words that rhyme. *Pat, bat, cat, gnat, sat, tat, chat, hat, shat, at, that, mat, rat, fat, vat* and DAT all rhyme in English and the list contains several minimal pairs (although note that it does not illustrate all the consonant phonemes of English). However, not all languages have a rhyming 'tradition' (English didn't a thousand years ago, for example) and the concept won't necessarily make sense to your consultants. You may need to give an example. Sometimes speakers will come up with their own pairs for you, so it is good to ask about 'words that sound very similar to this word'. For example, you could ask if the person can think of any words that foreigners mix up.

Another way to test contrast is to say two words from your list to your consultant (or play two sound clips) and ask if they start with the same sound, or a different sound. Ask for examples of words that start with the same sound (this is known as alliteration, and is also culture-specific).

Once you have this new data, you're in a position to go back to your earlier hypotheses and revisit them. Don't be surprised if your new data introduces contradictions, or forces you to revise hypotheses which you thought were already confirmed. You will probably need to do this several times. You may still come across new phonemes even when your fieldwork is quite well advanced. In English, for example, /ʒ/ is not very common, and occurs entirely in loan words. You probably wouldn't come across it in early field sessions.

3.3 More on transcription

Good transcription is time-consuming, especially when you first begin. Expect to spend hours over your first recordings. Early work will pay off later.

Make a rough transcription as your consultant is speaking. It is much easier to transcribe live than from a recording. For example, you can watch the consultant's mouth to see if their lips are rounded. Your ears can filter out background noise much more easily when you are hearing it live. When such noise is recorded on tape it is much more distracting because you can't make use of audio depth (sounds closer to you versus sounds further away) to tune out unimportant noise.

Ask your consultant to say a word slowly if you don't hear it properly the first time, several times if necessary. When people are asked to say a word slowly they will tend to syllabify it automatically. Slowing down pronunciation of course alters pronunciation, but it is useful for securing the place of articulation.[2]

One of the hardest aspects of transcription is not hearing the language through the phonological filter of your own accent. Be on the lookout for consonants which aren't in your own language. Train yourself to be aware of the allophones of phonemes in your language (for example, the aspiration of stops and vowel reduction in English).

Know the International Phonetic Alphabet (or another standard transcription system) thoroughly, even if you are not really interested in a phonological description of the language. Make sure you have a copy of it, you could stick it to the front of your notebook, for example. Once you've come up with a transcription system, either stick to it, or make sure that you make a note of the point at which you changed and the equivalences between the old system and the new, otherwise you'll confuse yourself and others who use your notes. Make a note of what system you're using if it's at all non-standard.

There might be conventions for your language area which are different from the IPA. For example, Abbi (2001:95) recommends dots for representing retroflection rather than the IPA characters (ɭ, ɖ, ʈ ɳ) – that's a regional standard for Indic languages, and is also found in some parts of Australia. Handwritten dots can be easier to distinguish than tails. A word of warning – they're easy to leave off and if your photocopier is dirty you'll get lots of extra dots. Underlining is safer. Neither underlined nor under-dotted characters are in the standard set of Unicode characters, although they do appear in some Unicode fonts. Be careful that you can tell all the glyphs in your handwriting apart. For example, in my writing, <l> and <ɭ> are almost identical, which caused problems when I was working on Ndebele.

Your transcription system should be easy to type. There are free Unicode IPA fonts, for example, which can be mapped to keyboards. There are other systems, such as web input, drop-down boxes and scroll-through menus, but as soon as you are typing even small amounts of data extra keystrokes or mouse clicks slow down data entry considerably. Ease of typing may affect your choice of transcription system. For example it may be that your language has a vowel system with primary realization of phonemes like this:

(4) i   u
    ɛ   ɔ
      ɐ

In this case, a, e and o would be good alternatives for ease of data entry over ɐ, ɛ and ɔ (once you're sure of the phonemes). There is more information about things to consider in transcription systems in §5.1.

3.4   Common errors and cues

I guarantee that early in your fieldwork you will made transcription mistakes. Everyone does. Learning to accurately perceive an unknown language is a challenging task. There might be phones you've never heard before, or sounds which are allophonic in your native language might be phonemic in your field language. The following list contains some cues for sounds that new transcribers (and not so new!) often have trouble with. It isn't complete by any means, but these are some of the most common problematic areas, especially for native speakers of English. The only way to improve is to practise.

Problems with consonants:

- Don't forget to write **aspiration** in your transcriptions; English voiceless stops are aspirated allophonically in syllable-initial position so we tend to register voiceless aspirated stops as simply 'voiceless'. Aspiration may be missed in codas and on affricates.
- English speakers often perceive voiceless **unaspirated** consonants as voiced. If the language has a three-way distinction between voiced, aspirated voiceless and unaspirated voiceless stops, you can learn to perceive the unaspirated series by elimination. The aspirated series and voiced series will be fairly easy; the unaspirated series, then, are the stops which you are not sure are voiced or not.
- Tense stops and **ejectives** are easy to confuse.
- **Nasalization** can also be difficult to perceive accurately. Nasal vowels can be perceived as sequences of Vowel + Nasal, or missed entirely.
- **Palatal** stops and palatal affricates are easy to confuse, especially as a palatal stop often has some affrication associated with it (i.e., the oral closure is not completely clean and the release has turbulence associated with it which can appear on a spectrogram like affrication). Listen for the affrication.
- **Voiceless laterals** and trills are often misheard as [s] or [ʃ].
- Initial **velar nasals** [ŋ] can be difficult to hear for speakers of European languages if they are not expecting it. It is typically misperceived as [m], [n] or [w].
- English speakers often have difficulties with coda [l], mistaking it for palatalized when it is simply not velarized.
- **Bilabial** and labio-dental fricatives can be easily mistaken for one another, but the difference in closure is easy to see, so watch your consultant's mouth.
- **Double articulation** is often missed, for example [k͡p] and [g͡b], etc. are often misheard for single [k] and [g].
- **Glottal stops** are very easy to overlook.

Problems with vowels:

- Undiphthongized **mid vowels** [e] and [o] are very difficult for English speakers to perceive accurately.

- In general, it is easy to ignore **phonation** type (breathy voicing and creak especially), or to transcribe it as something else.
- **Long vowels** in unstressed syllables often sound stressed to speakers of English, so before you write a rule that says that stress shifts to a long vowel, do investigate the acoustic manifestations of stress in the language to see whether the primary stress is, in fact, shifting.
- Vowel length may be misperceived as tenseness (e.g. the contrast between [i] and [iː] as [ɪ] and [i]).
- Some English speakers may have trouble with high front vowels before nasals (e.g., [ɪ] versus [e] versus [ɛ], particular if they speak a variety of English which merges these vowels).
- It is easy to overlook front rounded vowels, or to hear them as back rounded vowels (i.e., to mistake [y] for [u]).
- Unstressed vowels may also be misperceived. In English there are many fewer contrasts in unstressed syllables than in stressed syllables, therefore English speakers tend unintentionally to collapse contrasts in unstressed environments.
- **Voiceless vowels** are often missed at a first pass. They sound somewhat like a puff of air, or /h/.
- Consonant clusters may be misperceived; it is easy to miss epenthetic vowels or to perceive them when they are absent.

Tips:

- **Lip rounding** can be seen, although not all speakers round their lips to the same extent.
- **Retroflection** of consonants is most easily heard on the preceding vowel.
- The speaker's tongue can usually be seen during the production of **laminodental** consonants.
- There are web sites which have sound files linked to IPA charts. These are excellent ways to practise training your ears. You can also use them to ask your consultant which sound is a 'better' example of the sound you are investigating.

3.5   Data organization

You will be helped in discovering the phoneme inventory of the language if you have a good way to organize your data early on. (There is extensive discussion of this in Chapter 4.) When you have your wordlist and your preliminary transcription, it's good to start a database of lexical items as soon as possible. In field-methods classes, each student could maintain their own database or the class could maintain a single database which everyone works on.

If possible, I recommend working with more than one speaker early on, and getting a basic wordlist from several speakers. It's probably not possible to do that in a field-methods class, but it's a way of meeting new people in a field situation. It will also minimize the effects of idiosyncratic pronunciations. You can transcribe items side-by-side in a table, in a spreadsheet or simply on the same page of your fieldnotes. This is an example of Bardi words transcribed phonetically from three speakers. The phonemicization was added later.

English gloss	Speaker 1	Speaker 2	Speaker 3	Phonemicization
water	ˈuːla	ˈoːla	ˈuːlạ	/ˈuːla/
fish	ˈɐːlɪ	ˈɐːlɪ	ˈɑːl̪ɪ	/ˈaːlɪ/
grey hair	ˈɹɐbʌʎʊ	ˈdʒabʊʎʊ	ˈɹɐbʊju	/ˈɹabuʎu/

Make sure to leave plenty of space for notes, comments and questions.

I also strongly recommend segmenting the audio recordings of your wordlists so that it is easy to play multiple tokens of the same word. There are several ways to do this and some tips are given on the book's web site. Playing tokens of words one after another will help you get information on free variation.

Once you have hypotheses about the phoneme system and allophony, write them down! Make sure you keep track not only of your data, but also of your analyses.

3.6 What to record?

If you are doing fieldwork for a specific project, you will already have a good idea of what you want to do. If you are doing a general description of the language, or if you have not decided what area to specialize in, it can be difficult to know where to start. Start with the wordlist, and take things from there.

There is a temptation to spend most of your time collecting data, perhaps delaying transcription and analysis until you return from the field. If you are working on a highly endangered language, I think you should record as much good quality data as possible, even if you do not have time to analyse all of it. As you work on your data more, the unanalysed parts of your collection will become easier to deal with. You may be able to work with part-speakers later on in talking about the texts, and you have a lifetime to puzzle over your elicitations. But if the basic materials aren't there, they can't be recovered later on. This is not to say that you should just record and record with nothing else. Unanalysed streams of speech where we don't know any of the words are also not very helpful. If the language is in a precarious state, or if you are not sure that you'll have more than one fieldtrip, you should try to cover the basic phonology, morphology and clause structure as soon as possible.

Ladefoged (2003:8) reports an experience with a speaker who wanted to tell traditional stories rather than do the wordlists Ladefoged needed for his phonetic analysis. Don't let these opportunities pass by. Even if you have no use for the data, there may well be someone who will need it later on. In 1960 Geoff O'Grady met a Bardi speaker. He had no idea how many people spoke Bardi but assumed it was endangered (a safe bet in most of Australia). He was only there for a day and would not be able to use the recordings himself, but he thought there would probably be someone who would be able to make use of it, so he recorded the woman describing the pictures in a UN pamphlet in Bardi. It is a unique recording: there are very few tape recordings of people of that age speaking the language.

It is important to use your recorder as much as possible. You never know what will be useful later on. You don't want to miss anything, and digital data are easy to store, so unless recording would be impossible or inappropriate, record as much as is practical. That is, I disagree with Crowley's (2007:101–2) comment that you should use the recorder less as you get to know the language better.

In Appendix B, I have given a sample programme for a documentation/description trip. I don't recommend sticking to it absolutely, however. It's more an indication of the relative amounts of time to spend on different topics. If the morphology of the language is very complicated, you will need to spend time getting paradigms straight. If the phonology of the language is complex, the earlier stages of elicitation may take a while. A good general rule to follow is to start simple, but don't stay simple. Get gradually more complex, go back and check, and continue.

3.7 Summary and further reading

The following chapters extend the ideas and methods introduced in this chapter. Now that you have a small amount of data, it's a good time to think about how you're going to organize your future field data so that you can make the most of it. The chapters after that discuss elicitation of different topics in more detail, beginning with phonetics and phonology and moving on to the lexicon/semantics, morphology and syntax. It is somewhat artificial to present these chapters in this way, since you will work on more than one area at once. You will be getting syntax data at the same time that you're working on morphology, and even while eliciting with particular syntactic constructions in mind you may come across new morphology or more data points for phonology. You will continue working on the semantics of individual lexical items even after you have achieved fluency in the language. However, reference grammars are written with these categories in mind, and it's very common to have students write papers on the phonology, morphology and syntax of the language as though these categories are discrete.

3.7.1 Summary of procedures

Here is a summary of the procedures discussed in this chapter:

1. Elicit some words and record them.
2. Transcribe them while the person is speaking, using narrow transcription.
3. Go over your recordings later and correct errors.
4. Make a list of the sounds you have attested in your data.
5. Look for any minimal pairs. Make a note of them and add those phonemes to your list or chart of phonemes.
6. Look for obvious allophonic conditioning.
7. Make a list of 'unknowns'.
8. Get more data. Does this new data solve any of your unknowns? Does it create any new ones?
9. Now, for your ambiguous or insufficient data, go hunting for solutions.
10. Incorporate this new data. Go back to your phoneme list and add the new items you've discovered.

Finally, memorize the wordlists from early sessions as soon as possible. That will give you some vocabulary that you've already mastered, and it will give you a reference point for transcribing new words. For example, it will let you ask questions such as 'is this the same sound as the first sound in the word for potato?'.

3.7.2 Further reading

- **First Field sessions**: Hale (2001), Newman and Ratliff (2001); the website for this book has an example 'first' elicitation session (using Hungarian).
- **Phonology problem solving**: Clark and Yallop (1995).

THE INTERNATIONAL PHONETIC ALPHABET (revised to 2005)

CONSONANTS (PULMONIC)

	Bilabial	Labiodental	Dental	Alveolar	Postalveolar	Retroflex	Palatal	Velar	Uvular	Pharyngeal	Glottal
Plosive	p b			t d		ʈ ɖ	c ɟ	k ɡ	q ɢ		ʔ
Nasal	m	ɱ		n		ɳ	ɲ	ŋ	N		
Trill	B			r					R		
Tap or Flap		ⱱ		ɾ		ɽ					
Fricative	ɸ β	f v	θ ð	s z	ʃ ʒ	ʂ ʐ	ç ʝ	x ɣ	χ ʁ	ħ ʕ	h ɦ
Lateral fricative				ɬ ɮ							
Approximant		ʋ		ɹ		ɻ	j	ɰ			
Lateral approximant				l		ɭ	ʎ	L			

Where symbols appear in pairs, the one to the right represents a voiced consonant. Shaded areas denote articulations judged impossible.

CONSONANTS (NON-PULMONIC)

Clicks	Voiced implosives	Ejectives
ʘ Bilabial	ɓ Bilabial	' Examples:
ǀ Dental	ɗ Dental/alveolar	pʼ Bilabial
ǃ (Post)alveolar	ʄ Palatal	tʼ Dental/alveolar
ǂ Palatoalveolar	ɠ Velar	kʼ Velar
ǁ Alveolar lateral	ʛ Uvular	sʼ Alveolar fricative

OTHER SYMBOLS

ʍ Voiceless labial-velar fricative	ɕ ʑ Alveolo-palatal fricatives
w Voiced labial-velar approximant	ɺ Voiced alveolar lateral flap
ɥ Voiced labial-palatal approximant	ɧ Simultaneous ʃ and x
ʜ Voiceless epiglottal fricative	
ʢ Voiced epiglottal fricative	Affricates and double articulations can be represented by two symbols joined by a tie bar if necessary. k͡p t͡s
ʡ Epiglottal plosive	

VOWELS

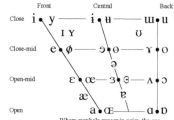

Where symbols appear in pairs, the one to the right represents a rounded vowel.

SUPRASEGMENTALS

ˈ	Primary stress	ˌfoʊnəˈtɪʃən
ˌ	Secondary stress	
ː	Long	eː
ˑ	Half-long	eˑ
˘	Extra-short	ĕ
|	Minor (foot) group	
‖	Major (intonation) group	
.	Syllable break	ɹi.ækt
‿	Linking (absence of a break)	

DIACRITICS

Diacritics may be placed above a symbol with a descender, e.g. ŋ̊

̥	Voiceless	n̥ d̥	̤	Breathy voiced	b̤ a̤	̪	Dental	t̪ d̪
̬	Voiced	s̬ t̬	̰	Creaky voiced	b̰ a̰	̺	Apical	t̺ d̺
ʰ	Aspirated	tʰ dʰ	̼	Linguolabial	t̼ d̼	̻	Laminal	t̻ d̻
̹	More rounded	ɔ̹	ʷ	Labialized	tʷ dʷ	̃	Nasalized	ẽ
̜	Less rounded	ɔ̜	ʲ	Palatalized	tʲ dʲ	ⁿ	Nasal release	dⁿ
̟	Advanced	u̟	ˠ	Velarized	tˠ dˠ	ˡ	Lateral release	dˡ
̠	Retracted	e̠	ˤ	Pharyngealized	tˤ dˤ	̚	No audible release	d̚
̈	Centralized	ë	̴	Velarized or pharyngealized	ɫ			
̽	Mid-centralized	e̽	̝	Raised	e̝	(ɹ̝ = voiced alveolar fricative)		
̩	Syllabic	n̩	̞	Lowered	e̞	(β̞ = voiced bilabial approximant)		
̯	Non-syllabic	e̯	̘	Advanced Tongue Root	e̘			
˞	Rhoticity	ɚ a˞	̙	Retracted Tongue Root	e̙			

TONES AND WORD ACCENTS

LEVEL			CONTOUR		
e̋ or	˥	Extra high	ě or	˩˥	Rising
é	˦	High	ê	˥˩	Falling
ē	˧	Mid	e᷄	˦˥	High rising
è	˨	Low	e᷅	˩˨	Low rising
ȅ	˩	Extra low	e᷈	˧˦˧	Rising-falling
↓		Downstep	↗		Global rise
↑		Upstep	↘		Global fall

4
Data Organization
and Archiving

Everyone has their own way of taking notes and organizing data. Some insist on hard-backed books, others swear by index-cards and folders, others use spare envelopes. Many transcribe and organize data directly on computer and use little paper at all. The aim of this chapter is not to tell you which notebook to use. Rather, I raise some of the issues in data collection and organization which you should think about. I also give a checklist for some of the metalinguistic data you should be collecting and some thoughts on how to store it.

Data collection, organization, annotation and analysis is a complicated multi-step process. Such processes are often described in terms of 'workflow' – that is, what happens to data as it goes through different processes, what order those processes should occur in, and so on. By now you've probably already done some work with a speaker and collected some data. You may have already made a copy of the recording and transcribed it. The order in which you complete the tasks associated with creating, processing and analysing materials is called the 'workflow'. A suggest workflow plan is given on the following page (see also Thieberger 2004). The rest of this chapter picks up on various components of this workflow diagram. The items in the square boxes are the main steps in the process, while the ovals are the tasks in each step.

This chapter assumes that you will have time during your fieldtrip to spend many hours per day processing data. It might be hard, if not impossible, to do this regularly. Many fieldworkers work in communities where it would be rude to leave a guest on their own. In that case, it's all the more important to take notes of your recordings as you make them, and to have some way of sorting out your data in the time you have. Note that in the diagram, there are many more tasks that take place after the session than during or before it!

Field workflow

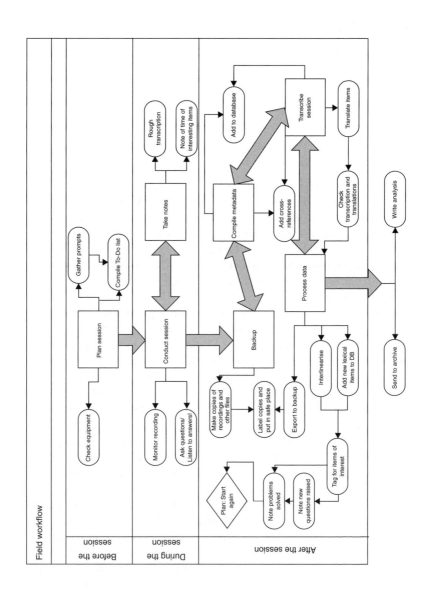

4.1   Before the session

In the previous chapter we talked about what to do in the early sessions, and we mentioned the importance of planning in advance. I recommend planning at least two sessions ahead. That way if things go quicker than expected or you have less time to plan than expected, you won't run out of material.

Fieldwork preparation is a little like class preparation. How detailed your written preparation is depends on your confidence and experience. Your ability to judge how long activities will take will get better, as will your confidence in explaining prompts and keeping to do lists in your head. Early on, though, it's better to write all of this down.

4.1.1   Notebooks

If you are handwriting much of your notes, write on one side of the page only. Use the other side for notes, later corrections and cross-references. Don't write on every line. If you cross things out or write glosses above words in your notes, you will not want to write on every line. Make a note of abbreviations and symbols used in the front of the book. Start each section of notes with the date, time and place, and speaker (see further §4.4).

When using handwritten notes, always use a notebook with a binding. Some recommend hardback notebooks because of the durability of the covers and the stability of the bindings. They are quite heavy, though. I prefer spiral bound A5 100-page notebooks with cardboard or plastic covers because they are easily balanced on my knee, and they aren't too heavy. They also fit into a standard size sealable plastic bags and are easy to photocopy or scan.

We want fieldnotes to last as long as possible, whether print or digital. There are some things you can do to make this more likely. Use acid-free paper and ink. Gel pens look pretty but most of them aren't acid free. Highlighter deteriorates rapidly. Everyone has their own opinions about whether to use pencil. Pencil doesn't bleed when the paper gets wet (unlike ink), but it does smudge if you're carrying your notebook around a lot and the pages rub against each other. Ball point pens seem to be more durable – the ink is smudge-proof and you can still usually rescue most of the information on a piece of paper that's been through the washing machine in a pocket.

Another aspect of durability and recoverability is making sure that pieces of paper are not lost (or put through the washing machine in the first place). Avoid the temptation of writing vocabulary items on the backs of envelopes, or at the very least stick the envelope into a note-book or copy the information to your fieldnotes as soon as possible.

There are several ways of organizing the notes themselves. Some people like to use a single notebook for everything, while others have several: one for elicitation, one for transcription of texts, another for miscellaneous queries. The most useful system will depend on how organized your field sessions are. I do lots of different things in my elicitation sessions so I would be constantly swapping notebooks if I had one for each area of fieldwork.

You need to be able to decipher what you meant when you come back to your notes later. Go over your notes after the session and add anything that you remember from the session that isn't in the notes (make sure you can identify what's a later addition), and annotate them for hypotheses about the data, questions, comments, and notes on cross-referencing. There are a couple of ways to keep track of this information – you can use highlighters or post-it notes and page markers (although bear in mind that highlighters aren't very archivally friendly) or different coloured pens (but that information will be lost when you photocopy your notes).[1] Or tag comments in your database electronically (this is preferable).

Avoid the temptation to make corrections by writing over what you first wrote. Perhaps you first write

(5) bubatj   'hair'

but you need to change it to *bupatj*. Don't just write over the *b*. It's surprisingly difficult to read this sort of correction unless you know what it should be. (That is, if you write over the *b* and come back to it in 6 months' time, unless you know which phoneme it should be it's usu-ally impossible to tell which was written over.) Cross it out and write above, below, or somewhere obvious. It is also useful to be able to see what you first wrote. You can take notice of this information to diag-nose your own frequent transcription errors or pronunciation variations among consultants.

(6) ~~bubatj~~   bupatj   'hair'

4.1.2 Structure of the project

It is a very good idea to work out a basic directory structure before you leave the field. That way, you will not be trying to organize parts and files the same time that you are collecting your first data. It is much easier to think about this in advance than to try to reorganize once you have a large number of files.

There are a couple of different things to consider. First is the directory or file structure that you will use. That is, where will you keep all the different files that you will be creating? The second question is what different types of software you will be using and what different files you will need in order to carry out work.

Some people like to keep all their files in a single directory. That way, they know exactly where everything is, because it's all in the same place! A set of directories is preferable. A possible directory structure would include different directories for audio files, transcriptions, budget forms and other reports, secondary analysis such as articles, assignments, or your dissertation; lexicon files, or other categories of this type that you find useful. A project structure might look like this:

Folder	Example contents
Articles, Talks	Articles, talks, seminars, conference presentations and so on that you give about the language
Audio	Audio (and video) files
Data files	Transcriptions of texts, fieldnote database files (e.g. Toolbox files) of elicitation
Genealogies	This material could be restricted and therefore should be kept in its own directory so it is not inadvertently given to others.
Housekeeping	Grant reports, applications for permits, letters written in relation to the project.
Learners materials	Lessons or school materials created as part of the documentation project (if appropriate)
Lexicon	Files associated with lexical elicitation and dictionary compilation
Metadata	Your metadata database and other associated documents (e.g. the explanation of your transcription system)
Miscellaneous	Anything else
Other people's work	If you have data that other people have collected on the language, it's good to keep it separate from your own data.
Photos	Fieldwork photos and associated metadata.

4.2 After the session

4.2.1 Make a backup

Make backup copies of your recordings as soon as possible.[2] This goes for audio recordings and any other files (e.g., your database where you keep all the information about what is in which recording). Make sure that the backup worked (i.e., that the copy didn't become corrupted). Never directly edit your original recordings. You could accidentally delete part of the recording, or resample it, or a file could become corrupted.

As soon as the media is recorded, make sure you can't accidentally write over it. (Slide the tab on the minidisk or DAT tape to 'read only', or break the tab on the cassette, or finalize the CD.) When transferring files make sure that you always know which folder is the original and which is the updated version. There are several ways of backing up your recordings and files. I recommend at least two different backups (stored in different places). Portable hard drives are not very expensive. Data DVDs are an efficient way of backing up large amounts of sound data. CDs are also good. Hard drives can fail so do not rely on them alone.

How often should you make backups of your data? How much data are you prepared to lose? I back up my transcription files each day in the field, and I burn CDs every three or four days (depending on how much transcription I've done). Audio gets backed up as soon as it's transferred to computer, and I post the backups every few weeks to my regular address.[3]

Document everything. Make sure you have audition sheets[4] for the recordings you've made and that your recordings are labelled in an informative way. Always keep blank media in a different place from recorded media. Some people have a special bag for recorded tapes; some use transparent resealable plastic bags. Others keep blank media in the same bag as the recording equipment and recorded media from that session go in another bag (e.g., with fieldnotes). However you do it, keep them separate.

4.2.2 Label the recordings

It's important to know what recordings you've made and where they are. Labelling is crucial. Write in permanent marker (not pencil). The least it should contain is the tape number, your name and the date, and preferably there should be other information such as language, speaker and key words. Write as much on the label as you can fit. The same information should be on the box. Record the same information on the tape itself. Ideally do it at the start of the recording. That way, if the label falls off and you lose the box, you will still know what's in the recording.[5] A script might be something like this:

(7) 'Tape number 10, recorded at One Arm Point by Claire Bowern on the 25th of July, 2005. Claire Bowern and Mary Smith are checking dictionary words.'

In reality I have always found this almost impossible to do. I don't usually know exactly what I'm going to record until I arrive at the speakers' house and find out who is around, if they want to work, if it'll be possible to record, etc. When we're ready to start I don't want to waste time with a spiel. There are a few ways around this. One is to leave a minute on the front of an analogue tape and record it later (but be very careful to make sure you don't record over what you've already done!) The other (which is easy with digital recording) is to record a summary of what's on the track at the end of the day.

Another crucial component to recording organization is having some sort of numbering system for your recordings. Some systems are:

- each tape or recording is numbered through your career (e.g., 1–1000)
- each fieldtrip has a number (1.1–10, 2.1–100) etc. – numbered by collection
- numbered sequentially by language worked on (B1–100, Y1–100)
- using the date of recording (20050107a, 50020107b, 20050411)

Whatever system you use, each recording should be uniquely identified. If you are using reusable media, such as compact flash cards, each session (or 'episode') might get its own number. Whatever the system, stick to it and document it.

A further possible consideration is how you will deal with other recordings. You might have access to previous linguists' recordings, or radio recordings, or recordings made by speakers themselves. You need to decide how these will be incorporated into your cataloguing system (or if they will be). Will they get the same numbering system as your own recordings? If so, how will you keep them separate (given that recordings made by others are the intellectual property of someone else)? If they are kept separate, will you be able to find things on them?

This all sounds like a lot of work. It is, but it's nothing compared to the pain of not knowing what you have, or accidentally deleting a recording.

4.2.3 Recovering information

The reason you are going to the field in the first place is to make a record of a language. Presumably you want the data to be accessible not only to yourself but potentially to other people as well, including other researchers and speakers of the language. At the very least you will want to organize your data so that you can find things in it later on. Therefore it is worth investing some time and thought in how you organize your fieldnotes. Don't rely on your memory; you won't remember what's in which recording in six months, or what a particular question mark meant. Did it mean that the gloss is suspicious, or that you aren't quite sure of the transcription, or that you want to check that the word is in your main database? Finally, the media should be durable. It would be a disaster if you lost everything because someone spilt a drink on your laptop, or you lose the piece of paper with your coding system.

4.3 Software for data processing

There is a lot of software available for linguists to use in data management. What you choose will depend on your level of computer literacy, issues such as font support, existing materials, and what you want to end up doing. The three most important aspects of fieldwork software are:

1. You must be able to get your data into the program easily. Fieldwork and data management are time-consuming enough without the data entry being difficult.
2. You need to be able to find things in your data easily.
3. You need to be able to get data out of the database, for example in producing reports for the language community, getting examples out of your database and into the text of your reference grammar, and when converting between programs.

Some software programs are easier to use than others. If you find mastering new programs difficult, use one that is on the easier end. There is no point in using a program with multiple capabilities if you know you won't be using any of them.

What fonts or keyboard input will you need to write the language? If the language you are working on uses a script that is written from right-to-left, obviously you will need to use a program that can handle data entry in that format. Will you have any special fonts you will need to use and can they be used in all the programs you will need without conversion? Thirdly, will others be able to use your data? If you are working in an area where the schools all use a particular font, can you share data with them?

Minimize the time you have to spend retyping or re-entering data between programs. Currently, there's no one method that will get your data into all programs, but there are ways of minimizing the wasted time. Ideally you should be able to transcribe your tapes and then move data around, annotate it and include it in a final write-up without having to retype.

Archiving should also be on your mind, even for your own fieldnotes. Is your setup one that others can decipher? The format for your working documents and those for an archive might be different, but you will save yourself a lot of work if you take archiving into consideration from the beginning, for example by transparent file naming. (See further Bird and Simons (2003).) Some specific software recommendations are given on the web site which accompanies this book. As a minimum, you will need:

- A digital audio (and video) player, preferably one which will let you align transcriptions with the audio
- A database to keep your transcriptions, lexical files and notes in, preferably one which allows for semi-automatic interlinear glossing.
- A word processor for writing articles, your dissertation, etc.
- Specialized linguistic software, such as for spectrographic analysis, vowel plotting, a statistics program, etc.

The simplest way to organize data is to type everything in a word processor. You could have one file for your fieldnotes, another for your lexicon, and a third for analysis. I don't recommend this approach, though. For example, perhaps you need to find all utterances by one speaker. You would have to go through all your data and pull out all the examples of that speaker by hand. A much better way to store your fieldnotes is in a database. There are programs which let you build a dictionary and export the records in a consistent format to another program. Even in the 'old days' before computerized database software, linguists used card files to organize their data before a dictionary typescript was produced. A computer database allows you to do the same thing as the card files. Formatting a dictionary completely by hand, as a Word document, with correct alphabetization, formatting and so on, would be very difficult to do, and if you wanted to do something as simple as displaying all the nouns in the data, you would have to go through the examples by hand.

A very commonly used fieldwork database program is *Toolbox*. It allows for the creation of a structured dictionary, semi-automatic inter-linearization, fieldnote compilation, and other tools such as corpus searching and wordlist building.

4.4   Metadata

Metadata refers to any information about the records you are making. That is, it is data about the data. It is useful to get into good habits about metadata early. Do an audition sheet for your recordings at the end of each day. It will save a lot of time later (if only for your executor)! It makes your data easily searchable; if you have a summary of your recordings with information about key topics, speakers, and so on, it is much easier to find a particular section than if you have to hunt through them all. It lets you sort out which transcriptions should be a priority. In field-methods classes, having a shared collection of metadata lets others in the class know what has been elicited already if they weren't present at the session. Linguists already use metadata when they make a note of the date of the elicitation session and who it was conducted with. This section extends that idea further.

Different types of metadata will apply to different parts of your collection. For example, you don't need information about sampling rates when you are providing metadata about your consultant, but such data are needed for digital recordings. Minimally you will have metadata which applies to the collection as a whole, to individual item types in the collection (e.g., notes, recordings and so on) and to participants in the project.

A set of sample tables for compiling metadata are given in Appendix A and further sample databases (and further links to information) are given online.

4.4.1   Project metadata

The project metadata includes information about the collector (you), who funded it, the language under study, the place the recordings were made, and other general information about the materials you have collected and the format of the items you are depositing.

4.4.2   Item metadata

Most of the metadata you compile will be about individual recordings (or 'items') in the project. Here is a list of common metadata categories, along with an explanation. These categories are used in the sample field session on the web page.

Name of category	Explanation
Unique Identifier	Each item in your collection should have a unique number (that is, so there's some way of unambiguously referring to each item)
Item Title	A title for each item
Collector	The person responsible for gathering the data in the first place. For your fieldnotes, this will be you
Place	The place where the recording was made
Subject language	The language under study
Contact Language	The language the item is in (and, dialect if necessary)
Speaker	the name of the speaker or participants in the item
Date recorded	The data the recording was made. YYYY-MM-DD format avoids ambiguity
Description	Description of the item
Links	Any cross-referencing, e.g., to recordings, video, photos and other transcriptions
Type of Item	What type of item it is (e.g., narrative, song, transcription, analysis)
Format	format of the medium (PDF, WAV, XML, etc.)
Recording information	For digital recordings, the sampling rate at which it was recorded, and other technical information
Rights and Access	Who has rights to the material, and whether access to the material is restricted
Comments	Miscellaneous comments

4.4.3 Participant metadata

There is additional metadata to record about the people whose language you are recording. As you get to know your consultant(s) you will find out something about their lives. You will want to know this metadata in order to pinpoint possible factors in variation, for example. Here are some suggestions for metadata categories pertinent to consultants:

Name of category	Explanation
Name	
Other names	Other names they go by, e.g., nicknames
Pseudonym	If your consultant is referred to by a pseudonym in your published information, record the pseudonym here
Social status	Clan/tribe/caste, social class (if relevant)
Age	Age or approximate age
Occupation	
Education	
Marital status	
Language background	Are they a native speaker of the language? If not, how did they learn the language? Other languages known (and how acquired)
Comments	Any other relevant information (e.g., relationship to other speakers in the collection)

Make sure that people are happy with what you've put in the public metadata. Some people might not want a lot of information about themselves in the public domain. Not all metadata needs to be publicly identifiable. It may not be appropriate to ask for all this information at once, and not as soon as you meet your consultants. But you could ask someone to tell you about themselves as part of a recorded narrative in the language, and make up one about yourself to test your knowledge of the language. Don't forget that people are probably just as curious about you as you are about them.

It is also possible that your consultants will not want to be identified at all. In that case you should have them pick a pseudonym which can be used. Only you and they will be able to identify the speaker from the pseudonym. You should still collect this information, but keep it safe.

4.5 Processing field data

The following sections contain some general information on points that you should take into consideration when organizing your field data. You need to consider what an 'item' is: Data could be organized around 'tracks' or 'episodes' within a recording. An episode might be a single session or a story within the session. Each episode would be an item in your collection. Giving related items the same file name makes associating data easier. For example, if your recording is given the number 150307-01 (first session on 15 March 2007), the audio file could be 150307-01.wav, the transcription 150307-01.eaf (if you are using the *Elan* transcription program to link audio and text), the Toolbox record would be 150307-01, and so on.

It is also very useful to be able to keep track of which pieces of raw data have been processed, particularly if you are not working on all sessions sequentially. If you have a database for your metadata, it is easy to have a field in the database where you can record whether the words for that session have been added to your master lexicon, or whether the transcription has been checked with a native speaker. It's helpful to have such annotations within the file (or at the top of the notebook page) too.

We've talked a lot about keeping track of your data and processing it. However, it's a good idea to be able to keep track of analyses too. Some people use a separate notebook to jot down ideas and notes about problems that need solving; others have a database, others note them in the fieldnotes themselves.

4.5.1 Interlinearizing

Providing interlinear glossing to texts adds a lot of value to your data. It makes them much easier for you and other linguists to use, and it provides an implicit working out of your analysis of the language.

You'll need to decide how much detail you want to give in your interlinearizing. If you're glossing examples of complex allomorphy for the phonology chapter of your dissertation, you are going to be more interested in the underlying representation and morphemes than for your chapter on discourse organization. If your target audience is language learners, using lots of abbreviations and terminology will be confusing. After you spend some time working on the language you will be familiar enough with it that you won't need glossing to tell you what the words mean. Fluent speakers, if they read, won't need it either.

Opinions vary on how helpful interlinearization is for language learners. I've been told by someone with a lot of experience in producing literacy materials that native speakers find it distracting, especially if they have limited literacy skills. On the other hand, I gave some inter-linearized texts to Bardi learners and they really liked it. The English word sometimes acted as a prompt for the Bardi word if they were having trouble reading that. It was less daunting than the text with no breaks. It was a huge help with learning grammar, but it would not have been useful to people who knew the language already.

Here's an example of a Bardi sentence with various levels of interlin-earization. Version 1 is what's used in the Bardi oral history book, where a few stories have interlinear glossing. There are no morpheme bound-aries marked and glosses are full English words or phrases. It is very similar to a free translation which has been reordered so that the words line up. Version 2 is what I use in conference papers and articles which I write about Bardi syntax. The glossing is more detailed and includes abbreviations. Version 3 includes a full morphological analysis (with rep-resentation of deleted segments) and all morphemes are fully glossed.

(8)	Nganjalagal	oorany	roowil	innyana	jaarla.
Version 1	I saw	a woman	walk	she did	on the beach.
Version 2	1SG-TR-see-PST	woman	walk	3SG-TR-'catch'-PST	beach
Version 3	nga-n-(ng)-jala-gal	oorany-ø	roowil	i-n-(ng-)nya-na	jaarla-ø.
	1-TR-PST-see-REM.PST	woman-ABS	walk+	3-TR-PST-'catch'-REM.PST	beach-LOC

'I saw the woman walking on the beach.'

4.6   Archiving

4.6.1   Reasons for archiving

There are two main reasons that raw field data should be archived. The most important is to keep the data safe. Original fieldnotes could get lost when you move house, or your house could be flooded or burn down. The notes and tapes could get mouldy if they aren't stored properly. Your computer could be stolen. Professional archives are designed to prevent data loss through catastrophes like this. After all, with so many lan-guages endangered, we don't need to add to potential loss of linguistic diversity by storing the only records of a language improperly.

The second reason is to let others know what has been recorded on the language. There are too many cases of duplicated effort because earl-ier work was either not known about or unobtainable (for an example, see

Bowern 2008). This allows communities, linguists and other interested parties find out what has been done on the language.

Archiving is not the same thing as just 'putting your materials on the web'. The purpose of archiving is to preserve the material for the future. This is not the same as making the material available on the internet. For example, digital audio files would normally be archived at a higher sampling rate than would be practical for uploading to the web. Files for distribution need to be easily accessible, whereas archived files do not. A web distribution would have to protect anonymity (if applicable) – for example if your consultants wished to remain anonymous, you would not publish the key to their identities and pseudonyms in the web materials distribution.

4.6.2 Places for archiving linguistic data

Your university library may have archiving provisions (e.g., a DSpace electronic archive), and there are several area archives and libraries, such as the Smithsonian Institutions, the Alaskan Native Language Center, Berkeley's Survey of California and Other Indian languages,[6] The Hans Rausing Endangered Languages Documentation Project,[7] the Australian Institute of Aboriginal and Torres Strait Islander Studies,[8] and the African Language Material Archive to name just a few. The participants list of the Digital Electronic Languages and Musics Archive Network (www.delaman.org) is a good place to start.

4.6.3 Archive contents

You should deposit your field recordings, original notes, audition sheets, and any secondary analyses (including conference papers). Also archive anything which is vital to the project which might not be easy to recover if it's lost. This would include any fonts which are vital to the project, for example. Don't include in your archive anything that's not related to the project. It is very easy to end up with personal letters and other such things in your fieldnotes.

You may also want to consider sending to an archive anything that you have worked on that has created 'added value'. For example, you may have gone through the text collection of someone who worked on the language previously, compiled metadata descriptions for it and annotated the texts. This document now has added value, because it contains much more information than it did before.

Archive anything that you would not want to lose, and anything that cannot be easily recreated from other materials. So, for example, you may not want to archive all of the individual drafts of your dissertation, and all of the drafts of your transcriptions, unless they contain lots of information which you cannot get from the final copy. You may also want to archive down-sampled versions of your field tapes if you spent a great deal of time compiling them, but since they can be easily created from the higher quality recordings, it's not vital that they be included in the archive as long as the original higher quality recordings are included. Likewise, any secondary materials, such as articles, web sites and your dissertation, should be part of the collection.

Find out in advance what formatting requirements the archive has. For example, some archives require digital files, whereas others prefer hard copies. Make sure that computer files are archived in a format that is recoverable later. Remember Word 2.0? How many of you can still read documents in that format? Do your best to ensure that your documents are readable in the future. You should save a copy of your files as rtf, plain text, or html as well as Word or other word processing programs. They are open-source formats and have a much better change of the data being able to be read in future. Have a printout of important notes on acid-free paper that's stored somewhere safe.

Work on a project is seldom done, so it is unwise to plan to wait until the project is completely finished before sending materials to an archive. Usually the best time is at the end of the grant period; archive raw data and everything that is finished at that point. You can always add to your collection later.

4.7   Further reading

- **Archiving**: Gibbon, Bow et al. (2004), Johnson (2004), Musgrave (2006), Robinson (2006), Trilsbeek and Wittenberg (2006).
- **Fieldnotes:** Emerson, Fretz and Shaw (1995).
- **Metadata**: Wynne (2005: ch. 3).
- **Software:** Antworth and Valentine (1998) (see also the book's web site).
- **Workflow:** Thieberger (2004).

5
Fieldwork on Phonetics and Phonology

In Chapter 3 we talked about basic analysis of early data, especially in working out a phoneme inventory. This chapter extends these ideas to discuss phonetic fieldwork (particularly in acoustic phonetics) and gives some suggestions for research design for phonetic analysis.

5.1 Broad and narrow transcription

In §3.2, we discussed a plan for discovering the phonemes of a language which relied on transcribing with as much detail as possible. However, there are different levels of detail in a transcription. The levels are often characterized as 'broad' and 'narrow', although of course it is possible to distinguish various degrees of 'narrowness' and 'broadness'. A broad transcription will be phonemic rather than phonetic. It may or may not include notation for stress or tone (if stress is regular, it would not be included in a broad transcription). A narrow transcription, on the other hand, would normally include stress and allophonic variation.

When transcribing your early data, use a narrow transcription. You don't know what features are going to be relevant. If you later find out that two phones you thought were separate phonemes are actually allophones, it's easier to collapse the transcription than to go through all your data later and work out which of the sounds you transcribed as *n* are really *n* and which ones are actually *ŋ*. Later on, as you gain familiarity with the language, broad transcription will let you transcribe data more quickly. A broad transcription also makes searching for all instances of a word easier (otherwise you would have to search for all instances of each allophonic realization). You can make notes on the narrow transcription of individual lexical items by using a transcription program with multiple tiers. The broad transcription would be done on one tier, while another tier would be used for more information about items of interest. For example, in English, word-final voiceless stops are frequently either glottalized, or not released at all. A phonemic transcription would represent them all with a voiceless stop symbol, but a phonetic transcription would show whether the stop was fully released, glottalized or unreleased.

There is a continual tension in fieldwork between the need to standardize for efficient searching on the one hand, and accurately representing what people actually say on the other. People produce all sorts of linguistic data, and they make speech errors. All of this is interesting for linguists on some level, but if you are transcribing for edited works, much of that will need to be standardized to make the work usable for speakers. If you have the same word transcribed in four different ways in a learner's book, it will be very confusing to those trying to learn the language or the writing system. They will not be able to tell whether spellings like <kev> and <gev> represent a minimal pair or two ways of writing the same word. Therefore, I recommend (contra Vaux and Cooper 1999:31) transcribing consistently and phonemically once you know what the phonemes are, rather than always primarily transcribing the speech forms.

5.2   Research design

In this section I have included some general principles of phonetic research design and experimental methods.

5.2.1   Plan your experiment in advance

Form the hypothesis you want to test, and formulate a way to test the hypothesis. Don't try to test too many things at once or you will end up with too much undirected data, and too many confounding variables.

Let's consider a simple example. You notice in your fieldwork language that vowels seem to be quite a bit longer before voiced stops than before voiceless stops. Your working hypothesis would be that vowel length is correlated with the voicing of the following stop. To test this hypothesis, you would not only have to measure vowels in the relevant environments, but you would also have to attempt to rule out other possible conditioning factors. Some of those factors might include the vowel length being the primary distinction, and the stop voicing being secondary. You would need to rule out speaker variation, and other factors, such as stress.

5.2.2 Design the experiment

In order to test your hypothesis, you need to design an experiment. In our experiment about correlations between vowel length and stop voicing, the logical experiment would be to record a controlled wordlist which included enough tokens of the relevant words, with the vowels before voiced and voiceless stops in a variety of syllable structures and stress positions, and then to ask several different speakers to read the words in a carrier phrase.

5.2.3 Picking research participants

It is a good idea to make initial recordings from several different people early on in your field session. This gives you a chance to hear the language from different speakers, and reduces the chance of you biasing your description of the language towards a single speaker's idiolect. It also gives you the opportunity to meet different people (hopefully several different families in the speech community) and lets you evaluate different speakers' strengths. Also, some people simply speak more clearly than others.

For phonetic research purposes, the 'ideal' speaker is not too old and not too young. They are a monolingual speaker of the language under study; they have all their own teeth and no speech problems. In practice, no speakers of the language may fulfil the 'ideal'. In many parts of the world multilingualism is widespread, so there may not be any monolingual speakers for you to record. If the language is highly endangered it might not be spoken by anyone young, or anyone with all their teeth.

5.2.4 The wordlist

The wordlist itself is important. A list with examples of all the major contrasts in a language can lead to very long wordlists. You need enough tokens of each word to produce statistically significant results, but not too many to bore your research participants. Three tokens of each word is usual, but you might not be able to get three all the time. Not everyone will see why you need to repeat the words, and they may get very bored quickly. Your consultant may be insulted that you do not accept what they say the first time. In that case explain why you need several examples (in case there is noise in the background, or you didn't hear it properly the first time, or that people might say the same word in a few slightly different ways, or that you just need lots of examples). Make sure that they know you are not questioning their ability as speakers by asking for repetitions. Another way to elicit repetition is to write down the word, and ask the consultant to say it again so that you can check that you wrote it down the right way.

Your wordlist should be randomized. Even if you compile it by grouping all the long vowels in monosyllables, make sure that all those words are not next to one another, or you could generate priming effects. If you have difficulty getting a consultant to repeat tokens, you can have words in the list more than once. This also minimizes the problem of list intonation on repetitions. If you do this, however, it is a good idea to tell the person that the words are in there more than once, otherwise they might think that it is a mistake.

You will also need to have some control words. For example, if you are mostly interested in the realization of a particular consonant word initially, you would not want to have all the words in the sample start with that sound because the consultant might realize why you have those words. Furthermore, if you are measuring coarticulation effects, you will need examples of all segments without the coarticulation targets so that you can examine whether coarticulation is present (i.e., in order to measure the extent of coarticulation, you need to have noncoarticulated samples to compare them with).

5.2.5   The script

Here is an example of a possible script:

(9) 'I am going to say an English word. After I say the word, please say the word with the same meaning in your language. Please say your word three times so that I can make sure I have heard it correctly. Ready?'

You:	Number 1: hair
Consultant:	...
You:	Number 2: foot
Consultant:	...

Avoid citation tone or quick repetition by explaining the consultants should speak 'normally' and clearly). You might need to embed the target in a frame, such as 'that's called *X*.' Don't always use the same frame in that case, although use one that is equivalent. If your language is a tone language, you should always embed the target in a frame. In the case of languages with extensive tone sandhi, it might be necessary to have several frames. In that case you might need to know quite a lot about the language before designing a wordlist that will be useful.

It is often recommended that the researcher does not say the word in the target language themselves. This is to avoid priming the speaker to use a certain variant if you use one variant over another. Avoid having the consultant read the list because of the possibilities for reading pronunciation. Reading intonation is different from speaking intonation. In practice, however, avoiding both of these can be rather difficult. Translating back into the target language may throw up a different word. For example, in Yan-nhaŋu there are three words in current usage for 'mother': ŋamarrku<u>l</u>i, ŋamuŋu, and ŋä<u>n</u><u>d</u>i. Any of these would be an acceptable response to the prompt 'say the word for *mother* in Yan-nhaŋu'. Having the consultant read the words avoids this problem, because they are presented with the word in the first place.

It is best to keep the recorder running throughout the session and to extract the relevant information later. Stopping and starting inevitably leads to missed information. Keeping notes of the time at which interesting things are said, or inserting track marks in the recording will help you find information more easily.

5.3 Further topics in phonetic research

5.3.1 Articulatory phonetics

There are a few ways to get information about articulation. One is to ask the speaker what they are doing with their tongue, lips and mouth when they say a certain word. That way you will be able to get information about the movement and placement of their active and passive articulators. Bear in mind, however, that they may not have terminology to describe what they are doing (most English speakers only know the term 'alveolar ridge' if they have done a linguistics course, for example). The descriptions might be ambiguous or hard to interpret. Here's where you can help with your linguistic knowledge. Give the consultant some alternatives to choose from. For example, you could ask 'where's your tongue, is the tip on your front teeth, or the ridge behind it, or further back?' Answers to these questions are not always reliable, but it's a good start, especially if you can point out some minimal pairs and ask about the differences between them.

Another way to attempt to find out about articulation is mimicry. Try to produce the sounds yourself and monitor what you are doing, and ask the consultant to tell you when you say the word the right way. This is also not very reliable. There are several different articulatory ways to produce the same sound, so you cannot be sure that your articulation is the same one as the speakers are using. Vocal tract differences which lead to differences in voice quality may make mimicry difficult. A 23-year-old graduate student will not sound like an 80-year-old even if their place and manner of articulation is identical. Speakers might also be quite tolerant of differences between your pronunciation and theirs, and accept pronunciations which deviate from theirs in several ways.

Watch the speaker's mouth. Many gestures are invisible because they are contained entirely within the speaker's mouth, but you can see lip rounding, lamino-dental consonants and labialization. It is also easy to see the difference between bilabial and labio-dental consonants. Videoing speakers from the front and in profile will allow you to study lip movements.

For more detailed information about articulation you will need extra equipment, such as a static palatography kit. The minimal kit includes a set of soft brushes, olive oil, medical charcoal, a light, a blunt-edged mirror which will fit inside the person's mouth, a way of sterilizing the equipment and a camera. Bear in mind that some of these techniques are quite invasive (such as sticking a tube down the consultant's throat to measure air pressure in the pharynx); even painting someone's mouth with charcoal and olive oil and taking photos involves touching the person's face, which might not be welcome or appropriate. If you want to make these measurements during a longer field trip, it is often better to wait until you and your consultants know each other well. That way you have built up trust between each other and you can gauge what their response to a request to do palatography might be.

5.3.2   Perceptual phonetics

Perceptual phonetics is the study of how speakers perceive sounds. Perceptual studies are seldom conducted as part of descriptive fieldwork, but some basic studies are possible to do in the field. It is possible to use a program such as *Praat* to present synthesized stimuli, to randomize the presentation, to record acceptability judgements, and to ask speakers to pick from several alternatives. You can do some basic perceptual work yourself. For example, you can present speakers with stimuli containing different allophones and asking them to rate their wellformedness.

5.3.3   Acoustic phonetics

Even if you aren't a phonetician, you should be familiar with basic tools for phonetic analysis, such as how to read a spectrogram. You shouldn't just rely on your ears, because perception is unreliable and conditioned by many different factors. Good training and extensive practice is very important, and knowing how to do a basic acoustic analysis is extremely useful.

At the very least, you should try to confirm your hypotheses about the phoneme system of your language by taking measurements and using spectrographic evidence. That is, if you argue that the language has two series of stops, one voiced and the other voiceless, make sure that this is the case. If you believe that vowels are lengthened in open syllables, check this by measuring the length of vowels in closed syllables, open syllables, and calculating whether the difference is statistically significant. A well-trained ear can pick up a lot of information, but (as we saw in §3.4), it is easy to be misled.

5.4 Suprasegmentals

5.4.1 Stress

Try to mark stress in your transcriptions from the beginning. If the stress system is complex you will need as much data as possible. Furthermore, the placement of stress almost always interacts with vowel length and quality, so you will need an analysis of the stress system in order to have a good analysis of the phoneme system.

Stress is manifested by a combination of intensity (loudness), duration (length) and pitch. Stressed syllables tend to be longer, louder and higher in pitch than unstressed syllables. Vowels in stressed syllables have different qualities from those in unstressed syllables. There might be fewer phonemic distinctions in unstressed syllables. The placement of secondary stress is also important, and may be determined by several different factors, including syllable weight and number of syllables in the word.

Both primary and secondary stress can be affected by prosodic constituents higher than the word. Words may have different stress when appearing in phrases. Compare:

(10) New York (in my pronunciation) /nʲu ˈjoːk/

versus

New York City /ˌnʲu ˌjok ˈsɪɾi/

Sentence focus affects stress too. Not all languages have stress, and of those that do, not all have lexical stress. In some languages stress regularly occurs on a particular syllable of the word (e.g., first, last, or second-last); in other languages stress may be unpredictable.

5.4.2   Tone

Tone languages are very common in Asia, Papua New Guinea, parts of North and South America and Africa. Field-methods classes tend to ignore tone, or be frightened by it. This is unfortunate; to ignore tone in a tone language is to leave out a major part of the phonological system. Furthermore, tone is often not only lexical; in some languages tone marks grammatical information, such as person or tense. Don't ignore it just because it might be hard to hear. After all, we make the attempt to transcribe VOT differences, even though they can also be hard to distinguish.

Some things will make tone transcription easier. Tones in some languages are accompanied by particular phonation types (e.g., in Acoma or Vietnamese). Therefore you have a double cue to the tone – the pitch and the voice quality – and can listen for both.

Secondly, speakers of tone languages will still often produce list intonation (or citation tone) when asked to speak words in isolation. Therefore it is important to embed your target words in a 'frame' (or short sentence). The frame may produce its own tone sandhi effects, so you may want to try several frames. One of the reasons field-methods classes often find tone work difficult is they try to elicit words in isolation, and the data are confounded by list intonation.

Not everyone will be conscious of tones in their own language, so you may have some difficulty getting overt information about tone levels and contours – that is, questions such as 'is this syllable higher than this one' may be incomprehensible to the consultant. Gerrit Dimmendaal (personal communication) has taught consultants to whistle tone patterns. Asking consultants to wave their hand may also work, or having them exaggerate the differences. Eliciting minimal tone pairs as reference points can also be very helpful.

Segmenting your recordings, tagging the clips and being able to play them back one after the other can make work like this easier.

5.5   Further topics in phonology[1]

In addition to work on phonetics, there is also much to be discovered in relation to the patterning of sounds in the language, that is, phonology. A minimal sketch of the phonology of a language should contain the following items. There should be a statement of the contrasting segments in the language, and this should be backed up by data, including minimal and near minimal pairs, and a description of allophony (see Chapter 3). The maximal-minimal pair list should illustrate contrasts in all syllable positions, in clusters and in different stress positions (if the language has stress).

A phonology sketch should also contain information about phonotactics, such as any neutralization of contrast in particular positions. For example, many languages have a reduced set of contrasts in syllabic codas. Your work should also investigate syllable structure. What are the maximal number of segments which can appear in a single syllable? Can onsets, codas or nuclei be complex? Are there any restrictions on vowel or consonant clusters? If so, what governs them? Are the differences between clusters within roots versus those across morpheme boundaries?

Thirdly, there are many possibilities for investigation in morphophonology. Perhaps use the phonological conditioning of affix forms across morpheme boundaries. Perhaps you have evidence for vowel harmony, or consonant harmony. Affixation may produce changes in the position of stress in the word. Perhaps the language has hypocoristic formation, or reduplication gives you evidence for phonological templates.

You will be able to obtain data on most of these topics by using regular elicitation strategies. That is, asking for particular words, or words in particular frames designed to elicit the morphology you're after, will work in most cases. Evidence for phonology can also be provided from language games (and the games are worth documenting in their own right). Asking your consultants to say words backwards can also provide interesting evidence for perceived segmentation, as well as whether they associate stress and/or tone with particular vowels or particular positions in the word. See the section of further reading for more information about these topics.

Finally, it is a good idea to try to confirm your analyses with phonetic data where possible. As an example, consider the interaction of stress and vowel length. You might have a theory that stress placement interacts in complex and interesting ways with vowel length. Before you publish such an analysis, make sure that stress is actually moving. Native speakers of English are accustomed to associate strength and vowel length, and it is very easy to assume that the stress moves to the long vowel, even when it is regularly on a short vowel elsewhere in the word.

5.6   Further reading

- **General:** Clark and Yallop (1995), Ladefoged (1997, 2003), Ladefoged and Maddieson (1996), Maddieson (2001).
- **Experiment design:** Scherer (1997).
- **Equipment:** Ladefoged (1996, 1997), Stevens (2000).
- **Phonation types:** Gordon and Ladefoged (2001).

- **Acoustic phonetics**: Fujimura and Erikson (1999), Johnson (2003), Ladefoged (2003: chs 5–7), Stevens (2000). The *Journal of Phonetics* frequently has articles of phonetic descriptions based on fieldwork.
- **Language games:** Azra and Cheneau (1994), Bagemihl (1995), Breen and Pensalfini (1999).
- **Stress and Tone:** Dimmendaal (2001), Hyman (2006), Yip (2002).
- **Transcription effects:** Bailey, Tillery and Andres (2005).

6
Eliciting: Basic Morphology and Syntax

6.1 Why do elicitation?

Being about to ask intelligible questions about language is one of the most important skills a fieldworker can have. How do you learn to ask people who haven't studied linguistics about their language? How do you interpret their answers and how do you frame questions in a way that they can answer?

Elicitation is not the only way to get data, as I have said before. But elicitation of various types is a very useful way of getting data quickly. Even if most of your data comes from recorded narratives (or 'texts') after preliminary work, you will still be working through those texts with a native speaker of the language and asking questions about them. This is also a type of elicitation. Some aspect of a language are only discoverable through elicitation – they will appear in texts so seldom that it will be almost impossible to get enough information about them.

6.2 First elicitation of sentences

In §3.1 we discussed the early field sessions, and I suggested that you begin with lexical items in isolation so that you can work out the phoneme system of the language and build a basis for the transcription of longer utterances. I also mentioned that it may not be possible for you to work from isolated lexical items. I recommend moving from individual lexical items or your very simple carrier phrases to slightly more complex phrases fairly quickly (perhaps after one or two sessions). It's not necessary to wait until you have the phoneme inventory analysed before you leave the elicitation of individual items. Some problems will remain for weeks, even months or years!

Think of your early fieldwork as similar to constructing data sets for linguistic problems. In introductory classes, you get a defined set of data and must work out what all of the individual words or morphemes mean, and describe the principles of clause or word formation. Your aims in early fieldwork are the same, except you construct the dataset yourself without knowing anything about what you'll find.

6.2.1   Where to start

Start with a simple sentence and elicit other sentences that differ minimally from it. It's important to vary a single item at a time. For example, don't change the tense of the verb and the number of the subject simultaneously, since you'll confuse yourself if these categories are marked cumulatively. Use words you already know. It's very tempting to move quickly into complicated constructions, but it's counterproductive. You won't know enough about the morphology to parse accurately and you won't know enough about the language to sort out the myriad of possible competing analyses. It will be more confusing than enlightening, and that will annoy your consultants because you won't be able to follow what they are telling you.

Part of an early elicitation session might look like this:

(11)   The cat is chasing the mouse.
       The cat is chasing the mice.
       The cats are chasing mice.
       One cat is chasing two mice.
       The cat is eating the mouse.
       The mouse died.

From sentences like these, you will be able to get much preliminary information about morphosyntax. You will get a first idea about number marking, and whether number is marked on the verb, on the noun phrase, both or neither. You might be able to find out something about argument structure too, and whether the language has an ergative or accusative case. You'll also get an indication of whether plural is marked in the presence of a numeral.

However, just as important is what you don't find out from the sentences. You cannot definitively conclude whether the language has ergative case marking. If the language has a split ergative system by aspect, it will be precisely these sentences which would not show it. If the language only has accusative marking on pronouns, you won't see it either. A verb like 'eat' often shows exceptional argument structure, so you can't conclude anything about the grammar of the language more generally from patterns on this verb alone.

Now you know what you need to test next. Perhaps you have an indication that number is marked on the verb. Now you would want to test other verbs and other participants to see whether the same patterns obtain. Perhaps you have discovered that number is marked within a noun phrase. You would also want to collect further examples of this, and see whether this is true for all types of nouns, or perhaps only animate nouns (and so on).

The next stage is to try and generalize what you know to words that you don't know. Your elicitation might go something like this (in this example, data in the target language are symbolized in angle brackets: <>):

(12) How would I say climb?
       <Answer>
       Can I say <the cat is climbing the tree?>
       <Answer>
       Could you say it for me?

The principles of elicitation work exactly the same way for more complex data. In each case, you obtain sample data, form a hypothesis, test it with more data, refine your hypothesis, and use the hypothesis to make predictions about how previously unrecorded sentences will be formed.

Another area to explore early in elicitation is basic elements of a noun phrase. That way you can build up complexity relatively quickly, by asking for some nouns, then some plurals (but don't expect the language to have morphologically marked plurals), some attributive adjectives (again, don't expect the language to have these), numerals, demonstratives and possessives. An exception would be if you are working on a polysynthetic language where most utterances consist only of a verb, in which case it may be more useful to work on simple verb paradigms.

(13) a cat
       this cat
       that cat
       two cats
       these cats
       my cat
       my cats
       my five cats

> my black cats
> your furry cats
> your five furry cats

In summary, early elicitation should concentrate on basic sentence structure. This will give you information about the basic word order of the language (if there is one) and will also give you a chance to build up vocabulary. It can be done even if your consultants cannot (or will not) give grammaticality judgements. At this point, it doesn't really matter what data you get, as long as you get something that you can transcribe and that you know the approximate meaning of.

From there, you will be able to make up some sentences of your own and test them. Make sure to back-translate your sentences,[1] as they might make sense, but mean something different from what you think they mean. It shows your consultants that you're serious about studying and learning the language, and that you've been listening to what they tell you. That is good politics as well as good linguistics.

6.2.2 Redundancy

Whatever your method of elicitation, you need massive overdetermination of data (as Bernard (2006) calls it) in order to be confident of your findings. Never build an analysis on just a few sentences. Incorporate redundancy into your elicitation. Use what you expect to be the same structure, with different words. Ask similar questions, introducing a new variable each time (e.g., different tense, different number of participants). Ask the same questions of different people. Once you've got your first set of data, think of as many analyses of it as you can (even potentially far-fetched ones). How will you choose between them? Use your hypotheses as the basis for your subsequent elicitation.

6.2.3 Working on multiple topics

You can use elicitation as a tool for getting vocabulary too, by varying the vocabulary in your sentences. Be a little careful with this, it can backfire and can distract your consultants if you use too many obscure words at once. If you have agreement in noun phrases, try to use phrases slightly more complex than a single noun, since this is a way of eliciting more morphology.

Hale (2001) recommends using example sentences for a dictionary as a basis for elicitation. Bouquiaux and Thomas's (2001) very detailed survey is in the same vein. This is useful for targeted elicitation, for expanding vocabulary and, potentially, for acquiring a wide range of language structures in a short space of time.

Go through your notes at the end of each day, work out what you learned, what you do not understand, and what you want to ask about in future (and how you will go about clarifying what you don't understand). At the end of every session you will have data that clarify, mystify and that seem to lead into yet more questions. Don't rely on your memory, write down your thoughts (it becomes somewhat like Agar's (1996) log book of 'deductions drawn' and 'questions raised'). You will also see what progress you have made (which is a good way to cheer yourself up when you feel that things are going badly) and whether the same problems keep coming up.

6.2.4 When to stop eliciting

Don't keep collecting individual words for months. It's boring for consultants, and you won't get far in semantics without knowing the grammar of the language. Start moving on to sentences within a few hours of elicitation time, certainly within the first few weeks of a field-methods class. It is very tempting to spend a lot of time eliciting vocabulary items and worrying about transcription issues. For example, Abbi (2001:68) advises about 20 hours of elicitation time to gather a 300-item list. That would be about five weeks of class under most field-methods courses and too great a time to spend without more complex data.

6.3 Types of data collection

There are many ways of collecting data, and elicitation is just one of them. Elicitation itself can take several forms. The following table gives a list of techniques, using Turkish as an example.

Technique	Example
Translation of sentences into the target language	'How do you say *I want to eat dinner?*'
Back-translating sentences you or other consultants have made up	What does *Ben de kitap okuyup durdum* mean?[2]
Manipulating data (changing one word in a sentence, or changing the order of items, to see how that changes the structure)	I've got a sentence *Ben de kitap okuyup durdum*. What would *Ben de kitabı okuyup durdum* mean?

Continued

Continued

Technique	Example
Asking for grammaticality judgements	Is this a good sentence? *Gülşat kitap okuyup durdum.*[3]
Asking questions about sentences already elicited, or from texts	I've got a sentence *Gülşat kitabı okuyup durdum* that's not grammatical. What should we change to make it a good sentence?
Using stimulus tools, such as pictures or videos	See §6.3.6
Semi-structured interviewing	conducting conversations in the target language to elicit certain words, types of construction, or discourse strategies Ethical reasoning tasks and problem solving are useful for this.
Creating questionnaires	see §6.3.3

Another data collection method is analysing previously published materials, or other people's field notes. This is discussed in Chapter 13.

6.3.1   Translation

The most common method of elicitation is to have your consultant(s) translate sentences into the target language. Start simple, and be specific. That is, don't immediately begin with large numbers of complex verb phrases with relative clauses and the like. Start with simple noun phrases (consisting of a single noun) and a verb in the present tense. Be prepared, too. Write or type the sentences in advance and leave a gap in your notes for the answer. Allow enough space for interlinearizing your answer (even if you do most of your interlinearization through a parser, you'll want to make notes during the session about what new items mean). For problems in translation, see §6.4.1.

6.3.2   Grammaticality judgments and negative data

Getting negative data (i.e., grammaticality judgements about acceptable and unacceptable sentences) is important. However, you might have to explain what you mean by ungrammaticality. Your consultants might not be clear on the difference between prescriptive and descriptive errors, so someone might say that a sentence is 'wrong' when it's not grammatically incorrect, it's just the wrong register. Consultants might also react to things that are grammatically correct but impossible in real world conditions. 'Colourless green ideas sleep furiously' is a 'grammatical' sentence but it is semantically very odd. It's well-formed but meaningless, and since most people are not quite so interested in the arbitrary relationship between form and meaning as linguists are, be careful using these sorts of sentences for elicitation.

If you are not sure whether a response of 'yes, it's fine' means that the sentence is grammatical or simply that your consultant is being polite, a slightly better question to ask is 'would a fluent speaker of the language ever say this?' This is a good way to weed out sentences that are technically grammatical, but are not preferred. If you get the response 'well, *you* could say it', that almost always means that there is something wrong with the sentence somewhere. Asking when someone might say a sentence like that can also produce interesting responses.

Be careful using this technique early on in your elicitation, because it is easy to make mistakes that have nothing to do with the grammaticality of what you're looking for (e.g., agreement errors). Ask your consultant to fix the sentence to so that it's grammatical. This gives you an idea of what they dislike. There might be several things wrong with the sentence.

People may be wary of correcting you out of politeness. Occasionally say things you know are wrong to check on this. In some areas, it is automatically assumed that everything an outsider says is bound to be incorrect (e.g., Wallace Chafe's comment at CLS, April 2005 on how some of his consultants would not allow him to make up sentences to test because he was not a community member). It can be quite disheartening to be constantly corrected, but it's what you want – you want to learn about the language. It's especially difficult in a class situation, where everyone is frightened of appearing ignorant in front of their colleagues.

Some linguists maintain that grammaticality judgments are useless, because 'any sentence can be grammatical with the appropriate context'. This simply isn't true. For example, there is no context where an English speaker will accept a phrase *house the* instead of *the house*. Variations in grammaticality judgments may point to further interesting topics for research. For example, English speakers differ on whether they consider *penguinly* a possible English word (as in 'he did a penguinly walk towards the dining table'). The fact that not everyone accepts this word (and others like it) potentially gives you interesting information about the productivity of the -*ly* adverbial/adjectival morpheme. Leading questions and other elicitation artefacts can lead to apparent problems with elicited judgements, but with appropriate care there is no reason why you cannot gain insight using these techniques, and avoiding them on spurious grounds simply leads to a poorer description.

6.3.3   Questionnaires

A large part of elicitation with consultants is equivalent to informal questionnaire use. You might design one for you to administer yourself, to multiple consultants. Alternatively, it might be a set of questions for someone else to administer, or for consultants to do on their own. This method of data collection is very good if you need a standard data set over multiple respondents, for example in examining potential variation, or if you are just starting to work on a topic and you are trying to gather data on potential points for further research.

An important aspect of questionnaire designing is to make the answers maximally useful; to do this you need to have a clearly circumscribed topic and try to anticipate possible analyses of the data. The question might be something like 'what is the behaviour of basic verbal agreement in this language?' This general question can be broken down into a lot of sub-questions:

- Does the language have verb agreement?
- For all persons/numbers?
- With which arguments?
- How is it realized?
- If there is multiple agreement, do the markers interact?
- Is agreement affected by tense, mood, or transitivity?
- Are there verb classes/conjugations?
- Does word order affect agreement?
- Is agreement ever optional?

In order to answer these questions, your questionnaire will need to contain:

- a variety of verbs with full NP arguments
- a variety of argument structure possibilities (verbs likely to be intransitive, transitive, and ditransitive)
- examples in different tenses

- verbs of different event structures, and with different types of semantic roles
- some way of working out the citation form of words in the clause (if you don't already know).

You will also need to provide instructions to the questionnaire taker and administrator. For example, can the questionnaire taker substitute a word if they can't think of a good translation for the one you've asked for? Do they have to translate literally, even if it sounds stilted in their language? Should they do the questionnaire in order or can they leave questions and come back to them?

The longer your survey, the greater the likelihood that you will get a small response. Therefore don't make the questionnaire too long; it should not take longer than 45 minutes to fill out.[4] This means that you need to devise a survey very carefully to answer well-defined questions. For example, in our mock verbal agreement survey above, it would not be possible to ask about agreement and causative constructions in any detailed way in a short survey, and even the question as posed may contain too many facets for adequate exploration in a single survey.

Questionnaires do not have to be done by pencil and paper (or even by computer text). You could ask your respondents to record their answers aloud, either on a recorder or through computer software (there is language-learning software which will allow you to give 'tests' where the 'student' can record audio answers to written or spoken questions).

6.3.4   Data manipulation

A further good way to get data quickly is to take sentences you already have and manipulate them. Here are some suggestions:

- Turn sentences into questions (and vice versa).
- Manipulate voice and valency possibilities; e.g., active – passive/ antipassive.
- Manipulate the tense of the verb. Ask for a sentence in the present, then get the same thing in past and future (or other categories the language has).
- Negative polarity – ask for a sentence, then get the same sentence in the negative.
- Manipulate the number of participants (e.g. singulars for plurals and vice versa).

Language games and 'exercises' can be used for elicitation:

- Take these words and make a good sentence out of them (give a noun and a verb at least, or whatever you want to test).
- Rearrange the words to make a good sentence.
- Fill in the gaps.

6.3.5 Controlled creative tasks

'Controlled creative tasks' require the consultant to be creative (the more willing a player your consultant is, the better the data will be) but they are also directed toward the acquisition of particular data. They work best when you have some familiarity with the language and can respond.

Language games can be helpful. For example, get one speaker to think of an object, and have them play '20 questions' with another speaker. Record the exchange and get them to translate it for you. You might need to explain the rules of the game. When I've played this game with consultants, it has often turned into a conversation rather than strictly following the rules. That doesn't matter – the aim is not to play the game *per se*, it's to get people speaking and producing questions and descriptions.

You can also make up short texts to elicit certain grammatical constructions. For instance you might want to see if the language has passive voice, but you haven't been able to elicit them directly. You might make up a story with lots of sentences which would be amenable to passives, such as high animacy participants being acted on by low-animacy ones or topic tracking across clauses in where the topic is a direct object (languages usually like topics to be subjects). I have listed a number of strategies for eliciting textual/narrative data in §9.3.3.

6.3.6 Use of stimulus prompts

Another way of getting data is to use stimuli, such as pictures or videos. Materials range from controlled experimental data to pictures of scenes where the consultant describes what is going on. Common stimulus prompts include the set of *frog story*[5] books by Mercer Mayer, and the pear story[6] video. Wordless children's books from the area are always useful. You can record your own prompts, or use readily available items (such as toys, sticks or other objects).

Make sure you have a way of recording which responses were given for which prompts. This is quite easy if you are videoing your work, but if you are manipulating objects and recording at the same time, it might be difficult to recover the configuration that your consultant was talking about.

If your time is limited and the language is endangered, it might seem very odd to record stories about small American boys and their pet frogs rather than traditional stories belonging to the culture you are studying. If that is a worry, you should probably stick to narratives from within the culture. On the other hand, constructing an unknown story from a set of pictures and retelling a well-known story from memory are quite different tasks. The *frog stories* are very useful because they have been translated into many languages, and the data can be used for cross-linguistic studies. There's no rule that says you can't do both.

Himmelmann (1996:29) argues that even so-called universal stimuli are culturally specific, and cites Du Bois (1980) as an example. Du Bois had several problems in showing the pear video to people in Mexico and Guatemala. However, Du Bois's problems were methodological rather than a product of the stimulus materials. First, Du Bois had extensive questionnaires about consultant information which was either sensitive or irrelevant (e.g., asking for occupation in an area where most people were not in structured employment). Find out about the area in advance and plan what type of questions you will need to ask, and how to ask them.

Another issue involved expected behaviour in an experiment. The viewers of the pear video did not know that they were expected not to discuss it with the other participants before being interviewed. Why should a group of Guatemalan teenagers know that a group of American experimenters expect them to watch a video in silence if that's not what they normally do? Tell your research participants if something like this is crucial.

There were problems in showing the video in a Catholic area, and thereby (a) making the project apparently tied to that group, and (b) excluding Protestants from the area who did not want to be associated with the Catholic mission. Your consultants can give you advice on such matters, since they have had some exposure to linguists and they know the local community and culture. Finally, Du Bois and his team lied or joked about where the money for the project was coming from. Don't joke about that sort of thing unless you know that it will be taken the right way. None of these problems has anything to do with the actual video or the task! They all arose from lack of awareness of local protocols.

If you are using a computer to deliver the stimulus materials in an area where people aren't very familiar with them, let them experiment with the machine for a while first, show them what it does, and get them used to how it works. Next, explain what the person will see and what they need to do. For example, for the 'PUT[7] project' materials I collected for Yan-nhaŋu, I said something like this:[8]

(14) ŋali gurrku nhäma video, gulkuruŋumiṯṯji. Nhunu gurrku nhäma yolŋuḻu ŋumun'thana. ŋarra gurrku djana'yun 'Nhapiyan nhani mana?', ga nhe dhu ḻakaram, nhunu waŋiyi ŋarrakuḻa, explain'im gurrku ŋarrakuḻa. ŋarra dhumuluŋa nhä buḻaŋgitj yänmiṯṯji waŋanaragu. Manymak?

> We're going to watch some short videos. You'll see someone doing something. I'll ask, 'what's he/she doing?' and you'll tell, you'll tell me, explain to me [what they're doing]. I don't know the right words (lit., 'a good way') for talking [about it]. OK?

For each video, allow plenty of time for the person to think about it and ask any questions. Expect to get different types of data from different people, ranging from a single word or short sentence to a full description of the participants and their actions.

Cultural appropriateness of materials was not a factor for the speakers I worked with, although the level of Indigenous or neutral content was overall very high. There's no Yan-nhaŋu word for *carrot*, so we just said *muru, yakarra* '*carrot*' (vegetable food whose name is carrot). For others we substituted equivalent objects (e.g., 'nail polish' was 'colour bottle'). Deciding what to call things was interesting in itself. Sometimes a loan was used, sometimes another word was extended, sometimes a generic term was used. Some of the actions in the videos were bizarre (why on earth would someone pick up a plastic cup with their teeth and carry it to another table?) but that simply caused some chuckling, and it became a running joke.[9] After all, as we tell students doing introductory linguistics courses, one of the key features of all human languages is that they can be used to talk about things that a person has never seen before.

6.4 Potential problems

While it sounds quite easy to get a consultant to tell you words in their language and to write them down, many things can go wrong. The best way to find out about potential errors is to make them! There's nothing like coming back to data later only to find that it's useless for one reason or another for learning how to avoid that problem in future.

6.4.1 Translation problems

Just asking someone to translate a sentence doesn't give very much guidance about what's required. One very common cause of confusion is whether the translation should be absolutely literal or free. It's very easy to produce gibberish by translating a sentence word-by-word. You may need to explain that you need a sentence which also sounds natural in the language. One way to check this is to read back the sentence, and ask whether it's something you might hear someone on the street say. You can also check the sentence with another speaker of the language, but be careful that people don't get the impression that you are checking up on them.

Your consultant may not want to provide isolated words. It's not a very natural thing to do, and if they haven't had much experience with linguists or education they might think it's ridiculous that you don't want whole sentences. You could point out that you are just learning the language for the first time and you want to be able to pronounce each word properly, and know what each word means. If that doesn't work, use a carrier phrase. That way, you still get data which you can use, and the consultant gets to give you the data in a way that is comfortable for them. Use the same sentence for each word, so you'll be able to identify which part of the sentence means what. If you're pointing at objects, don't forget to say what you're pointing at; if you have an audio recorder only and don't do this, you'll have a lot of recordings where you can't identify what you pointed at!

I once worked with someone who had great knowledge of the language, but never gave a straight translation of a sentence. For every sentence I asked, she would think of a context and make up a story about it. I once asked her 'How do you say "the dog bit me on the leg"?' Her answer was along the lines of the following: 'Maybe you were walking to the shop one day. You're young, you walk around a lot. *Bard arr mindan. Roowil miannyan* [I walked off]. And Mr Leslie's dog lives between you and the store and he leaves there it during the day. It's a really cheeky dog. *Biiligij ginyinggi iila* [it's a cheeky dog]. So maybe you were walking past one day and it bit you on the leg. *Nyiyambolon inarli-jjirri ginyingginim iila* [This dog bit you on the leg].' When I was just starting out it was invaluable, even though it wasn't what I asked for. Vica Papp and Anne-Marie Hartenstein, when they were working on Northern Moldovian Hungarian, worked with someone who would translate elicited sentences quite closely, but would also add an extra comment about the reason for the event in the elicitation prompt.

Think of this as 'added value' rather than translation errors – each elicitation prompts results in extra data even though it may be confusing at first.

It's natural to use the language that both the speaker and hearer have in common, so it's not uncommon for a consultant to repeat the word in English (or the contact language) rather than the target language. Gentle reminders or questions like 'Now how would you say that in Xish?' usually work. Occasionally I have had fully bilingual consultants say the English word with the phonology of the target language.

6.4.2   The gavagai problem and semantics

Imagine this: a pith-helmeted anthropologist/linguist is working on a previously undescribed language, when his consultant sees a rabbit run past. The consultant says *gavagai* and points. There are many possible interpretations of what *gavagai* might mean here – perhaps it is the word for 'rabbit' in the language, or perhaps for a particular species of rabbit or hare. Or perhaps it is a pet rabbit and *gavagai* is its name. Or perhaps it means 'look!' or 'hmm, they taste good' or 'they're a real pest'.[10] For every utterance you hear, you have to decode the language and relate the linguistic signs to what you know about the real world. It is only context which allows us to narrow down the range of possible interpretations and it is very easy to draw a different conclusion from what the speaker of the utterance intended.

Not only do you have to work out what your consultants are telling you, they have to work out what you are asking them and provide an appropriate response. There are many possibilities for negotiation in meaning to fall down, and for the intent to be misinterpreted and the imparting of the intended meaning to fail. The only way to avoid this is to do a lot of fieldwork; eventually you will gain experience in what sorts of questions commonly result in uninformative answers.

There are several ways that translation may be misleading. You might not get an accurate idea about what the word means – for example you may ask for the word for 'hand' and get in response a word which means both hand and forearm. The answer was a correct answer to your question, as you got the word used to refer to that body part, but it was also not the full story. Beware of regional variation – for example *cheeky* in Aboriginal English doesn't mean the same thing as it means in standard English. Agar (1996) gives the example of 'square' in New York junkie English versus its wider connotation.

You probably won't get a precise translation of your sentences. If you do, it might be worthless anyway, because it might be something that no one would ever say. Do not assume that every aspect of the contact language sentence will be reflected in the target sentence, and do not assume that the sentence you are given directly translates the participants or the tense of your target. Bear in mind the linguistic competence of your consultants, they might not be aware of the fine-grained distinctions that you are trying to get at. Even if your consultants are fully fluent in both languages, it is very easy to switch participants, or give a different tense from what is asked. Don't think of these as 'errors'; they are the inevitable consequence of this method, and a very good reason for not using it exclusively.

It's very common for consultants to switch first- and second-person translations. Those pronouns are shifters, the referent of 'I' or 'you' is different depending on who is speaking. Therefore it is common, when asked for a sentence such as 'I went to the shop', for the consultant to shift the referent automatically and give you the equivalent of 'you went to the shop'. Alternatively, you may be given the same form for first and second person (i.e., one will 'shift', but the other will not). One way to make sure you have all three persons represented in your data is to start with elicitation of third-person forms, rather than first person:

(15) He went to the shop.
     You went to the shop.
     I went to the shop.

Although the first- and second-person forms may still be reversed, this is a way to encourage the production of all three persons. It might take some time to establish which forms are first person and which are second person. A good way to elicit guaranteed first-person forms is to ask your consultant to tell a story about what they did yesterday.

Another common 'shifter' problem occurs with imperatives and questions. Questions are often answered rather than translated (so make it clear that you want to know how to ask questions, rather than the answers). Imperatives (at least when elicited through English) are often taken for the citation form, so you might end up with an infinitive or a present tense form rather than the imperative. Playing a game such as 'Simon says' with several consultants is a good way to get either imperatives or indirect speech!

Finally, consultants may refuse to translate sentences which are impossible in the real world. You can encourage the consultant to pretend, or ask something like 'what would you say if this were possible?' This might have unintended results. For example, you might end up with a lot of sentences in the irrealis! In most sentences, the actual words aren't very important. When you learn the language better you'll be able to come up with words that have the same morphological structure if that's what you're trying to test. There is no reason not to stick to real world events with semantically plausible participants early on.

6.4.3 Mistranscription

Mistranscription is inevitable. No one can transcribe an unfamiliar language perfectly at the first go. Don't expect it, it's implausible. In §3.4 there is a list of segments that English speakers find particularly easy to confuse, and looking at that will help you become aware of the sorts of mistakes that are commonly made. The only way around this is to continue to be careful and to check and recheck transcriptions until you're familiar enough with the language to be confident in the categories. In a field methods class, you can each transcribe individually and then compare your results.

6.4.4 Language problems

Your consultants might not be native speakers of the contact language (or you might not be). They might have an accent, or they might not be able to understand your accent all the time, and that may lead to confusion. For example, for someone who speaks Australian Aboriginal English, *chin, skin* and *shin* are likely to be pronounced identically, as are *hid it* and *hit it*. In some cases people might think of the words as not homophones, but one polysemous word; for example, *judge* and *church*, or *grub* and *crab*.

Back-translations will help avoid these problems. Be prepared for your early data to be riddled with errors in transcription, semantics and parsing. It's important to revisit your earlier data once you know more about the language.

6.4.5 Multilingualism

Occasionally, you might get the wrong language completely. This is pretty rare, but sometimes it happens that consultants either don't speak the language you think they do, or they do speak it but they prefer to give you another language instead. The most extreme case is illustrated by the doculect of McDonald and Wurm (1979), where their consultant was being interviewed for materials in Garlali, but he preferred to speak Punthamara, so that is what he gave them. The mistake was caught just before the book went to press. As it turned out, it didn't matter much, since Punthamara was also almost undocumented! A less extreme case is where a consultant will provide a single word in another language. This is especially common if more than one language is in common use in the speech community.

Vaux and Cooper (1999:42) have some discussion of the topic of multilingual consultants and the 'problem' of consultants who borrow freely form the superstrate language or languages in their informal (or formal) speech. This is quite common in multilingual areas. You could include the loans in your database, but mark them as assimilated or unassimilated, or find out about when they are most often used. You could include them with their non-borrowed variants in your own database, but not include them in any published or distributed materials.

Be wary of assuming that similar forms must be loans. For example, Spanish *mucho* and English *much* mean the same thing, but one is not borrowed from the other (in fact, they are not cognate). Therefore, be wary of excluding words that you suspect are borrowings simply because they appear similar. You could work on a historical linguistic project using data of this type.

Multilingualism can be problematic in syntactic elicitation too. You might get sentences in more than one language, or sentences with obvious calques (or occasionally, sentences in the wrong language entirely!). Loan words might have their own morphological patterns, as they do in languages like English and Romani. The only way to ensure that this is not happening is to know all the languages spoken in the area (which might not be feasible), or to ask several people the same sets of questions.

6.4.6 Boredom and tiredness

Watch for boredom. Work out when to give the topic a rest and go on to something else (or have a break). In general, don't work for more than an hour without a short break. Data accuracy goes down rapidly when the consultant is tired, and your transcription and alertness are also an important factor. Sometimes things simply aren't going to go well. Don't worry about just taking a break sometimes.

Consultants sometimes feel bad if there's no word in their language for a concept in the contact language. It's worth reminding your consultant if things are going badly that the absence of an equivalent is not a reflection on the language under study. This is where your knowledge of typology can be useful; for example, in assuring people that it's ok that they don't have a different word for 'blue' and 'green', because plenty of languages don't make that distinction.

Some people like this type of elicitation, though, because it makes them think about their language and the relationships between words.

Others may be happy to do paradigmatic elicitation, but may dislike playing around with language, inventing words or testing permutations of sentences. They might not see the point of it and think that you are trying to trick them. You might need to do paradigm elicitations in small batches on different days, combined with other topics. Making your sentences funny sometimes helps, but it can also be distracting.

6.4.7   Question formation

Avoid leading questions if at all possible. It's a type of priming (setting someone up to produce a certain answer). Question formation is itself culturally specific. Agar (1996) has an interesting discussion of leading questions in anthropology; he makes the point that all questions are, to a certain extent, leading. The fact of asking a question implies that there is something about the answer that will interest you. Leading yes/no questions have an 'easy way out' response, which is just to agree with what is being said. For example, if you ask about a phoneme using the question 'is it *b* or *p*? It's *p*, isn't it?', you set up an 'easy' answer. Just saying 'sorry, I didn't hear right, was that *p* or *b*?' will result in the same information without the potential bias.

6.4.8   Wrong type of data

It is all too easy to compile elicitation questionnaires which do not cover all the information you need. It is very difficult to design a good set of elicitation prompts – it is much more difficult than just coming up with a set of sentences. Chances are that you will brainstorm sentences of very similar structure. Planning your elicitation carefully and taking into account factors like animacy of participants, number, and similar things will help reduce this problem.

6.4.9   'Helpful' comments

It's quite common for consultants to give you information about the analysis of a word or construction. This is a good thing! You want your research participants to be engaged in what you're doing. Never take anything at face value, though. This goes for your own analyses too, as much as for those offered by consultants.

In my first ever field-methods class, our consultant knew some grammatical terminology, including 'tense' and 'person'. She labelled anything to do with the verb 'past tense', including applicatives and associated motion. Think back to your introductory linguistics class and the misconceptions that you were disabused of in the course of the semester.

While you shouldn't take a consultant's comments on analysis at face value, do take note of them. They are often helpful in forming an analysis, or helping to think of ways in which to distinguish between competing analyses. Many people, particularly people who are attracted to consultant work, are in a position to offer you valuable information. After all, some linguists also place great store on their own intuitions and introspection is their primary method. The intuitions and comments provided by your consultants are another data point, and like all data points, some are more useful than others.

Listen to what your consultants want to tell you. Some consultants will take on the role of language teacher. While we are often accustomed to think of this as a negative approach, since we associate language teaching with prescriptivism, teaching and learning styles, even informal ones, vary greatly from culture to culture. Part of respecting your consultants is taking into account the way they interact with you.

6.5 Summary

6.5.1 Overview of method

In general, I recommend approaching morphological and syntactic elicitation as though it were a set of class problems. Use the following steps:

1. Gather initial data using some speculative sentences designed to capture the major morphological/syntactic constructions in the language (spend perhaps half an hour of elicitation on each topic).
2. Analyse initial data; transcribe the sentences, parse them as best you can. Make a note of any morphology you can't parse, and check that the other morphology behaves as you expect it to. If it doesn't, make a note for further testing.
3. Form an initial hypothesis (or, better, several hypotheses) about the structure of the sentences.
4. Work out how you would tell which of your hypotheses is right. What type of data would you need to falsify one hypothesis, or prefer one hypothesis over another?
5. Design another data-gathering task designed to answer those questions.
6. At any point, you should have a number of different competing ideas in your head about how things work; be prepared to evaluate them on the fly and come up with new questions in your protocol.

7. Transcribe, parse, work out what you don't know, discard hypotheses which are no longer tenable and make up new ones.
8. Expect to do this many times over the course of a field trip.

To make sure that you have examples of many syntactic phenomena, you can go through a checklist, such as the one in Appendix D, or make your own list of things that you want to investigate. You could start with the table of contents of a grammar of a related language. Make this list before you leave for the field; you will certainly add to it and refine it while you are working actively on the language. Even if you don't invent your questions until the night before you ask them, have a good idea of the topics you will investigate before you leave.

6.5.2   Further reading

- **Documentation/Description:** Ameka, Dench and Evans (2006), Gippert, Himmelmann and Mosel (2006), Shopen (1985).
- **Elicitation:** Kibrik (1977), Payne (1997), Samarin (1967).
- **Interviewing:** Patton (2002: ch. 7).
- **Stimulus materials:** Bouquiaux and Thomas (1992), Vaux and Cooper (1999).
- Further information is available on the web site.

7
Further Morphology and Syntax

In this chapter, I address further topics which arise in working with morphological and syntactic field data.

7.1 Elicitation of paradigms

As your collection of elicited sentences grows, you will acquire a collection of inflected words. However, you may not know what the citation form for all of these words is, and you probably won't know all of the different ways that they inflect. There will be lots of gaps in your data. Therefore, fairly early in your fieldwork, it is a very good idea to bring some systematicity to this data collection.

The first thing you need to do is to work out what you don't know. The easiest way to do this is to compile a the list of all of the inflected words in your data. That way, you will know what words you have with which morphology. This also serves as a handy check for variant transcriptions.[1] Next, work out which data are missing. For example, you could compile a table of the nouns in your data arranged by inflection. It might look something like this table of data from the Cushitic language Qafar (Hayward 2001:635).

	nibd- 'awake'	*duf-* 'push'
1sg	*nibd-iyoh*	
2sg		*duf-tah*
3sg masc	*nibd-ah*	*duf-ah*

3sg fem		*duf-tah*
1 pl	*nibd-inoh*	
2 pl	*nibd-itoonuh*	*duf-taanah*
3 pl		*duf-aanah*

Now, you need to go about filling in the missing cells in the table. You may not be able to ask directly. Questions such as 'what is the ablative of *house?*' or 'what is the third-person singular feminine imperfect of the stem *nidb-?*' are seldom productive ways of talking to non-linguists. There are two main ways to get this data. Either make up a sentence to translate the word in a context which is likely to produce the relevant form, or make a guess as to what you expect the word to be based on your previous data and see if it's right. For the example in the table above, you would want to ask something like this:

(16) I am pushing.
  We are pushing.
  You are awake.
  She is awake.
  They are awake.

You may also want to have a go at eliciting full paradigms, without waiting for words to come up in context. The easiest way is to collect a set of words in a simple frame.

(17) 'He Xed today.'
  He worked today.
  He smiled today.
  He saw a cat today.
  He went to school today.
  etc.

Then, alter the frame slightly, for example

(18) 'He will X tomorrow'
  He will see a cat tomorrow.
  He will go to school tomorrow.
  etc.

People often find this type of task repetitive and boring. Making up stories can make the elicitation a bit less tedious. For example, to collect examples of allative-case marked nouns you could make up a story where someone goes to a series of places. A child has lost a favourite toy and they go *to the shop, to their grandmother's house, to the bus stop, to the car, to school,* and so on in order to look for the toy. Stories where someone has lost something are great for locational phrases in general, for example the child could look *under a stone, in the rubbish bin, on top of the table, beside the bed, next to the tree.* Such elicitation forms also make good children's books.

When checking forms in paradigms in isolation, however, check the forms of the same word, together. Don't do all past tenses, then all present tenses. It seems to cause confusion. Don't try to work too fast either, and only ask for one form at a time. There's a strong temptation to ask for several forms at once, but it often results in confusion. Avoid framing questions like 'How do you say "he is singing" and "I am singing"?' Your consultant may catch on to what you are eliciting and will give you the paradigm without further prompting after a while.

Once you have a good idea of the way words inflect in the language, when you come across a new word, do spot-checking of paradigms to make sure of what morphological class it belongs to. You will need to become adept at parsing on the spot. Work out what forms you need to determine paradigm membership early on in your analysis (if possible); for example, for knowing the full conjugation of a Latin verb, you need the infinitive, the past tense, and the passive participle; all other forms can be predicted from those three. Such key forms are called 'principal parts'.

7.2 Productivity

Not all morphology is productive, however, data on the extent of productivity will take a while to gather. You'll need some familiarity with the language to know what you need to test for. Productivity is partly associated with frequency. That is, if you come across a morpheme frequently, on many different items in the same word class, that's a good indication that it's productive. However, some morphemes might be rather rare, but still productive, and there may be some morphemes which occur on high-frequency items, but are not generally productive. If you have an electronic corpus, you will be able to search for instances of a given morpheme to see which items it can occur with. This is another reason to interlinearize your corpus.

To test productivity, come up with a sample set of words which you think might be able to take the morpheme and see if the resulting forms are grammatical. If they all are, it's not completely safe to assume that the morpheme is productive. You might just have been lucky in the words that you chose. If only some of the items are grammatical, see if you can see what they have in common. Is it a semantic class, or is it something to do with the phonological shape of the word, or is it something else? You can also ask your consultant to think of other words that have that ending on it. You might need to give some examples, rather than asking about the morpheme directly. Wug-testing also provides clues to productivity. Make up some words and see if consultants will accept derived or inflected forms (don't forget to check what they would mean).

It's very tempting to ask about productivity directly. However, questions like 'can this ending go on all words, or just on some?' can be very misleading. For example, your average English speaker when confronted with this question in the street ('are there lots of words in English with the ending -ness, such as kindness and happiness?') may either answer 'yes', depending on whether they happen to be thinking about Anglo-Saxon adjectives, or 'no', if they happen not to think of a couple of words off hand. People seldom have reliable explicit knowledge about productivity or frequency.

7.3 Selected topics in morphology

7.3.1 Derivational morphology

Not all languages have extensive derivational morphology, and some have none at all. Testing for topics such as number marking is quite easy if you're using a contact language which has this type of morphology. It can be tempting to add a numeral or quantifier to make explicit that you want a plural item, but this may distort your data. Some languages only mark plurality when there is no numeral or quantifier present in the phrase. The language may mark more distinctions than the contact language. For example, some languages have both a dual and a plural, or a paucal. In some languages, paired body parts are always dual, while in others they are exceptions and take plural marking. Be on the lookout for a distinction between mass nouns and count nouns too.

You should also test for definiteness marking. It's best to do this in context, and to ask questions of your consultant about the implications of a given sentence. Do not expect the translated sentence to necessarily have the same definiteness values that you implied in the prompt.

It can be quite difficult to work out markings for definite and indefinite noun phrases. It helps to elicit them in the context of other quantifiers. It also helps to start with deictic marking, using the items that you can see and manipulate.

Eliciting derivational morphology which results in a change of word class can also be done through the contact language. It's easiest to do this if you point out the relationship between roots explicitly, rather than asking for words in isolation. You might say 'English has all these words which describe people doing actions: a *runner* is someone who runs, a *singer* is someone who sings, and so on. Can you think of similar words? For example, I remember that *sing* is *ḍar'ṭaryun*. What's the name for a singer?' Sometimes this technique results in paraphrases, so you might need to ask specifically if there is a single word. A list of common derivational categories it is included in Appendix D.

7.3.2   Class, gender or category marking, and conjugation membership

Some languages have gender systems, or inflectional classes for open word classes. There are strong a-real tendencies, so if you are studying a language in an area where noun class systems are common, you should be on the lookout for them and test for them. Noun classes often arise with numerals, with inflection marking, and on accompanying adjectives or modifiers. Therefore, you can test for them by using the same modifier with nouns of different shapes, size, texture, animacy or other feature. For more information about such systems, see Corbett (1991) and Aikhenvald (2000).

The discovery procedure for inflectional classes is exactly the same as for other morphology. That is, get examples of different words in similar syntactic contexts, and see how they differ. Keeping track of different inflectional classes can be quite difficult if the system is complex. The easiest way to do it is to compile charts with all the morphology, and keep a list handy of which words appear to belong to which class. Memorize as much as possible. Number the classes and include that information in your lexicon.

7.3.3   Suppletive morphology and accidental gaps

Languages often have suppletive morphology (such as English *go* versus *went*). Suppletive pairs are easily missed early on. You will have so many gaps in paradigms that it might be very difficult to tell whether potential suppletion is that, or a word with similar meaning in a paradigm that you haven't yet fully recorded. The problem of identifying suppletion is compounded by the presence of accidental gaps in paradigms. That is, a particular word might not have an inflected form in a particular cell of the paradigm. Over time you may notice systematic gaps in certain paradigms. For example, in Khoekhoegowab (also called Nama), paired body parts take singular and plural morphology, but no dual marking.

The studying of paradigmatic gaps is not something to be concerned with early on in elicitation. It is difficult to ask directly about paradigmatic gaps, since it is easy to accidentally 'coerce' a speaker into producing forms through overgeneralization. The best way to test for gaps is to get speakers to do a survey-like task where they are required to produce suspected gaps in a sentence. If there is a lot of disagreement in which form is produced, that is a good indication that there is a gap.

If this is common in the language you are studying, you should develop a way of marking genuine gaps from data gaps in your corpus.

7.3.4 Case marking

Basic information about morphological case is easy to elicit. Ask your consultants to translate a set of sentences with different argument structure arrays (varying the semantic roles and grammatical relations). Take note of case frames, including any irregular case frames for certain lexical items (e.g., place names frequently have zero locatives in some parts of the world, or if your language has ergative case marking, there is likely to be a split somewhere in the morphology. In that case, it is quite easy to elicit sentences which do not give you meaningful information about the case frames of verb). For example, if the pronouns in the language are marked on a nominative/accusative pattern, and nouns on an ergative/absolutive pattern, subject pronouns will not tell you if the verb is transitive or intransitive if no object is present.

Going beyond the basics, however, is trickier. Your sample sentences are just the beginning of more advanced exploration of case semantics. You should test for optionality of marking, and possible interaction with constituent order. For example, in a good number of languages, overt marking of direct objects is optional, but the presence or absence of the case marker has effects on where the argument can appear in the clause, and whether it is obligatorily interpreted as definite.

7.3.5 Tense and aspect marking

There is more to tense marking than elicitation of basic paradigms. Working out exactly when a certain tense is likely to be used can be quite difficult. There can be a *sequence of tense* effects, for example, where the tense of the verb in a dependent clause is determined by the

main clause. Present tense may be used in narrative to give an imme-
diacy to the narrative, and tense, aspect and Aktionsart (roughly, the
temporal structure of the event denoted by the verb) may interact in
different ways. For example, in Yan-nhaŋu, the 'past' tense forms are
also used to mark resultant states which may persist to the present
(cf. *mukthun* (present) 'to be quiet, to become quiet'; *mukthana* 'to have
become quiet, therefore to be quiet'). Be aware of the relationship
between aspect and Aktionsart and design your elicitation questions
to include verbs of different event structures. If you see an unusual
example of TAM marking in a text, tag it and see if you can find similar
examples.

Be aware of the role that aspect can play in elicitation. For example
don't try to do aspectual elicitation on a verb such as *die*, which is often
irregular.

Tense can interact with temporal marking elsewhere in the clause, so
be sure to test verbal tense marking both with and without temporal
adverbs or other temporal marking.

7.3.6 Variation and optionality

It is not uncommon to find considerable apparent variation in morphology. Perhaps you have examples of a suffix which appears to alternate
in free variation with another suffix. For example, you may have an
antipassive construction where the demoted object can be either in the
dative case or the locative. Or, you might have examples where a particular morpheme appears to be optional, and its presence or absence
does not appear to affect the meaning of the clause.

Such variation may be due to several factors: perhaps different speakers have different preferences where more than one choice is possible.
Different speakers could have understood your prompt question in different ways. Alternatively, the difference in morphological marking
could be due to age-based or other dialectal variation. There might be
genuine variants which are conditioned by a factor that is not obvious
from the data you have so far. Finally, it could be an error of some kind,
either a speech error, a transcription error or something else. Usually,
the only way to sort out such variation is to wait until you have more
data.

Make a note of variation in your data early on. It's worth coming up
with a tagging system for your notes, or a set of keywords that you can
use to annotate your field notes and transcriptions. Using a program that
has a concordance generator will help you easily find other examples of
a particular word without hunting through your notes each time.

7.3.7   Discourse-based morphology

Some types of morphology are almost impossible to elicit in a planned fashion. You will come across them as language is used spontaneously. This is yet another reason why it's a very good idea to learn to speak your field language, and to listen for the way language is used around you even outside of structured elicitation sessions. One example of this is the way that morphology and intonation interact in vocative constructions. In many Northern Australian Kimberley languages, when someone is calling out to someone they lengthen the vowel of the last syllable of the person's name (or the word), and they add a suffix -*w*, which may itself be held for a considerable length of time. In transcriptions, this might be represented as *kaliyawwww* 'Byeeee!' (in Nyikina). directly eliciting something like this would be almost impossible, so make sure that you are aware that you cannot conclude from elicited data what categories are not present in the language. Other similar discourse-based morphology will, of course, only turn up in discourse.

7.4   Handling unknown morphology

It's not uncommon in the first few months (or years!) of fieldwork to be constantly assailed by new morphology, or by new uses of familiar morphemes. In early elicitation, it is also very common to miss morphemes completely. That is, you will treat as morphologically simple words which are, in fact, morphologically complex. It is also possible to overgeneralize, and to find apparent morpheme boundaries in words that are actually simple. There is no way to solve this other than to increase your knowledge of the language.

If you don't know what a morpheme does, ask your consultant for other sentences which contain the inflected word (e.g., if I have an example of *nhälil*, and I know what *nhä* means, but not -*lil*, I might ask 'Could you tell me some other sentences/things to say which have *nhälil* in them'). Try to generalize the morpheme to other words and ask your consultants to put them in sentences. If you are not sure if the word is morphologically simple or morphologically complex, try to inflect the word yourself and ask your consultants to put it in a sentence. If the word is actually simple, your form will probably sound to them like a language joke. For example, for some speakers of English the word *integral* appears to have the prefix *inter*- (and, in fact, this is a very common spelling error). If you are doing fieldwork on English and wanted to test whether integral did in fact have this prefix, you might ask whether there was a word *intragral*.

In other cases, you might have identified a morpheme but you might not be sure what conditions the allomorphy. Your data might be misleading. Here is an example from my field-methods class in 2005–06. Eastern Armenian has two nominal plural allomorphs, *-er* and *-ner*. Based on our class data it was possible to say (with a few exceptions) that *-er* was used for consonant-final stems and *-ner* was used for vowel-final stems. On the other hand, the data also supported an interpretation where *-ner* occurred on words of more than one syllable, and *-er* on monosyllables. In fact, the exceptions were covered by this latter rule. Subsequent testing showed that the number of syllables is the important conditioning factor. This illustrates the need to revisit hypotheses if you start finding exceptions. While many rules have exceptions, does not mean there is not a better generalization.

7.5 Common problems

There are some problems that come up exceedingly commonly in analysis of previously undescribed languages. One is clitics. Is a given form a clitic or an affix? You might have some evidence that points one way, and some that would lead you to the opposite conclusion. The important thing to do here is to work out what evidence you have one way or another, and then try to work out what it would take to decide in favour of a particular analysis. What would you need to know in order to discover which of your two hypotheses is correct?

It is very common to misparse words. It is very easy to be misled along particular morphological analyses early on in the description of the language. Expect this to happen. It is the result of not having enough data (or in some cases, either having too much data, or not having enough of the right type of data). Don't feel discouraged, the most important thing is to be able to keep track of your analysis in your head, and to recognize when you get information that confirms or contradicts it.

It is very tempting to regularize transcription to your citation forms. You may do this, however, at the risk of overlooking conditioning and regularizing your data. Be very careful. This is why it is a good idea to make notes on realization if you're transcribing phonemically.

It is also very easy to set up a pattern and then to have consultants overgeneralize. (This is another instance of priming.) It is possible to prime consultants to set up a particular response by giving them a pattern. Try this yourself by asking an English speaker for the past tense of the following verbs:

(19) sing   (sang)
    ring   (rang)
    ping   (*pang*)

You can avoid this problem by not doing too much elicitation at one time, by using the forms yourself in sentences, by eliciting with two people there to check each other, or by randomizing forms in paradigms. (I don't recommend the last one, as it is confusing and tiring to consultants.)

The biggest problem that tends to happen with elicitation is that it is difficult to realize the degree of reliance placed on existing structures in the analysis. That is, it is quite difficult to move away from assumptions from the languages you know well to see what it is that is going on in the language you are studying. There is a strong default assumption that things will be the same unless you have evidence to the contrary. Therefore it is very easy to overlook potential differences, simply because you assume they will be the same as your native language.

7.6   Further topics in syntax and semantics

7.6.1   Constituent order

Early on in your elicitation you will get data on constituent order. However, it is quite easy to be misled by elicitation on this topic. For example, if your language has no basic word order (i.e., discourse determined word order as is found in many languages in Australia and native North America), the same order will probably appear in the prompt and translated sentences. Therefore, if you're using English as your metalanguage and all your responses are SVO, you cannot be sure that SVO is the basic word order of the language. You should try early on to move constituents around in the sentence. Another common pattern in free word order languages is for common discourse participants to receive topic position in sentences. That is, the elicitation itself creates a discourse context.

Even if you do not work in the syntactic theory that generates sentence structure from rules, it is a good exercise to try to describe your data in those terms. It gives you a good idea about potential gaps in your data, possible ambiguities, and allows you to make predictions about what possible and impossible sentences might look like.

Some progress can be made in constituent order discovery through elicitation. That is, you can take a sentence, switch the order of constituents, and ask if the result is still grammatical (and what it means). However, your best clues to constituent order will come from textual data.

7.6.2   Scope

Scope is a core topic in the generative literature. However, it can be very difficult to elicit scope judgements, or even to get people to see that there's a difference in scope readings. For example, a non-native speaker of English might not realize without prompting that 'every child caught a fish' is ambiguous between wide and narrow scope readings (one in which every child caught one certain fish, versus the reading in which each child of a set ended up with a fish, but not necessarily the same one). The best way to elicit these types of judgements is to set up pictures (or scenarios) and ask for translations. Do it in a small group and allow for the participants to discuss the possible meanings. Try to have something concrete to illustrate the different meanings if possible. For example, you could have a set of coins and ask about the sentence 'every child got a coin'. Have consultants illustrate whether such a sentence in their language implies that each child got a different coin, or whether they only received one, or whether either interpretation is possible.

7.6.3   Causative constructions

Not every language has causative constructions; some have both simple and complex causatives, and others have only one. Some languages distinguish direct and indirect causation. Causative marking might be morphological as a derivational device only, or it may be more productive. Some languages distinguish reasons from causes. That is, the reason for an action might be marked differently from the cause (or causer) of an action. Eliciting such constructions can be quite difficult at first. If the language has both an analytic causative and a morphological causative, eliciting through the English analytical (make) causative often primes consultant to produce analytic causatives. It is also quite difficult to get a sense of the semantics of such constructions through elicitation. If you're having trouble finding such constructions in the language, it may be worth to wait until you have textual materials. Or, you could use a set of stimulus materials which have causers in them, such as videos where one participant makes someone else do something.

7.6.4   Commonly missed constructions

Some constructions cause particular problems in field-methods classes, particularly constructions which are not very common in European languages and which are not covered in standard classes.

Numerals and number marking often interact. That is, it may be that number is only marked on a noun phrase when the numeral is present. This can cause intriguing conclusions, because a tempting way to try to elicit plural marking is through including a number. The numeral system itself is worth documenting, by collecting not only lower numbers and decimals but also larger numbers, and ways of describing multiplication, addition, subtraction and other mathematical operations.

Reflexive and reciprocal marking may occur even when there is no overt reflexivity of the action (see Gerdts and Hukari (2006) for an example). Applicative marking and antipassives can also cause problems. Kroeger (2004) has a good description of applicatives. Copular clauses are often not investigated extensively. Remember to test for different types of predicates (e.g., with a nominal predicate, as in *my friend is a teacher,* as well as adjectival and other types of predicates). Tense marking and negation can also interact with copular marking.

It is very difficult to get translations of deictic markers, since they can be used not only spatially and literally, but also metaphorically in many languages. There is a tendency to assume that there will be a precise translation for *this* and *that.* It is very tempting to assume that the lexical category (or part of speech) of an item will be the same as it is in English. This is a very dangerous assumption to make. You will need to come up with your own tests for parts of speech in the language. Subclasses of nouns may behave in different ways with respect to case marking. Personal names in place names many inflect differently from common nouns (or may have a reduced number of case possibilities).

It is common to spend much less time on the syntax of languages that have complex morphology than on languages with simple morphology, and that can lead to a lopsided description. For example, some grammars of northern Australian languages have a hundred pages devoted to morphology, but only ten or so to syntax. Don't fall into this trap.

Another area that frequently causes difficulties is complex predication, or clausehood more generally. It may be initially very difficult to determine whether a given string of words comprises a single clause, or more than one. There are syntactic tests for this, however. For example, negation marking is clause bound; therefore if you have a single negation marker which takes scope over both verbs, that is a good indication that the verbs belongs to the same clause (for more tests, see Bowern 2006).

7.7   Where to from here?

7.7.1   The next step

If you work this way with elicitation material, you will have a fairly good idea about some aspects of the language. You'll know how to form basic sentences, and quite a lot about less basic structures as well. You will have acquired a knowledge of various (more and less useful) vocabulary items. You'll have a lot of data which will be useful for phonetics, phonology, morphology and syntactic work. You'll probably also have a lot of unresolved questions. It's also important to realize what you don't have. You don't have much data about pragmatic factors of language use. You probably have a lot of items glossed 'particle', 'emphasis', or '??'.

The next stage is to expand your data collection methods. As discussed in the introduction to Chapter 9, elicitation doesn't give you the full story. Textual data will help to clarify some of these questions and will probably give you yet more puzzles.

The best way to explore topics for morphology is to have a good grasp of the literature on morphology, morphosyntax and typology. There are numerous overview volumes dealing with different morphological and syntactic phenomena, including Aikhenvald, Dixon and Onishi (2001), Comrie (1989), Corbett (2000, 2006). General morphology textbooks, such as Haspelmath (2002) and Bauer (2003) may also be useful here. Collect examples of the construction[2] and work out what you think the essential features of the construction are. Then go hunting in the literature for something similar (and ask colleagues and your advisor), then work out in what ways the construction you've identified is similar, and how it differs.

7.7.2   What if none of this works

It may happen that none of the methods described here are useful to you. Your consultants might not be comfortable working with elicited sentences, and may refuse to translate. You may not find anyone who speaks the language fluently, and so the materials you've prepared might not work.

In that case, perhaps your best option is to be guided by your consultants and learn what they can teach you. For example, if your consultants are not comfortable working with elicitation, they may have their own ideas about how to teach a language. That may still give you a great deal of data if you are patient and can extract the relevant generalizations from the materials you're given to work with.

Moreover, while I have stressed the importance of negative data, elicitation and grammaticality judgements, it is possible to do a great deal of work and get a great deal of data from positive materials alone.

7.7.3 Working in the field language

During your field trip it may become desirable or necessary for you to work in your field language. I have not included information on monolingual elicitation here – see Everett (2001) for more information. You may wish to work with monolingual as well as bilingual consultants, though. It's possible to do this even without fluency in language, and I recommend it highly as a way of helping you to increase your fluency quickly.

Your early aim in working this way should be simply to get people talking. You'll be able to go through what they said and transcribe with bilingual consultants later on. If you have some ability to respond in the language, you will probably get fairly simple structures, as people will use foreigner talk to you.

Some techniques you can use include asking very general open-ended questions as a way of encouraging discussion. You can also present stimulus materials. Asking for vernacular definitions is also very easy to do with monolingual consultants.

7.7.4 Further reading

- **How to set out an argument**: Harris (2000) is an excellent example; see also Green and Morgan (1996).
- **Auxiliaries:** Anderson (2005).
- **Semantics:** Evans and Sasse (2005), Matthewson (2004, 2005).
- **Quantifiers:** Enç (1991).
- **Experimental design**: Crain and Thornton (1998: chs 16, 17, 24).
- **Various morphosyntactic categories**: Aikhenvald (2004), Chafe and Nichols (1986), Comrie (1976, 1985), Dixon and Aikhenvald (2000), Dixon (1994), Lyons (1999), Palmer (1986).
- **Syntax**: Bouquiaux and Thomas (1992), Levinson and Wilkins (2006), Payne (1997), Shopen (1985), Thomas (1975).
- **Word order and (non)configurationality:** Austin and Bresnan (1996), Jelinek (1984), Kiss (1998), Mithun (1992, 2003).
- **Parts of speech:** Schachter (1985).
- **Monolingual fieldwork:** Everett (2001).
- **Typology:** Comrie (1989), Haspelmath, Dryer et al. (2005), Nichols and Woodbury (1985), Shopen (1985), Whaley (1997).

8
Lexical and Semantic Data

In the previous chapters we have discussed sentences, morphology and grammar. However, we should also talk about the documentation of the lexicon of a language. Lexical documentation can be something done in conjunction with other work on the language, however dictionary making is also an extensive enterprise in its own right. You could just wait for lexical items to appear in the course of your other work (e.g., in text collection); however, the returns on this method diminish rapidly as you gain familiarity with the language (i.e., the number of new words in texts drop off rapidly).

8.1 Getting vocabulary

One way to collect words is just to ask for them. We discussed basic lexical elicitation in §3.1.3. Those methods can be extended to more detailed and less common vocabulary within various semantic fields. Collecting antonyms, converses and hyponyms at the same time as a lexical item can be useful. For example, when you ask for 'little', ask for its opposite at the same time. (Don't just ask for the English opposite, in this case 'big', ask for the 'opposite'.[1]) You may also want to branch out early and ask for 'very little', 'littler' and 'littlest'.

I've always found it easier to do vocabulary elicitation in small groups (three or four consultants). Consultants prompt each other and the arguments about definitions are usually interesting and good sources of conversational data. In a field-methods class this probably will not be feasible. Don't worry if your consultant can't remember a word, you can always come back to it later. It's easy to forget the word for something if put on the spot.

Get your consultant to take you on a tour of their house, street or village and name every item. Interlinearize your texts soon after transcribing and make a note of any new words. A technique that I have found useful is to ask your consultants to pretend that they are speaking to a Martian who crashed their spaceship near the community and who wants to find out what different things are called in the language. This Martian doesn't know anything, so needs to know what absolutely everything is called. Phrasing the task like this provides a bit of light relief from your endless questioning.

8.2   Lexicon compilation

Even if compiling a dictionary is not your main intention, keeping a lexicon database file is very useful. The list of words will help you study phonology, including variation. A wordlist is an excellent source for interlinear glossing, and it is also a useful item to return to the community at the end of your field trip if a dictionary has not yet been compiled. You can compile a wordlist using just about any format – card files, Word document or Excel spreadsheet. But a database is easier than a flat file because you can store information hierarchically and it's easier to code and search.

Here is a list of information that it is useful to have in a dictionary or wordlist. However, even a headword and gloss will be useful. Further information about dictionary compilation is given in §14.8.

- the **headword** sorted by semantic field or alphabetical order – many database programs allow for variable sorting
- **parts of speech** (be very careful about creating parts of speech labels on the basis of the gloss of the word. This is very misleading.)
- phonological **irregularities**; **pronunciation** if unpredictable from the standard orthography
- a single-word **gloss** for interlinearization
- a more detailed **definition**
- morphological **paradigmatic** information, such as gender, class or conjugation.
- any notes on comments your consultant made about the semantics of an item
- **encyclopaedic** information, e.g., information on an item's usage or ethnographic information about the cultural importance of the item. This could be accompanied by a picture
- synonyms and antonyms, hyponyms or other information about how the word relates to other items in the lexicon
- **example sentences** illustrating usage, with translations

- the source of the word (e.g., if a borrowing; etymology, if known)[2]
- **semantic field(s)** of the item
- any **usage** information – e.g., if it is slang or taboo
- a **reversal** field (so that you can compile an English–Language find-erlist from your data)
- **sound clip(s)**, and example sentences
- derived words
- the source of the information (e.g., who told you the word)
- questions for further research.

8.3   Specific domains for lexical elicitation

Here is some discussion of some particular lexical domains for elicit-ation, based on the list of semantic fields available on the web site. Note that semantic domains are highly specific to region, especially for flora and fauna, so an out-of-area list may need adaptation.

8.3.1   Body parts and products

External body part terminology can be elicited by pointing to the particular body part. For internal organs and body products, you may need to use terms in the contact language or anatomical diagrams. In some cultures it is not appropriate to show pictures of naked bodies (or anatomical diagrams), so find out in advance if this is all right. It may also be frowned on to show pictures of naked members of the opposite sex.

Try to get baby terms and slang terms for body parts as well as the regular terms. Possessive marking can be elicited at the same time as you do body part work. If the language has inalienable possession, this is a place you are highly likely to find it.

It might be easier in some cases to get detailed anatomical informa-tion about animals rather than humans. For example, hunter-gatherer groups often have very detailed knowledge of (and terminology for) the anatomy of the animals they hunt, but developed human information might be less detailed.

8.3.2   Artefacts and everyday items

The best way to elicit information about artefacts is in procedural texts (which may be videoed). Get your consultant to explain the use of the item, how it is made, and who uses it. You may need to consult a special-ist within the community. For example, most English speakers don't know much weaving vocabulary unless they are a member of a craft guild. Your average English speaker is highly unlikely to be able to give you an accurate definition of a warp thread.

Ask about everyday items as well as the exotic. Don't just concentrate on traditional items. If you are trying to learn to speak the language, you will also need to know the words for everyday items.

8.3.3   Flora and fauna

Books with pictures or illustrations of local flora and fauna are useful elicitation prompts. People might not always recognize the item from the picture, though, or they might be misled by the colours in the picture. Collaboration with trained botanists, and so on, will be necessary to make sure identifications are correct, but you can do some on your own. Glosses of the type 'kind of tree' are better than no word at all, but more information is better still!

Flora and fauna can be a great source of simple language elicitation. I have used both to elicit vernacular definitions (see Casagrande and Hale 1964). The set of questions can be used to turn just about any single word into a little story. They are particularly useful for flora and fauna but can be adapted to most items:

- Tell me all about X:
- What does it look like?
- Where is it found?
- What does it eat (and what eats it)?
- How is it different from things that look like it?
- What's it used for?
- If it's poisonous, what happens to you if you eat it?

The advantage of this type of data collection is that it involves preserving cultural knowledge at the same time as getting general language data. The texts make nice little story books too. Each book, or page, can be illustrated by photos (or children's drawings), or they can be made into short video clips.

You might need to gloss species through a third language. The species might not be named in the contact language. English is pretty poor in names for species outside Europe (and even then many people don't know those words). Not every species will necessarily have a name, and often multiple species will have the same name. Don't expect the names to match up to English names or to Linnaean taxonomy. Multiple species might have the same name, or the same species might be called by different names at different stages of its life cycle (e.g., English *goose*, *gander* and *gosling*). For further information, see Cotton (1996) and Berlin (1992), amongst others.

8.3.4   Place names

One area of the lexicon that doesn't often receive much attention is place names. In the Western lexicographical tradition, place names are left out of dictionaries, confined to specialized dictionaries or omitted altogether from linguistic research. Place names should be included in a documentation. They are useful for historical linguists, they often have different syntax from other items, and they are a wonderful cultural resource and a prompt for storytelling and deixis elicitation.

To do site mapping, you'll need a GPS and the best maps of the area you can find. Getting detailed maps can be difficult; often 1:100,000 scale maps can be the best you can find, and they are too small for accurate site mapping (although they can be enlarged on a colour photocopier and you can add detail by hand). Aerial photographs or satellite images may give you more information and may be more useful if good maps of the area are not available.

If your consultant isn't very mobile (or if you are working a long way from their traditional lands), it is possible to elicit place names by asking your consultant to give directions, telling you how to get from point A to point B and what you'll pass on the way. Or you can ask them where their favourite places are for different activities. Unless your consultant is absolutely amazing, you'll get omissions and mistakes (to see how hard this is, try it yourself – try to list all the streets you pass between your home and your university).

It's much better to take a small group of people to the area and get the data *in situ*. Try not to be the driver though; you'll need to write (recording is almost impossible unless you're in a quiet car on sealed roads and even then if you're driving you'll have enough to think about).

8.3.5   Kinship terminology

It's useful to master kinship terminology in your field language. You can observe what people call each other, how kinship affects interaction, and can use them as a prompt for kin-related language (e.g., wedding ceremonies).

Eliciting kin terms can be quite confusing. It's best to use real family situations – your consultants will probably be able to do complex kin calculations in their heads, but you'll get confused without practice.[3] Try to establish the range of each term. Who can be called *son* or *daughter*? Who can be called 'granny'? Elicit information from different people and compare the results. The scope of kin terms can be very difficult to define, for example, when eliciting from English, as the English kinship system is impoverished compared to many standards. Draw family trees. Ask different members of the same family. Reckoning may be different for men and women (e.g., for languages which classify children according to the sex of the parent, not the sex of the child; cf. Bardi *aala* 'man's child' and *bo* 'woman's child', not 'son' versus 'daughter').

8.3.6 Other domains

There are many other domains for lexical exploration. A few others that are useful or often overlooked are:

- Occupations (and social structures more generally)
- Value judgements – how to talk about evaluation
- Sounds, textures and the like
- Religious or other ceremonial terminology
- Musical terms; other specialized knowledge
- Abstract concepts (ethnophilosophy, moral reasoning)
- Mental vocabulary (thinking, forgetting, etc.)
- Mathematical concepts

8.4 Frequent lexicographic pitfalls

As mentioned in §6.4.1, it is very difficult to know whether the inferences that you have drawn about the meaning of a word are the same as your consultants' inferences. Discovering what a word or sentence means is not a trivial task! Here are some commonly encountered problems specific to lexicographic work.

8.4.1 Preliminaries

Multilingual consultants may give you a word in a different language. This doesn't mean that they don't keep the languages separate when they are speaking naturally, but it is quite difficult to do so when asked point-blank for vocabulary. Factual errors also occur sometimes – that is, your consultant may simply give you the wrong word. You've probably been in the situation where someone has asked what you call something, and you might not be able to remember (although probably came to you later on). If this happens in fieldwork and your consultant can't remember the item, don't worry, go on to the next item. They will probably remember later on and tell you. (See also the comments on translation in §6.4.1.)

8.4.2 Polysemy and homophony

Don't ever assume you've got a complete description of a word's meanings. For example, if someone tells you that Eastern Armenian *tʰɛrt* means 'sheet of paper', don't assume that this is the only meaning of the word (in this case, the word also means 'newspaper', but this was not the context in which the word was originally elicited). Sometimes a consultant will volunteer multiple meanings. It can be worth asking if a word has any other meanings, but the answer to this question is not necessarily reliable.

Sometimes consultants will say that two homonyms sound different. If you ask if two words are the 'same' (with the intention of discovering if they are homonyms or a minimal pair), the answer tends to be 'no' if the words have very different meanings, whether or not they are homonyms. A less ambiguous question to ask is 'are these the same word, or are they different words which happen to sound the same?' – that will elicit the consultant's feelings about polysemy versus homonymy, and will reveal if the words are not in fact homonymous and you have made a transcription error.

8.4.3 Descriptions instead of definitions

Consultants will often give a description of when a word might be used, which is not the same as the meaning of the word itself. Consider the following Bardi word:

(20) *manbin*
'soft rain'
'dry season rain'

In Aklif (1999), *manbin* is given as 'soft rain'. In fact, a more accurate meaning is 'dry season rain' (i.e., rain that falls in the dry season); such rain is usually light (in contrast to the heavy wet season storms), so the definition is not incorrect, but it is not the core meaning of the word; after all, light rain in the wet season is not *manbin*. A further example from Yan-nhaŋu is given below:

(21) *baḻgurryu*
'waistband'
'from string'

Here the *real* meaning of this word is 'from string'. It is the word *baḻgurr* 'string' in the instrumental case. A waistband is an example of something that is made from string. In other cases, the word may be both a descriptive item and have a more abstract meaning. For example, in Yan-nhaŋu *maɳutji-bu* means both 'something associated with eyes' and, specifically, 'glasses'.

Be on the lookout for times when your consultant says 'it's like when ...'. That is a good indication that the information you are getting is a description rather than a definition. (Of course, descriptions can be useful information too – and if they are given in the target language, they are an excellent sources of similes, short sentences or examples with the semblative case (if there is one) .)

8.4.4   Discourse context

We tend of think that elicitation is 'discourse free', in that there is not the discourse context that is created in narratives or conversational data. However, elicitation can still create its own discourse contexts, and this can interfere with your data. For example, if you use the same participants for each sentence, this greatly increases the likelihood that one or other of them will be identified as a topic (and therefore marked for topichood, by word order, intonation or morphology). One way to try to prevent this is not to have the same participants in two sentences in a row. This increases the artificiality of the elicitation, but it avoids potentially confounding variables like topic tracking.

8.5   Further reading

- **Kinship**: Holy (1996), McKinney (2000: ch. 14).
- **Lexicography**: Mosel (2004), Nichols and Sprouse (2003).
- **Lexical semantics and fieldwork**: Evans and Sasse (2005), Hellwig (2006).
- **Other types of documentation**: Austin (2005), Barwick (2005), Barz and Cooley (1997), Post (2004), Toelken (1996).
- **Ethnobotany**: Berlin (1992), Cotton (1996).
- **Indigenous knowledge systems**: Bicker, Sillitoe and Pottier (2004), Sillitoe, Dixon and Barr (2005).

9
Discourse, Pragmatics and Narrative Data

Field linguists are often told to rely on naturalistic data as much as elicited data. By this we usually think of recorded narratives. However, a comprehensive description of a language should be built not just on elicited data, but also other types of spontaneously produced speech. Narratives and discourse data are covered in this chapter.

9.1 Working with texts

Elicitation will allow you to make a lot of progress, but it will bias your data towards the constructions you chose to ask about and ones that are easy to translate. Also you can't do anything with frequency working from elicited data because there frequency is determined entirely by what you ask. Therefore, you should also use spontaneously generated data.[1]

9.1.1 Text genres and register

It is usually easy to get people to tell stories, but there are many other types of discourse and other genres and registers in languages too. If the language you are working on is regularly used, you should have no difficulty obtaining samples of different registers, genres, and types of interaction. You might be able to record a religious service (Christian sermons are often wonderful data sources for similes, imagery and prohibitions). Is there community radio or TV? You might be able to get tapes and transcripts.

Don't neglect written sources if the language you are working on is regularly written. Sometimes newspapers will have sections in regional languages (e.g., *The Namibian* has a section in Oshiwambo each week). Get people to write stories for you, or to write you letters (and write back in the language yourself). Make sure you collect a range of styles.

9.1.2 Text complexity

Don't be surprised if your early texts are very simple. It's very common for speakers to simplify their speech if their interlocutor isn't fluent. This might actually be a good thing early on. Think of such texts as linguistic bikes with linguistic training wheels, but don't be fooled into thinking that you are getting the full range of syntactic complexity in the language. If you continue to get very simple stories you might need to do something about it, such as asking people to pretend that they are telling stories to a fluent speaker who comes from a different place and hasn't heard them before (or getting your consultants to tell stories to each other with you absent). Such texts are also appropriate for producing learners' materials.

Different cultures have different ideas about what constitutes fluency. In English we tend to think of it as a mastery of the collocations and idioms of the language. In Bardi someone who's 'fluent' is someone who can conjugate a verb. Mastering the phonemic system with a good accent might also get you labelled as 'fluent' even if you can't put a sentence together. Sometimes you'll never be considered fluent, no matter how well you speak. Knowing some complex morphology might also increase your perceived fluency. All these things will encourage speakers to use more complex language to you, which in turn will expose you to it and allow you to master it.

9.1.3 Text brainstorming ideas

There are several ways to elicit texts. I have never had a problem getting people to tell stories when the speakers have been fluent, but it was much more difficult when working with part-speakers (cf. Austin's (1981) comments on his work on Diyari grammar). Here are some ideas:

- **Children's stories**. They are useful when first learning the language as they tend to be repetitive and fairly simple. They are also easy to tell and often have fairly limited vocabulary. Bed-time stories fall into this genre.
- **Picture prompts**, such as the frog stories or other pictures of scenes, will get people talking. Get them to tell you the story behind a picture. You might need to make one up yourself to demonstrate.
- **Instructions**. Get your consultants to tell you to do different things; these can get quite complicated (and this can be a lot of fun). It could be the steps involved in making a traditional item, a recipe, or the rules for playing cards, or directions for how to get to a landmark, or even shopping lists.

- **Descriptions of places, events and activities**. If you haven't seen your consultants for a day or two, ask them what they did. Tell them what you did.
- **Vernacular definitions** (see §8.3)
- **Traditional narratives**. All cultures have traditional stories (e.g., folk tales).
- **Personal reminiscences**. Biographies and autobiographies, anecdotes, oral history.
- **Jokes and insults**.
- **Proverbs**, and their explanations.
- **Translations of other stories** in the contact language.
- **Speeches**, oratory styles.

Not all of these ideas may be appropriate. For example, community members may be unwilling to translate stories from another culture into their own language. It may also be seen as inappropriate or insulting to continually ask for information about the 'old days' if no one lives like that anymore.

9.1.4   Acquiring textual materials

Make the most of your good storytelling consultants. Often others will defer to them. However, you might have very senior people who are deferred to for stories who might be very difficult to understand, or they might tell very short versions of the story, or they might not actually be very interested in language work. You should always respect this.

It's possible to get others to tell stories for data by asking them to explain a text. For example, I worked with an elder who told very telegraphic versions of texts which I could not follow. I asked another person to retell and explain the story, because I did not know the details and could not appreciate what I'd been told by the elder (which was true). I ended up with several versions of the story. Dickinson (2007) reports the rapid progress made by working with literate native-speaker teams. If your consultants already write the language you're working on, this can be a great way to get a lot of new data quickly.

Talking into a recorder with no audience is very difficult and not many people will do it well. It's much easier for someone to tell a story *to* someone, either to you or to other speakers of the language. Even if you don't understand very much, listen attentively, don't spend all your time writing. It's good for your language practice to try to understand as much as possible. When the text is finished, you could try to tell the story back (in the contact language or the field language). It has the dual function of showing that you are a good listener and understood the main points, and allows you to have a summary. It also gives you the chance to ask for key words and vocabulary.

Ideal storytelling situations are seldom ideal recording situations. In most cultures stories are not told in isolation, and so there might be a lot of background noise, talking, shuffling, eating and so on. These are the situations where a lapel microphone is useful. You can also exploit the advantage an audience brings. Bring some of the good storytellers together, and get them an audience. If I wanted to record the oral history of my family, I would get a group of my elderly relatives in a quiet corner of the local pub and let one-upmanship take its course.

Part-speakers or rusty speakers may find the idea of telling a full story really daunting, and may not want to do it (or may be unable to do it). There are some ways around this. They can practise first, so they can think about the words. Turn the recorder off until they're ready. Get them to tell it in the language they are more comfortable in first, and then retell it. You could also treat the story like a translation exercise. Once they have told the story in the language they are comfortable in, transcribe it and work on a translation sentence by sentence. This can also be done in groups. A 'story' told that way is a rather different type of object than one told spontaneously, but presumably if you are contemplating this type of storytelling, any data at all will be valuable for the documentation.

9.2   What to do with the materials

Now you're collecting all these language samples, you'll need to do something with them! Remember back to §4.5 (and that chapter) where we talked about the workflow for data processing. The same applies to textual materials. Make a backup, add the metadata to your database, transcribe the text (with help), check the transcription and translation, parse it, and then use that data to ask questions about what you didn't understand.

It's not uncommon to collect more raw data on a field trip (and in class) than you can possibly deal with. It takes about an hour to transcribe a minute of text when you first start, and although you will speed up, it will still take many hours of your time to fully process even relatively short stretches of language. You'll want at least some of your texts fully glossed and translated. Resist the temptation to keep recording without doing much processing, interlinearizing and analysis in the hope that things will become clearer by themselves.

9.2.1   Text transcription

Transcribing and annotating (and interlinearizing) texts is very time-consuming. If you are not working on your native language and don't have someone who can transcribe texts for you, you will need to find someone to go through the recordings with you. I highly recommend using a transcription program where you can link text to audio. This allows you to time-align your transcriptions and it makes it much easier to check what the person said (rather than having to sort through the whole recording). See this book's web site. Transcription formats vary, but for narratives I recommend doing it phrase by phrase, that is, using fairly short chunks of text. Early on you will not be able to keep much language in short-term memory. If you are transcribing by hand, the main rule (and only rule!) is to leave lots of space for annotations.

There are some ways to speed up the transcription process, or at least to maximize the utility of the time spent with your consultants. One way is to go through your text with a speaker and get them to repeat it slowly, line by line. Have two recorders. Use one to record your consultant's answers. Use the other to play back the text you're transcribing. Don't write much, just ask about phrases you don't understand. It means more work for you later in the day to transcribe the second recording, but it saves quite a bit of time during the session, and it's much easier to transcribe from the slow version. It only works once you have some facility in the language, though. It's too hard in early sessions. Another way to speed up transcription is to do a first rough transcription by yourself, then check it with a native speaker. This is useful once you know the language better or if your speaker speaks slowly and clearly.

Conversation data is hard to transcribe – there may be lots of fast speech phenomena that make it difficult to parse what people are saying, there may be slang expressions and overlap (speakers talking over each other). Most of these difficulties are actually why we want to record this type of data – we want information about fast speech production, we want to know about the slang and informal register, and how speakers actually use language. You may have trouble getting someone to help you transcribe conversation data, as your consultants may feel that transcribing conversations is a waste of time compared to working with more high prestige language.

9.2.2   Compiling a corpus

In its loosest form, a corpus is a collection of linguistic data. In compiling materials for a documentation of a language, you will be implicitly creating a corpus of material. There are good practices to follow in corpus creation, most of which have been mentioned already, implicitly or otherwise.

A corpus should be *representative* of the area of language you want to study. So, in order to study informal speech, you need a collection of informal speech: it's not possible to study the features of this genre from planned narratives. Therefore in designing your documentation you need to make sure that you gather appropriate samples of different speech varieties.

Secondly, you need full 'texts', and not samples or snippets of language. That is, using a corpus of elicited sentences or overheard phrases will not allow you to draw adequate conclusions about the language.

Each item in the corpus should have appropriate metadata attached: the speaker, circumstances of recording, and so on. See §4.4.2 for more information. Corpus data is more useful if it's annotated. That allows you to search for more detailed environments. It also allows you to create sub-corpora (e.g., a sub-corpus of all your planned narratives, and another of spontaneous speech; that would let you search for differences between the two genres).

Finally, we need to consider the size of the corpus. In general, the more the better, but don't be put off by the discussions of million-word corpora. That is unfeasible for a single linguist working on a previously undescribed variety. You can still make use of data in a corpus of much smaller size: a properly transcribed, time-aligned and annotated corpus of even 40,000 words very useful (and more than many documentation projects achieve).

9.2.3   Editing texts

If you put the texts that you've recorded into a book, you may need to do some editing, in consultation with your consultants. This is simply because the transferral of language from speech to the page changes our expectations and conventions. For example, in spoken language, self-repair and hesitation is common, but in writing we do not start a word and stop halfway through.

In many cultures written discourse and spoken discourse are quite different. This is true in some cases even when the language has not been written for very long and there are no formal written genres. At Milingimbi for much of the 1980s, for example, people spoke

Djambarrpuyŋu as their everyday language, but writing was usually done in Gupapuyŋu, a similar but distinct variety of Yolŋu Matha. Written/spoken diglossia are very common in Indonesia, the Middle East and India. Therefore it might not seem appropriate for you to use spoken language as representative of written language without heavy editing.

In converting transcriptions of spoken language to edited textual data, it can be helpful to use a transcription program with multiple tiers. If you are doing discourse analysis, you want the raw text with no changes. For your own notes, you need to use a transcription close to the original (but with notes on what people say is ungrammatical, or bad style, or a hesitation, or code-switching). If the texts are to be published, people will probably want to edit them more. How much repetition you take out is an important consideration (the papers in Murray and Rice (1996) provide further discussion).

9.3   Discourse data

9.3.1   Why should you record spontaneous/conversational speech?

You might wonder why it's worth recording conversational, informal, or spontaneous speech. After all, people make all sorts of speech errors, they use fast speech figures, they talk over one another; in short they make the linguist's job of transcription and analysis much more difficult. Why not make things easier for yourself by working with cleaner and more manageable data?

The most obvious answer is that in using only one type of data, you are missing out on documenting many aspects of language structure and use. How people actually speak in quotidian situations is usually quite different from how they translate elicited sentences or tell a story. Elicited sentences and narrative usually only contain one data from one speech register, whereas language users have access to many different registers and speech styles.[2]

Secondly, many elements of language are only explicable and describable in terms of language use. Not everything is; it's possible to describe agreement morphology in almost all languages on the basis of elicited data, but you won't make any headway on all the particles you've glossed as 'discourse particle' without reference to discourse. Thirdly, not confining your study to one type of data will improve your own language skills. Studying other people's conversations is useful for you when learning how to speak fluently and naturalistically.

Recording only narratives and elicitation creates problems for language revitalization/teaching classes. If that is all that has been recorded, students must learn a variety of the language based on narrative style, and it sounds weird or incorrect to speakers of the language when they import that style into other domains of language use. It also leads to large chunks of missing vocabulary and speech acts, for example, how they introduced a friend to someone new, or how they greeted each other, or the polite and rude ways of asking for something. Therefore, even if you intend to write a traditional descriptive grammar based largely on narratives and elicited data, make sure you also record other types of data too as far as is practical.

If you are working on a highly endangered language conversation data might be very difficult to obtain. People might not speak the language on a daily basis, or they might feel uncomfortable about speaking spontaneously while being recorded. People may also feel that it should be the formal standard language that is recorded and described, rather than colloquial speech. This may be seen as helping you to make the best possible description of the language. This is particularly common in areas where the colloquial variety has low prestige compared to the standard language, and where both are widely used (such as in Indonesia, and many parts of the Arabic-speaking world). You might need to spend some time working around diglossia like this.[3]

9.3.2   Getting naturalistic data

Naturalistic (non-elicited) data comes in many forms. When we think of 'discourse' we tend to think of conversations; however, there are many types of naturalistic linguistic data. Here are some of the types of non-elicited data you should try to collect as part of a general description of the language:

- Narratives in different genres (see §9.1.1)
- Conversations, with or without you as participant or observer
- Semi-structured or unstructured interviews, with you or a consultant or speaker as interviewer (see §6.3.5 and §9.3.3)
- Semi-monologic data (e.g., talk-back radio)
- Written language, such as diary entries, newspaper opinion columns, and blog posts.

For descriptive purposes we can divide this sort of data into planned and spontaneous data. Spontaneous data is more likely to have speech errors, slips of the tongue and repairs. Planned or edited data will have fewer errors like this. However, edited or normed data probably also has other things taken out that you might want included in a description. In areas where code-switching is common, planned data often contains much less code-switching than spontaneous speech. There may be register interferences. Therefore it is good to get a range of data of different types.

9.3.3   Manufacturing discourse data

If you cannot record naturalistic discourse data, there are some ways to manufacture it. Of course, using manufactured data is not the same as spontaneous speech, and should be a last resort. For example, your consultants could translate dialogues about some subject. This is still planned speech, but it is more likely to have topic chaining and other features than elicited speech.

Finally, you can encourage exchanges by carrying out tasks which require negotiation:

- 'What am I thinking of?'
- Problem solving
- Ethical reasoning
- Games, e.g., blindfolding and giving directions.

9.4   Topics for investigation in discourse and pragmatics

The possibilities for discourse and pragmatic study are endless: here are some suggestions for preliminary investigation of a diverse range of phenomena:

- Silence, turn-taking (e.g., pauses in speech and conversation)
- Chunking: what information is 'chunked' together in discourse, how does it relate to constituency? Etc.
- Repair: self-repair, hesitation, points at which repair can occur
- Overlap: how much overlap there is in conversation, where it occurs
- Narrative structure
- Formulaic language, formulas for greetings, closings, hedging, etc.
- Information structure: where does old information appear in the clause? How is new information signalled?
- Repetition: what chunks of speech tend to be targeted for repetition? When does it occur? What does it signal?
- Intonation (including main clause, interrogative, focal and list)
- Gesture

9.5   Further reading

- **Corpus linguistics:** Johnson (2004), Kennedy (1998), McEnery and Wilson (1996), Samarin (1967: ch. 55).
- **Discourse:** van Dijk (1997), Foley (2004).
- **Folklore:** Toelken (1996).
- **Translation:** Baker (1992).
- **Oral history:** Murray and Rice (1996).
- **Transcription:** Edwards and Lampert (1993), Edwards (2001).
- *Frog Stories:* Strömqvist and Verhoeven (2004).

10
Consultants and Field Locations

There are two important guidelines for choosing a field site. First, go somewhere you want to be (since it's you who's going to go there, you should have some reason for going, even if it's a fairly vague reason). Secondly, go somewhere where people would like to work with you (or at least wouldn't mind).[1]

10.1 Field-methods classes and the field

Field-methods classes tend to have the aim of preparing students in data elicitation techniques. That is, they give students practice at forming hypotheses and testing them by questioning a native speaker of an unfamiliar language. As we saw in Chapter 1, however, the analysis component of fieldwork can sometimes be rather small. As part of a field-methods class you get some practice in collaborative research, and some idea about data organization, but you are generally not required to do any of the ancillary work that arises in fieldtrips. The instructor does the administrative work such as applying for ethics approval, finding the consultant, and organizing payment. In the field, **you** do all of this.

In the class the speaker lives in your country, and is more or less familiar with the norms of social interaction in your culture. That is not necessarily true in fieldwork. You will be the ambassador for your culture, not the other way around. Field-methods classes often have highly educated consultants (e.g., graduate students or undergraduates at the university), and some may have training in linguistics. You cannot count on this in the field.

When you take a field-methods class it's usually one of several things you spend your time on. On fieldwork, the fieldwork is what you'll be spending most of your time on, and that can cause fatigue and over-work. Elicitation time is very limited in the class setting. The class may have only a few hours a week, if that. In the field, you might be getting that much data every day (which means much more processing time and greatly increased chances of information overload). In class, you have the support of your colleagues when your analysis doesn't work and you're stuck.

You will probably work with a single speaker in a field-methods class, which will give you a fairly coherent and consistent picture of the language. In the field, you will probably be working with several people, which will almost certainly lead to internally inconsistent data. Finally, most instructors forbid the students from looking at documentation for the field-methods language so that students get practice in working out a basic analysis on their own. That's a good skill to have. In the field, however, you should have an intimate knowledge of what other people have said about the language.

10.2   Choosing a field site and preparation

10.2.1   What makes a good (and a bad) field site?

There are some obvious factors that make a bad field site. Some groups do not want outsiders working on their languages. If no one wants you there, don't go. There are plenty of speakers of endangered languages who are worried that their language is not being passed on and would like to work with a linguist. As difficult as it might be for linguists to accept, it is up to the speech community to decide on the fate of their language, and we have to respect that.[2] We need to separate the activist role of linguists from the consultant role; it is not our job to tell speakers what should happen to their languages.

Another bad site choice is one where you will be in physical danger. Life is intrinsically dangerous; you might be run over by a bus crossing the street. However, sites in war zones are rather more dangerous than your average field location. Areas where kidnappings for ransom are common aren't recommended – they put you, your consultants, your government and your parents in a difficult situation. Sites where your presence would add to tensions or where you would simply be a burden (e.g., another person eating food in an area of scarce resources) are not a good idea.

As in all things, there is a calculated risk, and you will not necessarily know until you get there whether there are serious threats to your personal safety. One example is travel as a single female. In some places this brings obvious risk, although it may be possible to reduce the risk by being sensible and taking the usual precautions.

Sites that are impossible to get to are not very practical – if it's going to take you three weeks to walk there and three weeks to get back, and you have an eight-week summer grant, that's probably not a very good place to go for a first trip. However, it might be a great (if challenging) place to go for a year.

What makes a good field site, then? The best field sites are places where people want to work with you and where you want to be. Everything else follows from this. The best field sites don't necessarily have electricity and running water, and they aren't necessarily easy to get to.

There is nothing to say that you have to work on an endangered language. However, given the large number of languages in danger of disappearing, the relatively large proportion of community members of such languages who would welcome the opportunity to make a permanent record of their language, and the small number of linguists who are trained to do this, there are good reasons to do so. It makes sense to prioritize description so that languages which can't be described later (because there are no longer any speakers) are worked on first. On the other hand, there is also an incentive to record languages while they are viable, since the type of information that can be gained when there are very few speakers is quite different from the possibilities when there are many speakers.

Many students continue to work on a language that they have begun research on during field-methods classes. Others first begin work with speakers who live near their university before going to the field. Both of these techniques are very useful, although they are no substitute for the field trip itself.

10.2.2   When to go

Think about the time of year you will be able to go to the field. Monsoon seasons are not a good time to do fieldwork – the afternoon rain disrupts recording, it's very hot and humid which is bad for equipment, and in Australia at least, it's school holidays so the people you want to talk to might be away (and there'll be lots of kids around creating noise and distractions during recording sessions).

In an agrarian community, doing fieldwork during harvest time is a bad idea because your consultants will be busy all day, with priorities other than talking to linguists. Going in summer to do oral history is a bad idea if the group has a prohibition on storytelling during that time (see ,e.g., Toelken 1996:118ff.). In winter, it might be too cold, or it might be hard to travel to your site (e.g., it might be snowed in).

10.2.3   The one-language, one-linguist rule

In many parts of the world there's an implicit assumption that you will not work on 'someone else's' language (i.e., the language that another linguist is already working on). There's no point in going to a place where you will be duplicating another person's work and creating more work for their consultants. On the other hand, there's no rule that once a language has been worked on by a linguist, no one else can touch it. A language is never fully documented and there is always more to discover, and it's easy to make inaccurate generalizations, so you might discover something new! Also, languages change, particularly during language death, so the variety you describe might be quite different. Furthermore, if you are interested in a specific subdiscipline of linguistics it may help to work on a language where there is some documentation already. For example, if you are primarily interested in syntax, it will be easier for you to make progress if you do not need to work out the phoneme inventory and basic morphology from scratch.

The best way to resolve this is to contact other linguists who have worked in the area. A team approach may be best (where you work with another linguist with different interests). Alternatively, you may want to pick a different field site for the same language, a different dialect, or a different language. A language with a decent description may not be the best use of your time given how many undescribed languages there are.

10.2.4   How long to go for?

The length of the trip needs planning. How long will your university let you go for? There might be problems if you have not fulfilled your residency requirements at your university, for example. How easy/expensive is it to get to the site? Will you be able to go more than once? If not, your trip should be as long as possible.

How much money do you have to live on while you are there? How long you can afford to go for is important. What time of year will you be going? If you are likely to have lots of disruptions (e.g., funerals, travelling consultants), planning a short trip might be counterproductive and not let you get your work done. If you only have a few elderly speakers to work with, it is not a good idea to go for a long period of time unless you can work in such a way that you will not tire out your consultants (even though you run the risk that each trip will be the last opportunity to work with them). Will you be able to analyse your data as you go? If so, it makes more sense to go for a longer time. If you can't bring a computer or won't have anywhere to work, it might make sense to go for several shorter trips (cf. Crowley 2007:66).

In doing a three-year research-only PhD (as in Australia and the UK) graduate students generally go for an initial trip of about six to eight weeks, to get basic information on the language, to find out general community reactions, check out the field site,and so on. They then come back and process that data and make a detailed plan for a long fieldtrip, which lasts anywhere from four to 12 months. Then they come back and do the bulk of the writing up and analysis. There is then time for a final shortish trip to clean up final questions, deliver community materials, and so on. This implies that it's possible to do three trips with the budget, and that other considerations don't trump this plan. In countries where the PhD also involves coursework or a shorter thesis (such as the Unites States), there is usually an initial summer trip (in the second or even third year of the PhD), then a longer trip, perhaps over a semester, and then a shorter write-up period. However, there is a great deal of variation in length of trips. Being able to work with someone before you go to the field (or being able to keep in contact with your consultants when you return) will let you clear up some of your questions between trips.

10.2.5 Preparation

Preparing for a fieldtrip begins more than a year in advance. Choose your field area and read about the language. Talk to others who have worked in the area – they will have useful suggestions for priorities in documentation, tips for who to contact, and knowledge of what permits are required. Next, apply for research funding and start preparing your materials. It's good to have a database structure before you leave, and at least a week of materials prepared. It may not be possible to keep to your prepared materials (to be honest, it probably won't be) but it will give you a basis from which to work and will give you something to depart from, rather than having to start from scratch.

You need to be very familiar with your equipment before you start work, especially if you will be using both audio and video recording, or needing to set up multiple recorders. Know what the settings do and know which pieces of equipment and which cables go together. You may want to label your cables and adaptors, since video monitor cables and stereo audio cables look very similar, and sometimes the only differences between two transformers is the voltage. Many of Crowley's (2007:123ff) horror stories could have been avoided by fully testing the equipment before the fieldtrip. Pack your equipment so that it will survive the journey. Packing all your equipment together makes it easier to keep track of, but if that bag is lost or damaged you will have lost all your equipment. Therefore it is a good idea to pack your backup equipment in a separate place if possible.

Finally, remember that in going on fieldwork for any length of time you will need to take care of any obligations in your home location, such as making arrangements for bill payments, mail collection and apartment rent while you are in the field. This can also be extremely time-consuming.

10.2.6   Travel documentation

If you are travelling to a foreign country, you will almost always need a passport, and probably a visa. Don't assume that because you have been to a country as a tourist and didn't need a visa that you will not need one for research. You might also need the permission of the local group as a whole too. In Australia if you are working in an Aboriginal community, you often need a permit to stay in the community, although how these are organized depends very much on the individual community. If you are working with a Native American or Canadian First Nations group, you should get the support of the tribal council (if you have contacts with consultants in the community, they may be able to help organize this). In Brazil, you need the permission of FUNAI (Fundação Nacional do Índio) and the support of a Brazilian university.

If you do not have permanent residence or citizenship of the country you normally live in, make sure that you will not have difficulty returning after your fieldtrip. If you are leaving for an extended period of time (e.g., a year in the field), make sure your travel documents are still valid for re-entry. This varies from country to country. It is important, however, to talk to your university's international office, and that they realize that you will be gone for however long you're going for, and that you might not be in a position to receive mail or faxes.

10.3   Choosing a consultant

10.3.1   The ideal consultant

If you've ever taught (or been in) an introductory linguistics class, you know that it's possible to divide the class in three. Some students intuitively understand all the content and find linguistics as a whole fascinating. Others can work out how to do the problems and follow the lectures but for them it's just another class. The third group find it very difficult to think abstractly about language. This variation isn't just true of introductory linguistics classes, it's also true of the community at large, and the best people to find to work with are those with an intuitive understanding of using language to talk about linguistic structures. This skill isn't correlated with formal education, and people who possess it inevitably make the best consultants.

Ideally the consultants should speak the language you are studying fluently and as their primary mode of communication. There are, however, many situations in which it will not be possible to find such a speaker. For example, the language may be already moribund, and all everyday discourse might be in another language. Or there may be no full speakers of the language at all. The last speakers may be fluent, but old and frail, and not able to work for long periods. Or everyone may be multilingual and the language in question may be just one of the languages they regularly use.

The ideal consultant is a native speaker of the language under study, and an excellent second-language speaker of the contact language. Ideal consultants have healthy, obliging, and like-minded friends and relatives who don't mind being asked questions and being roped in work too. They have no speech impediments, they are fluent storytellers, and like thinking about and being creative with language. They have very clear articulation and infinite patience. The ideal consultant has no other demands on their time, they never get sick, and neither do their relatives. They never vary the loudness of their voice.

If you ever find such a person and are able to work with them, let me know. The 'ideal consultant' I've just described is a myth. Do not give up on someone immediately if you aren't understanding one another (e.g., if they don't understand the types of questions you are asking). It takes practice to think about language in the way that linguists do – you've been doing it throughout your career as a linguistics student so be patient and be prepared to try different things. It also takes practice to be able to ask questions clearly. Consultants also tend to have different strengths, so you may not want to work the same way with everyone. In my experience, anyone who wants to work with you for any reason other than money will be useful in your project. That is, enthusiasm is the sole absolutely necessary criterion for a consultant – everything else can be worked out.[3]

10.3.2   Finding speakers

How you find a consultant will depend on the area you are working in, local cultural and political factors, and what you want to achieve. In

Aboriginal Australia, I have never turned up anywhere without an introduction and the name of someone who is willing to do language work (and the permission of the Community Council). In other places, making contact before you arrive might be unfeasible.

Consultants will often find you – once you've met some people in the community you will inevitably be a topic of conversation and people who are interested in language will often seek you out (see also Macaulay 2005). In all my fieldtrips, I have never worked solely with the person I originally made contact with. They have always introduced me to other family members and friends and it has been possible to work with several people from early on in the project. Consultants will have their own reasons for wanting to participate in the project. This applies in field-methods classes as much as in the field. Speakers might want to work with you because it sounds like fun, as a chance to share their language, because their friends are involved too, because they're bored and have nothing better to do with their time, because they are worried about their language being passed on to their children, because they're interested in linguistics, and so on.

You might have trouble finding people who admit to speaking the language. There may be political reasons why they might not want to say they speak it, or they may not feel they speak it well in comparison to other people in the community (see further Crowley 2007:86ff). Establish your credentials and your motives, and be patient.

10.3.3   Consultants and literacy

Some linguists (e.g. Vaux and Cooper 1999) advise that when given a choice, it is better to work with non-literate speakers. The argument goes that literacy increases prescriptivism, or at least that schooling (which increases literacy) encourages prescriptivism. I don't agree. Everyone has views about how language should and should not be used, what should or should not be recorded, who in their speech community speaks 'properly' and who speaks 'badly', and which other languages are 'better' or 'worse' than their own. That is not an artefact of literacy and schooling, it's a fact about human interaction. Written materials may have high prestige value for non-literate (or less literate) speakers of the language and so may promote feelings of prescription.

Literacy is an extremely useful skill and working with literate speakers can save you a great deal of time. Literate speakers can help with spelling and transcription. In areas where literacy is comparatively rare, literacy might have some status. It might also have been acquired at some cost.[4] Such people might be grateful for the chance to use it, and to have a hand in the description and first recording of their language.

Non-literate speakers might know more about the oral history of the culture you're working with, because they might have been learning that rather than going to school. However, think about what message it sends when a university person goes to a community and seeks out the people with the least education, particularly in areas where education is strongly pushed as a means of economic advancement. Working with a team of people has benefits here.

Don't rely on the people who traditionally interpret the culture to outsiders. They may be the easiest people to make contact with initially. Having someone who is bicultural and who knows what is going on is useful and reassuring. You may be expected to work with them, but they may not have the time to spend with you that you need. Remember also that you are probably asking different questions from most of the people who ask them things about their language and culture, and you may not be satisfied with the answers you get, which have been developed for a different audience.

10.3.4 Knowing the regional lingua franca

So far, I have implied that you will be working through either English or your native language, but that is not the complete list of languages you may need. There are advantages to knowing the regional lingua franca, and many advantages to having a language in common for elicitation. It will make interaction with people apart from your consultants much easier (if they primarily speak a language other than your field language).

There can also be advantages to being unable (or unwilling) to speak the local lingua franca with your consultants. It may improve your chances of people speaking your field language with you (as Alice Harris (personal communication) found in Georgia; the only situation in which people would speak Georgian rather than Russian was if they did not know that she spoke Russian).

You'll probably pick up some of the lingua franca anyway, whether you make an effort to or not. There will usually be little reason to spend a lot of time and energy learning it from scratch in the field – that energy is better spent learning and using the language you came to study.

10.3.5 Consultants and gender

In most places it's easier to work with someone of the same gender as you. It's often expected. For example, in Aboriginal Australia the women tend to hang around together and camp together, and the men will be off somewhere else in a different camp. Trying to circumvent this aspect of the culture could cut you out of excellent data and opportunities to meet people. My hanging around all the time with men at my field site would probably lead to disrespect to me and comments on my lack of morals; it would ruin my relationship with the female relatives of the men I was hanging around with, and it could cause tensions in the family homes of the people I work with. In short, even though it cuts in half the number of consultants I can work with, trying to do anything else is not feasible.

There are often language differences between genders, though, so if you only work with a group of one gender there will be aspects of the language you will miss. Women can be more conservative speakers, especially in areas where men tend to travel to cities for work but women don't (this is true for many traditional languages in Iran and Afghanistan, for example). Abbi (2001) discusses a number of the relative merits of male versus female consultants in India, and Milroy (1980) makes the point that in 1970s Belfast, only a female outsider could be integrated into the social network to do the type of observation she was doing.

There are ways around gender taboos without upsetting anyone. There may be socially sanctioned settings where men and women can interact. A meeting for interviewing might be all right if there is a third person there, such as another of your consultants (ask someone who is highly respected in the community). You can give your recorder to someone else and give them a list of questions to ask, or you can work in a team with another linguist of the opposite gender.

Another issue which comes under the broad category of 'gender' and 'fieldwork' is what happens if you fall in love with one of your consultants. Vaux and Cooper (1999:16, *passim*) provide considerable discussion of sexual interest between consultants and linguists.

10.3.6   How many people to work with?

Some tasks are easier to accomplish with one person (such as recording wordlists), while others seem to work better in pairs or small groups. If there are few speakers, it's a good idea to try to work with as many people as possible. It cuts down the likelihood of part-speaker effects and partial fluency. It makes it more likely that your analysis holds for more speakers than just your main consultant. It also minimizes feelings of slighting other speakers, and puts less stress on the person you're working with. You can collect data faster this way.

People have different linguistic talents. Some people are natural linguists, others are not. Some are fantastic storytellers, others are not. Some people are really good at explaining things, others aren't. Sometimes you may need to work with particular people for political/ social reasons. There might be an expectation that you will work with community leaders, or the oldest speakers, or people your own age and gender. The expectations may not be directly mentioned to you. Working within or around such restrictions so that everyone is happy can take some time.

Phonetic/phonological elicitation is *always* better done one on one if at all possible. It speeds things up, it minimizes the potential for external noise (such as the person who isn't talking getting bored) and it makes it easier to use a head-mounted microphone. Some people prefer telling stories in a group, and the group dynamic is useful to keep conversation going. Others may not want an audience. I have always found semantic discussions and wordlist checking easier in small groups of about three people, since it allows discussion of intuitions.

10.3.7   Getting consultants to turn up

Being 'stood up' by consultants is a frequently reported problem. It's unavoidable to a certain extent – after all, consultants have their own lives and priorities. While you're in the field, your data collection is your main obsession, but for your consultants you are just one other thing they have to be concerned about. It sounds stereotypical (and obvious), but don't expect people without clocks and watches to be concerned about very specific times of the day. It's pointless arranging a meeting for 10:30 when no one has a clock. It's much better to be flexible in your work hours. Be aware too that in some cultures an agreement to meet isn't like making an appointment, it's a polite way of leave-taking (see Hill 2006) and doesn't necessarily obligate the person to turn up.

Make the work something your consultants will look forward to, not just a transaction (see also Milroy 1980:48–9). Have added incentives for people to work with you, such as inviting them to lunch and work afterwards. Don't try to work too much. If you tire out your consultants, they probably won't be enthusiastic about coming to work with you. Don't try to work at times of the day where your consultants have other activities. Consultants aren't going to turn up if there's a better option. (Neither would you, right?) Try to work with people with lots of free time (e.g., retirees).

Don't rely on one person; if you have several people you can talk to, there's more chance that someone will be available. Pick your consultants up or go to their house rather than waiting for them to come to you.

10.4   Linguist-consultant interactions

No one likes being disbelieved, or constantly being interrupted, or patronized. There are some commonly reported complaints from consultants about their interactions with linguists.

One of the most common is a feeling of not being given time to answer the question that the linguist asked. It's important, once you've asked a question, to give the consultant time to answer it. Rephrase the question if it's unclear, but don't keep talking. If you move on to another question, be clear you're doing so; it can be confusing if you have gone on to ask another question but the consultant thinks you are still talking about the previous topic. Pauses in conversational turn-taking might be different between English and your field language, and so what seems to you like a long uncomfortable pause might be quite normal for your consultants.

If you are going to the trouble to ask the question, it's because you don't know the answer and you think the consultant might. Therefore be careful that you do not contradict or correct your consultants. You may want to follow up on what they say, and ask more questions if what your consultants say isn't congruent with your current hypotheses about how the language works, but there are ways to do this without coming across as insulting or overbearing. Crowley (2007:175) mentions a linguist who corrects the language of his consultants. Never do that! Why would you be on fieldwork in the first place if not to learn from your consultants?

Mithun (2001) and Rice (2001) report the impression that a linguist gives of not caring or not listening. Consultants may also feel that they are being patronized. This is particularly an issue when there is a big difference in educational level between the linguist and the consultant (e.g., university faculty working with someone who's never been to school). You're on familiar ground with recorders, writing and linguistic analysis, but it might be very foreign to the consultant. Think of how you feel when you go to a seminar or conference presentation and the speaker gives a very technical talk and then gets annoyed if someone didn't follow.

Don't assume that things that you find fascinating will hold the same level of interest for your consultant. Boredom is an issue that comes up fairly frequently. You can avoid this by working with several different people, by not working for too long in any particular session, and by being sensitive to what your consultants want to work on.

Broken promises are something that my consultants in Australia brought up. People of European descent have a widespread reputation in Aboriginal Australia of breaking promises or not meaning what they say, and of not being trustworthy. Promises and trust are complex cross-cultural areas (see the discussion in Hill (2006) on promises, for example). Related to this is specifically the case of not seeing results. That is, the linguist does all this work and then goes away and the people who worked with the linguist feel they didn't see any results for all the effort they put in. Don't promise things you can't deliver, and make sure you follow through with the promises you make.

The process of decision making and consultation can leave consultants feeling that only lip-service was paid to their opinions. No one likes being asked for their input in a way that makes it clear that it won't be paid attention to. Consulting the wrong people in the community, or apparently pressuring consultants to a particular decision may also leave a bad feeling.

Finally, be careful about the rhetoric of endangered and 'dying' languages. We are accustomed to play up the perilous state of the world's linguistic diversity. It helps linguists both to get (much needed) grant money and to raise the profile of a serious issue if we talk about mass extinction, doomed languages and rapidly disappearing communities. The communities themselves, however, might be surprised and displeased to find their language and culture being described in the same terms we use for flora and fauna extinction.

10.5   Working with semi-speakers

It may be that you cannot find any full speakers of the language and you will be working with semi-speakers (also called part-speakers or passive speakers[5]) instead. First of all, it's really important to be extremely patient and never make the person feel ashamed that they don't speak the language fluently. There might be all sorts of reasons why they aren't full speakers, from having spent a long time away from their families through education or work, to being removed to a boarding school, to growing up in an area where the language was already moribund, to identifying primarily as a speaker of a different language group.

Semi-speakers have valuable knowledge – they may be the only direct link to the language as it used to be spoken. They may be the only people able to give the context and interpretation of old materials. Semi-speakers can have many different skills. Someone might not be able to tell stories but they might still know traditional practices, or have a large vocabulary of single words and phrases. They might not be able to make grammaticality judgements, but they still might be able to translate. It's more important than ever to make sure that you make the most of a person's natural skills. It is possible to make a lot of progress this way. The Kalkatungu grammar (Blake 1979) was compiled from several semi-speakers, some who could put words and phrases together, others who knew lots of different words. Kim and Park-Doob (2005) provide several good examples of including non-fluent speakers in fieldwork.

Part-speakers often increase in fluency as work progresses. Long-stored memories take time to surface and a person's language skills could be very rusty if they haven't spoken the language for a long time. Going through wordlists and previous materials often sparks memories. Cultural artefacts may also be useful. Discussing things in the contact language may also jog memories, so don't feel that just because you aren't getting any language information, you're wasting time. It may take a very long time, though, and it is easy for both you and your consultant to get frustrated.

If possible, get several people together to brainstorm. Different members of the group will probably remember different things, and can help each other. Don't immediately give up if they can't remember something (don't push it too hard, but don't give up as soon as you've asked something). Luise Hercus and I worked with part-speakers in Queensland (Australia). We had one session where it took almost 20 minutes to translate the phrase 'the boys are going for kangaroo'. It was worth the persistence, though, as it opened up a lot of memories and we were able to record at a quicker pace after that.

Don't necessarily record everything. An informal discussion with the recorder off may result in much more material than a situation where the consultant feels under pressure to perform. Take notes – you can always go back and ask for a recording at the end of the session if it's appropriate. Even taking notes might be off-putting (try talking to someone who is always looking at a piece of paper and not interacting with you). If it's not possible to take notes at the time, write down as much as you can remember as soon as the session is over. (This is a learnable skill and you will get better over time with practice.) Don't use a structured elicitation style to start off with. Have some questions in mind, but there is nothing more discouraging than a blank piece of paper with a list of unknown topics. A good place to start is by chatting about the people your consultants used to talk to (or learnt the language from).

If you are working primarily with semi-speakers you should be aware of potential differences between their grammar and the language as it was traditionally spoken. For example, there is a strong tendency towards regularization among semi-speakers, even when they might otherwise produce fluent speech (cf. Maiden 2004). There might be unsystematic gaps in their knowledge of paradigms. Another effect of language death noted in the literature is rapid restructuring in the final generation of speakers; for example Thurgood (2003) has recorded the creation of new opaque conditions on passive allomorphy, and Pensalfini (1999) has discussed the reanalysis of case morphology in Jingulu as discourse markers.

A very interesting issue (from many points of view) is the development of what have been called 'young people's varieties'. Speakers of these varieties are fluent; however, their language is often very different from their elders. Some varieties approach 'mixed language'' or creoles (see, e.g., McConvell and Meakins 2004). It is relevant to fieldwork in several ways. One is that you might obtain very different data sets from different speakers. Secondly, there might be tensions within the community over the way that different people speak; older people might feel that the younger speakers 'do not speak properly' (a perennial complaint across the world). If you are preparing teaching materials, you will have to decide which variety to use. If you use the 'traditional' speech of the old people, you might alienate the people that the materials are designed for. On the other hand, if you use their variety, you might be accused of perpetuating fallen standards and making a substandard record of the language (cf. Florey 2004). Therefore which variety or varieties form the basis of the documentation and language programme may need to be negotiated.

10.6 Living in the field

Where you live has an effect not only on your data collection but also on your analysis, your relationship with your consultants, and your sanity. Macaulay (2005) also makes this point – that is, your living conditions will have an effect on your state of mind and your ability to cope with your fieldwork.

10.6.1 Accommodation

You could live with a **host family**. This has the obvious advantage that if they speak the language, you will have many opportunities to observe how language is used and to practise speaking. It also provides you with people who can guide you in the community. However, it can also be quite stressful, for both them and you.

Hotels or **hostels** are another option. These aren't available in many places, but in some locations they might be the only option. Hotels will be very expensive if you are staying in the field for a long time, and some hostels have limits on the length of stay. **Rental houses** (short term or long term) might be cheaper than hotels, but it might be hard to get a short-term lease, or the house might be unfurnished, and in some communities there is no accommodation of this type. Many remote communities provide houses for community teachers, nurses, store owners and other service personnel, and sometimes it is possible to stay in such houses if you are there when one is vacant. Convents, mission buildings and schools sometimes have places to stay too. If you have your own camping equipment, staying in school classrooms can be a good alternative to camping in the rough, since there are often bathrooms, desks and so on.

10.6.2   Food

As Macaulay (2005) discusses, food looms large in discussion of potential fieldwork problems. In remote communities there are usually no restaurants, and food deliveries might be infrequent. You might not have good cooking facilities where you live, or the food might be packaged for large families while you are looking for things you can buy to cook for a single person. Cooking might be extremely time-consuming, and the food itself might be nutritionally very poor.

Be prepared for people to give you things that you would not normally eat. Refusing might be really offensive. It's probably not as bad as it looks. I think risking the occasional upset stomach and gross-out is worth it so as not to offend people, and you may even find the food delicious!

It's good to have food and drink available during your work sessions (although you may want to have defined breaks rather than just laying it out, as people sometimes chomp through the recording session!), especially in areas where feeding your guests is hospitable.

10.6.3   Health

Make sure that you get advice about the appropriate vaccinations and other health precautions to take. You might need certification of vaccination to enter some countries, or to return to your home country. Seek advice from a travel medical centre rather than your local doctor, who is unlikely to have the relevant expertise. You will not have immunity to the local diseases, so you may find yourself getting sick more frequently than usual. This section includes some frequent general health concerns for fieldworkers. It's too general to be useful in most cases: you should obtain reliable information about your field site before you leave.

More general health issues could include sunburn[6] and dehydration. Or, if you're working somewhere very cold, be careful of frostbite! Make sure you have access to rehydration salts and other basic first-aid items. In an emergency, boiled water with a small amount of salt and sugar can substitute. Sores and cuts can get infected easily in tropical areas so don't ignore such things, even if you're normally healthy. Use an antiseptic cream and keep them covered. Serious cuts may require stitches. Carry wound dressings in your first aid kit. For bad cuts, apply a pressure bandage to stop the bleeding and get help.

Clean water may also be hard to obtain. If the local water is not drinkable and there's nowhere to buy water, there are heavy duty camping filters available which use iodine and charcoal to kill parasites and filter impurities. (Don't use iodine-filtered water for long periods though, as it can cause thyroid problems.) Boiling water for 10–15 minutes will also kill most things.[7]

Take any medication with you, including anything you take regularly, and a broad spectrum antibiotic (if it's unavailable locally). Some customs officials will be suspicious if you take a lot of medication, so keep copies of the prescriptions so you can show that it's for you.

You should have some idea of the most prevalent infectious diseases in the area you'll be working. **HIV/AIDS** is widespread in parts of Africa, Asia and Oceania. It's spread through contact with infected fluids, particularly blood and semen. Luckily it's quite difficult to catch, but there's no vaccine and no cure. **Hepatitis** is another common disease; the different strains vary in infectiousness, seriousness and treatability. The most likely way you could be exposed to HIV or Hepatitis B is if you're asked to treat open wounds and you have an open cut on your hand. Hepatitis A can also be caught from unsanitary washing facilities or drinking water with faecal matter in it. A vaccine is available.

Malaria is spread through Anopheles mosquitoes, and there are several different strains. Check which one(s) is/are prevalent in your area. The choice of anti-malarial drugs depends on places visited, length of stay, activities planned, availability of health care, and drug allergies and age, so you will need to ask your doctor which one is most suitable. You should use a mosquito net and an insect repellent but don't use a very strong concentration of DEET repellent for long periods, since it's a neurotoxin.

Bacteria and amoebae such as salmonella, giardia and cholera, which cause vomiting and/or diarrhoea, are common everywhere. The usual treatment is rehydration and rest. More general nutrition problems are also common among fieldworkers. It can be hard to get fresh food and a balanced diet. Multi-vitamin tablets (including iron) are a good idea, even if you don't normally take them. Cook or peel all food to avoid food poisoning, if possible. Make sure food is thoroughly cooked right through and hasn't been sitting around. Washing food won't help if the water itself isn't clean.

Bites are common: not only snake bites and poisonous creatures but also things like sand flies (midges) and other irritating insects. The bites can get infected, so don't scratch them, and have antiseptic available. Leeches and ticks can be a problem – never pull them off, but make them release their grip. For ticks, touch the hind end with an irritant such as iodine or kerosene. For leeches, hold the burning end of a cigarette close to it or drop a few grains of salt on its body. Long sleeves, trousers (as opposed to shorts), and closed shoes help, but very thin fabric can be useless as mosquitoes can bite through it. Crocodile bites are a serious business and will not be prevented by any of the above.

If you're going anywhere remote for any length of time, you should take at least a basic first-aid kit containing Bandaids, Electrolyte solution for dehydration, hand sanitizer, broad pressure bandage/snake bite bandage (also good for sprains and RSI if you work too hard on your computer), pain killers, tweezers, scissors, sunscreen, insect repellent, a broad spectrum antibiotic (if you won't be near health facilities), antiseptic[8] and antifungal cream, and an antihistamine.

Some diseases may not develop until after you've returned from the field (e.g., many people develop symptoms of malaria after they've returned from the field and stop taking their prophylactics) so if you find yourself getting sick when you return, see a travel doctor and make sure they are aware of the countries you've visited.

10.6.4   Fear and culture shock

Practical aspects of life in your field community should also be part of your planning. Being scared about fieldwork is no reason to stay home, but equally there is no point in going to a community where you will be so freaked out that you won't be able to do anything useful. If you turn blue at the thought of living without electricity for a year, don't go for a year at first. Go to the area on holiday for a few weeks with a friend first. You might find that it wasn't quite so bad after all, you made some great friends and the language has a wonderful set of ergative affixes. Or you might decide that three weeks was all you could stand and there's no way you could go for longer.

It's normal to be in a blue funk about fieldwork. There are a large number of unknowns. Dissertations and theses are stressful enough without removing yourself from family, friends, advisor (in short, your support structures) for large parts of the process. Talk to people who've gone to the area and find out about their experiences (remember too that linguists love their field stories, especially about the dangerous animals they saw and the horrible things they ate, and that snakes tend to get longer and longer with each telling of the story). Further common feelings include fear of failure (that you will not be able to handle the work, or that you'll waste time), frustration at lack of progress, and loneliness.

Abbi (2001:8) makes a comment in passing on working in India that those going to the field must be prepared to interact with others of different social status. Part of going on fieldwork is living in a different culture and interacting with it. Some culture shock is to be expected, and the best way to lessen it is to know something about the culture before you go, and to be prepared for everything to be different.

Don't work all the time. This may sound like strange advice, since your time is limited and you want to make the most of your stay. However, lack of sleep and overwork will drastically reduce the quality of your data. You'll be too tired to respond to new data, you'll make errors, and it will likely magnify any other problems. You'll also miss a lot of interesting things if you spend all your time at your computer. Make sure you bring things to do in your free time, take off at least one day a week, and don't work all the time.[9]

You will be an object of curiosity. It will be irritating at times, but there's not much you can do about it. You will probably have little time to yourself which (depending on the sort of person you are) can be extremely stressful. In small communities, everyone **always** knows where everyone else is and what they are doing.

10.6.5   Personal safety

Trust in fieldwork is very important and you will not have a good time or an easy time making friends if you don't trust people. However, if you are in an unfamiliar place, you will probably feel out of your comfort zone, and staying safe is also important.

Depending on where you work, you might have to deal with 'unwanted attention', harassment or another threat to personal safety. Dealing with such attention is a life skill and not only applicable to fieldwork. However, being on fieldwork makes things more complicated. First, the dividing line between 'work' and 'non-work' is not at all clear for most fieldwork, so the 'unwanted attention' could have implications for your working relationships in a way that harassment from a random stranger in the street or in a bar at home might not. Secondly, because you are in an unfamiliar culture, your strategies for dealing with the attention might not work the way you intend. Thirdly, what you might classify as 'unwanted attention' may be accepted behaviour for the community, so people might not understand why you feel uncomfortable.

A product of being a visible outsider in a community is that someone will probably not like you for your gender, sexual orientation, education, race, age, or looks, and your high profile can make you a target, no matter who you are. On the other hand, your status as a guest in the community could also provide protection. A further potential danger is that as a stranger to the area you might be unaware of other dangers, such as poisonous plants and animals, dangerous river currents, or risky activities (such as which roads are dangerous to drive on).

Many of the 'problems' mentioned in this section on living in the field can be dealt with by asking your consultants. Make friends, tell people you're clueless about where to go, what to eat and what's poisonous. Talk to other linguists who've been to the area before about what likely dangers there will be and how to avoid them. For example, harassment in some areas might be avoided by wearing a wedding ring (or referring to your partner as your spouse).

10.6.6 Dress

There are only two rules for dress: be comfortable, and be appropriate. Don't be the only female over 16 wearing jeans, or the only male wearing shorts. Cover the right amount of flesh (and this is true for both men and women, although women usually have more restrictive dress codes). It's best to be conservative if you don't know the area. Your life as an outsider will be complicated enough without having people form the wrong impressions of you because of inappropriate dress. You should find out what the temperatures are likely to be so you have the appropriate clothes if you don't plan to buy things locally. How much clothing you take is up to you, but field equipment is heavy so you might not have a lot of room for lots of clothes.

10.6.7 Gifts

It is a very good idea to bring some gifts for your consultants and their families, especially for when you leave. What you give depends, of course, on where you are going. Don't confine yourself to the 'gift' section of the local bookshop, and try and find out in advance what would be appreciated. The list below is based on some of the most popular presents to older people in Aboriginal communities. It might give you ideas for non-traditional gifts; anything that's popular but difficult to obtain locally usually makes a good gift.

Non-prescription pain killers and muscle rub are good to have on hand. Other practical items include good quality batteries (the ones available in stores are universally old and bad), torches (flashlights), screwdrivers (flathead screwdrivers in particular, are very useful for all sorts of things), axes or sharp knives, penknives and sharpeners (but axes are hard to get through airport security).

Reading glasses[10] are also often excellent gifts, since they often aren't locally available in remote areas. If you have consultants who live in a strong exchange network where they won't necessarily keep the glasses (even if they need them), you could keep a pair or two with you which long-sighted consultants can borrow during your sessions. Clothes, especially caps and T-shirts, are always popular.

Other 'fieldwork' gifts include paper, coloured pens or markers (but not the ones which give off sniffable fumes), picture books and magazines (more appropriate in some places than others, but even people who don't read sometimes like looking at the pictures). Craft items can be useful too, including crochet hooks and thread, paint and knitting needles. Music CDs in different genres are popular. The most popular CD I owned on one north Australian fieldtrip was a CD of Uzbek folk music. You might not only be a representative for your culture, but also for 'global' items. Eva Lindström (personal communication) takes an inflatable 'globe' beach ball, which is useful as a game, a present, and for showing where she comes from.[11]

10.7 Coming back from the field

10.7.1 Leaving the field site

Your luggage will be packed full of bulky, heavy and very valuable stuff – your field notes and original recordings. Never put original recordings in checked luggage. Sweet-talk your way onto the plane, pay for excess baggage, but don't let them check your bag. If you're on a small plane with strict luggage restrictions, ask the check-in staff to weigh you along with your luggage. They might allow you to take as luggage some of the weight difference between yourself and the large mining executive sitting next to you. Sending your materials through registered post is an option if you're working in a country with a functional postal service, but even that is not recommended. Back up data on computer in case of problems or theft. Post the backups, don't carry them with you. Planning how to get your data back is important. Think about it and make plans as soon as you can (see also Robinson 2006). You've gone to the trouble of collecting and processing all these materials – don't run the risk of destroying your project because of a misplaced checked bag.

Find out what the protocols are for saying goodbye, and make sure you say goodbye to everyone you've worked with. Make arrangements for keeping in contact if you can.

Will you be returning to the site? If so, it is often useful to start negotiations for your next trip before you leave. For example, if you are likely to need a letter of permission from the community to apply for a grant, it is usually easier to organize it in person. It also reinforces your commitment to the community and makes you less open to accusations that you will take the language materials and won't return.

10.7.2   Reverse culture shock

You may experience reverse culture shock when you return from the field. That is, in returning home you may experience some of the same symptoms of culture shock that you had when you first left. You may feel overwhelmed by the amount you now have to do, or feel let down that no one understands what you experienced, depressed that you have no one to talk to about the language and your experiences. You may view your own culture more critically and feel disenchanted by the artificiality of social structures and rules. This is normal and usually passes.

10.7.3   Dealing with materials

When you get home there are things to do with the data you collected in the field. Is it backed up well? Did you promise to send anything to your consultants? Deal with these promises as soon as you get home, otherwise you'll forget.

When you unpack, you'll have lots of things to do! Make a list of the work that needs doing on the project, make note of dependencies in the list (e.g., items that need to be completed before other items can be done) and prioritize. Deal with archiving earlier rather than later. Not all archiving needs to wait until the end of the project. For example, if you have your field recordings already catalogued with the appropriate metadata, these could be archived straight away. Returning from the field also usually brings with it a great deal of non-linguistic activity, such as catching up with all the mail you received while away.

10.8 Further reading

- **Confessional ethnography:** Clifford (1980, 1983), van Maanen (1988).
- **Danger:** Kulic and Wilson (1995), Lee-Treweek and Linkogle (2000), Moreno (1995).
- **Health:** Werner (1993).
- **Language death and endangerment:** Crowley (2007:181ff), Florey (2004), Harrison (2007), Nettle and Romaine (2000), Tsunoda (2004).
- **Role of the researcher:** Whitehead and Conaway (1986).
- **Living in the field:** Macaulay (2005), Schreier (2003:Ch 4).

11
Ethical Field Research

11.1 Preliminaries

11.1.1 What is ethical research?

How can we define ethical research? A broad definition might be 'a way of working that you, the research community and the language community think is appropriate'. We can consider the question of ethics broadly, or more narrowly, in the sense of 'what type of research is approved by university ethics boards?'

We are comfortable with the idea that ethical considerations are inherent in medical research. For example, most people would agree that it is wrong to try out a new, untested treatment on patients without warning them of the fact and receiving their consent to participation in advance. There are ethical considerations in linguistics too, including recording research participants, the potential for inflicting harm, gaining permission to work on a language and observe people, and identifying research participants.

Since linguistic elicitation by nature involves working with humans, many linguists are accountable to overseers – grant agencies, university ethics boards and academic advisors. In some countries, including the United States, Canada, Australia, the United Kingdom, Israel, Scandinavian countries, Japan and many other countries in Europe, most linguistic research is subject to approval by a University ethics board (in the US, this is called an Internal Review Board or IRB). Many grant organizations require certification that your University's ethics board has approved or exempted your proposal before you are funded.

The topics raised in this chapter will still be relevant to your research whether or not you are legally required to obtain ethics approval. All linguistic fieldwork has ethical consequences and there are ethical issues which require thinking about. Ethics aren't just an issue when working on endangered languages either. You are not exempt from ethical issues because you are working on a language with many speakers. This chapter discusses a range of ethical considerations in linguistic fieldwork, ranging from the broad 'what is the right way to behave' to 'how does my research fit into the legislation?'

11.1.2   What can be researched?

Like other social researchers, [anthropologists] have no special entitlement to study all phenomena; and the advancement of knowledge and the pursuit of information are not in themselves sufficient justifications for overriding the values and ignoring the interests of research participants.

(American Anthropological Association 1998:§3.6a)[1]

The same comments apply to linguists. We do not have a special entitlement to study any language we want to. This can be hard for speakers of major languages to appreciate. We don't really care who learns English; it's a global language. The language itself is not anyone's cultural property in particular. Common words aren't owned by particular groups. But that view does not apply to many of the world's languages, particularly highly endangered languages. For example, in 2005 speakers of Mapudungun[2] in Chile threatened to sue Microsoft because the group had not been consulted about the development of a local version of Microsoft software.

11.1.3   Who decides what's ethical?

Compare the previous quote to the following:

[i]n ethical research…there is a wholly proper concern to minimize damage and offset inconvenience to the researched, and to acknowledge their contributions.…But the underlying model is one of 'research *on*' social subjects. Human subjects deserve special ethical consideration, but they no more set the researcher's agenda than the bottle of sulphuric acid sets the chemist's agenda.

(Cameron, Frazer et al. 1992:14–15)

The people being researched may not agree and they may not take kindly to having no say in the research agenda. It may be perceived as disenfranchisement if they have undergone land or rights dispossession in the past. The community may feel that their contribution to the research should not be limited to answering the questions that you think up for them.

So far I have talked about ethics as though there is just one ethical way to behave in research, and one system to satisfy. That is not true. Ethics are strongly a function of culture, and what may be considered ethical in one community would be unethical in another. For example, in medical ethics, informed consent must be documented in writing unless there are strong extenuating circumstances. Other communities may think it's not right to make someone sign a piece of paper in order to work with you.

11.1.4 Who owns the research outcomes?

Who owns the data that is going into the project? Who owns the physical recordings? the intellectual content? the words themselves? Is it possible to 'own' a language in the same way that it's possible to 'own' an idea, for example? Not all cultures agree on this, and your consultants might have opinions about these matters which both differ from yours and amongst themselves.

Copyright and intellectual property law is very complex (and varies greatly from country to country). Superimposed on the legal structure are local views of intellectual property, which may or may not be in agreement with the law (e.g., in Aboriginal Australia there is a widespread view that a language can be copyrighted; this isn't true under Australian law). If this is likely to be a concern, seek advice and consult within your field community about the desired outcomes.

11.2 Ethics of recording

You are not only recording language samples when you turn on your recorder, you are also recording people and personal information. What will happen to the information and the recordings when you have finished your fieldwork?

11.2.1 Illicit recording

Having a recording device trained on you is a barrier to producing naturalistic speech, as we all know. It might therefore be very tempting to record people without their knowledge in the interests of gaining better data for your research. Dixon (1983), for example, records going away while leaving his tape recorder running without the knowledge of his consultants. Wray and colleagues (1998) condone illicit recording, although they discourage it in most circumstances.

Recording people without their permission is unethical. First of all, it is illegal in some places to record someone without their knowledge. Secondly, it can destroy the trust that you've worked to build up between you and your consultants. If you said you wouldn't record them without them knowing and then you break that promise, why should they trust you about other things you've said? You may also make it difficult for other researchers later on. If a community has had a bad experience with one linguist they are less likely to be favourably inclined to future research requests.

Furthermore, it is not acceptable to record people without their knowledge, but then ask permission in retrospect. That is also a violation of trust. Some textbooks condone this practice (Wray, Bloomer et al. 1998:154), but it violates several ethics standards. For example, the American Anthropological Association's ethics standards make it clear (§III.A.4.) that consent in retrospect is not informed consent. Therefore, always, without exception, ask permission before making recordings.

11.2.2 Alternatives to illicit recording

There are other ways to get naturalistic data. One is to leave your tape recorder going and go somewhere else for a while – with the speakers' permission. The participants in the conversation have given permission for recording to take place, but after a little while (usually ten minutes or less) speakers will relax and begin to talk naturally. This works particularly well if part of the culture involves people sitting down talking together for long periods.

Another way to get this type of data is to ask for permission to record at some future time without the person knowing. That is, they know that they will be recorded in the future, but they don't necessarily know when it will be. You should always tell the person immediately after you've finished recording to give them the chance, while they still remember the conversation, to embargo any parts of it. They should also be given the opportunity to listen to the whole recording (or to read the transcript) in all circumstances.

11.3 Ethics and archiving

Data storage is also an ethical (and common sense) issue. Presumably one of the reasons you are working on an undescribed language in the first place (and one of the reasons that your consultants are working with you) is to make a permanent record. You therefore have an obligation to look after the data to make sure that it is stored safely and can be used in the future. The American Anthropological Association's ethics guidelines (III.B.4–5) include a clause that places an obligation on the researcher to make a good-faith effort to preserve the materials collected, and to make their results available in a timely fashion. This is particularly important when the language is endangered and the researcher's fieldnotes may be the primary record of a language when it is no longer spoken.

In archiving your data it is important to be clear about the permissions for access. This includes the intent of your consultants in giving you the information, and your intentions in collecting it. It also includes their views (and yours) regarding others' access to the data. For example, do they mind if others want to listen to your field recordings? Or make copies of your notes? or just view them? or write up their own analysis based on your fieldnotes?

11.4   Acknowledging speakers

Researchers have various ways of acknowledging the input of their consultants. How you do this depends, as always, on the type of work you are doing, what your consultants want and the expectations of your grant. There is a widespread expectation that you will acknowledge the time and effort your consultants have put into helping you. In some places there will be an expectation of overt acknowledgement. In other places, consultants may wish to remain anonymous (see also §12.4.2).

Co-authorship is one option for acknowledgment. Many linguists have co-authored grammars, articles and other materials with their consultants. It would be highly unusual, however, to have a co-authored linguistics PhD. The consultants might not feel that it's appropriate and your committee probably wouldn't be very happy either.[3]

Another way is to acknowledge the contribution of speakers by name in the acknowledgements section of a book or the first footnote in an article. This is good form, even if your consultants wish to remain anonymous (don't identify them by name but thank them for their input). Marianne Mithun gives the speaker's name for all examples she gives in linguistic articles. Others use speakers' initials as a way to reference examples in their fieldnotes, and they include explanation of the abbreviations in publications.

11.5   Permissions

Part of negotiating to work on a language is to obtain permission for your work. Such negotiation is an ongoing task; there may be need for renegotiation throughout your fieldwork as circumstances change, consultants' opinions on linguistic research change and the project changes. Consent must be 'informed' – that is, consultants should know what they are agreeing to.

11.5.1   General permission

A generic consent form is given in Appendix E. It covers audio and video recording, dissemination of recordings, primary data (such as transcriptions) and secondary work (such as articles written on the basis of the data elicited in class). It covers internet and print publication. The permissions script I use for working with Aboriginal people in Australia is a little different. It covers the same topics, but it is worded in much more colloquial English (and has been translated on the spot into several other languages for discussion with senior community members who do not speak English). It is also explicit about cultural knowledge, narratives and photographs. It contains a section on the appropriate archiving and distribution of gender-specific material. I have given a sample script for obtaining oral informed consent in the Appendix.

I mentioned in several earlier sections the need for wide consultation amongst endangered language speech communities. However, there may also be cases where this is too simplistic. For example, on a recent field trip in Northern Australia one of the senior Yan-nhaŋu women was angry with a group of anthropologists who had been working in her country. They had done what we would say is the 'right thing' – they had asked many community members to a meeting and had strongly encouraged everyone to give an opinion on the process. This angered her, as in that part of Arnhem Land, land tenure is held by families and clan groups, and in asking 'everyone' the anthropologists were giving equal weight to people who would not have traditionally had a say. Therefore, make sure that you are seeking permission from the right people.

11.5.2   Working with children

If your fieldwork involves minors, you will need additional ethics clearance. You will need the parents' consent before you start. You may well need their parents to be there. In some places, you might need police clearance to work with minors.

For linguistic descriptions, unless you are doing acquisition work you will probably not be working with young children, but you may want to do some work with teenagers if you are interested in differences between younger and older people's speech.

Different communities have different views; there might be suspicion about getting children to sign forms. It might be appropriate for you to work with children on the condition that it's 'casual', that is, that they are not paid and they do not have to sign forms. You will need to negotiate with your ethics board to find a solution that is acceptable to everyone.

11.5.3   Secondary use of materials and the 'research agenda'

There are also ethical issues concerning the secondary use of materials. When linguists collect language data, they usually want to use it for several different projects. After three months of fieldwork they do not expect to write a single book based on that fieldwork, but also conference papers and articles, and no doubt examples will also find their way into class and seminar handouts.

However, some ethics boards require that data be used solely for the purpose for which it was originally collected. This is to protect research participants and to make sure that 'informed consent' is truly informed. It is to prevent situations where confidential data are collected for a particular purpose and then used for quite a different purpose; the participants may have agreed to the original proposal but not to the subsequent one. The immediate implication of this is that if you collect material for a specific purpose, you can't necessarily use it for future projects.

The easiest way around this is to ask permission at the time of negotiating the original informed consent to use the primary research materials for future projects. That is, include in your permission statement a clause to the effect that the language data may be used for ongoing research on the language, and phrase your original ethics proposal sufficiently broadly that it will cover future similar work. Most speakers will be happy to agree to this, and in fact will expect that the information they provide will continue to be used. After all, they have invested a lot of time in talking to you and explaining their language to you.

There is nothing wrong with collecting data for multiple uses as long as everyone is clear about what those uses are, and that they agree to it. Indeed, data collection for multiple purposes is one way to get a lot done on a field trip and to ensure that both the community and the researcher agree about the outcomes of the fieldwork. For example, your consultants could read the text of a children's book – that would provide both a talking book for community use and data for your phonetic research.

Another potential 'secondary use' of materials concerns collaboration with other researchers. Perhaps you will be going to your field site at the same time as an ethnobotanist, and you could collaborate on research on local plant use and nomenclature. Perhaps a colleague is interested in some aspect of your field language and has asked you to get some data. Again, these situations potentially involve passing on primary material and may need to be cleared with your consultants. In general, these interdisciplinary fieldwork collaborations are well worth the effort. The ethnobotanist can benefit from the linguist's skills in transcription and elicitation of information; the linguist will certainly benefit from accurate identification of species and the specialist knowledge of the ethnobotanist in asking the right questions to record the richest information possible.

11.5.4   Ethics of gaining permission

If community permission to work on the language is denied, there is not much you can do about it. Try to find out informally why permission wasn't given – perhaps it was for a reason that you could negotiate about. Perhaps you asked the wrong people.

A further source of potential problems is officialdom. You might not receive ethics approval, or you might have the permission of speakers and your university, but not a government research permit. The best advice in such situations is from others at your university, or researchers who know the area well. Again, try to find out what the cause of the problem is. You may need to alter your research proposal a bit, or you may be able to negotiate a favourable outcome.[4]

11.6   Other ethical issues in research

This section contains a set of common ethics problems regarding interaction between linguists and community members. Some of these issues will be more pertinent in some areas than in others. Not all of these issues are legal ethical issues, but they come under the rubric of broadly defined ethical behaviour.

11.6.1   The researcher effect

As much as you try to minimize the 'researcher effect', it will still be present. That is, no matter how much you are able to include community views in your research, to consult with the language community and to negotiate mutually beneficial outcomes, at some level you are still a researcher conducting observations on the language and its speakers. The longer you are in the community, the greater the likelihood that the intrusion of a researcher will cause tensions. Minimize the intrusiveness of your presence and your research. You'll have an impact whatever happens. This might be anything from not monopolizing the only public phone to not taking up all your consultants' spare time. Looking after a researcher is a tiring business.

As discussed in Cyr (1999), some people believe that the linguists working on their language have hastened language death. That is, that instead of aiding the documentation and revitalization of a language, the linguist has killed it. While this might objectively seem rather unlikely (after all, it would imply that the linguist had a considerable degree of influence over the community), the perception is very important. Perhaps the language was already seldom spoken and the linguist, by working in the community, made that obvious. Perhaps the linguist worked with consultants who were already involved in revitalization activities, and the linguists' presence took time away from revitalization. Perhaps the community had high and unmet expectations (or the linguist's expectations of the work were different from what the community thought the project was about).

11.6.2   Alternative knowledge systems

In §1.5 we discussed fieldwork and identity, and the idea of compartmentalizing identities; temporarily suspending one's own belief system in order to objectify and quantify the interactions under study. We also mentioned that the researcher may do this, but the community under study will not necessarily suspend their views of you and your culture, race, profession, gender or religion just because you are there as a researcher and not as a private individual.

Furthermore, there may be an uneasy relationship between researchers and community members, in part because the community sees the scientific method in conflict with their worldview. Your research outcomes and research procedure may directly contradict local accepted knowledge. For example, Linnaean taxonomy is perceived by some to be a contradiction of Indigenous classification systems – that is, that Linnaeus was 'right' and other systems are 'wrong'.[5] Indigenous origin stories often conflict with the archaeological record. The group may have a belief that their language has always been spoken in that place, which may be contradicted by historical linguistics.[6]

Many Indigenous communities have a history of 'experimentation' and exoticization that is deeply resented, and 'Western Science' (of which linguistics is a part) is seen as perpetuating the practices which caused the resentment in the first place. Not everyone has the same view of the status of Western science that students and faculty at universities tend to.[7] As we have seen (e.g., in the public debates on the status of evolution in the US school system), there is a widespread perception that Western science is as much a set of beliefs and agreed practices as a religion is. Furthermore, while practitioners of Western science may look upon research as providing knowledge for everyone, not everyone agrees; neither does everyone, in fact, have access to that knowledge.

There is another side to this question. A complaint also frequently heard is that researchers do not share their knowledge with the community that adopts them. That is, the researcher gains a lot of knowledge from the community (knowledge of the language, culture, belief systems), but the community does not get access in return to advanced scientific knowledge, and that itself may be interpreted as disenfranchisement. If It's worth thinking in advance about how you might react and what your views are should you encounter these views on your field trip.

11.6.3   Exoticization

As fieldworkers, we study language and culture from the outside by objectifying it, analysing it and quantifying it. To others, this may be seen as exoticizing the group, their language and culture. However much you try to counteract these views, the very nature of research on minority languages often leads to a perception of exoticization. Unfortunately, linguists themselves sometimes reinforce this view, for example by including encyclopaedia entries with the title 'Bible translation into exotic languages' (Brown 2005).

Added to this is a large and freely available nineteenth- and early twentieth-century ethnography which places an emphasis on the exotic and the different. For example, each chapter of Page (1938) has a chapter devoted to a different 'primitive' race. Indigenous groups may primarily associate anthropological and linguistic research with this tradition, even though it has changed significantly in recent years.[8]

Remember that linguists' views of language are rather different from most popular views of language. Calling something 'cool' or 'weird', while a compliment in linguistics, might be taken as offensive or derogatory by others. Compare, for example, Bill Poser's experience related on the language blog *Language Log*[9] about his description of Carrier pharyngeals and uvulars as exotic to English speakers and the very negative reaction he received from a correspondent. Be mindful of these feelings. Be enthusiastic about the language by all means, but don't overdo your enthusiasm about all the wonderfully rare linguistic features you are finding in your fieldwork. Save that for other linguists.

11.6.4   Conflicts of interest

We tend to think of conflicts of interest as primarily monetary; that is, the researcher has the potential for monetary gain if the research has a certain outcome. While few linguists directly gain financially from their research, we stand to gain a great deal from good research in terms of publications and promotions. Perhaps a PhD rides on the outcome of the fieldwork. Therefore there *is* the potential for conflict of interest in linguistic research when what is in the researcher's interest might not be in the best interest of the consultants.

One way to avoid conflicts of interest is to be upfront about your interests in the first place. Tell your consultants who funds your work and what they expect out of it. Tell them what you expect and work with them to negotiate a research programme that everyone will support.

Another type of conflict of interest is where the research goes badly; for example, perhaps you were banking on a particular set of results that did not eventuate. Perhaps you had published an analysis which you find to be incorrect when you have more data. It is in the interest of your pride (and maybe your career) for the mistake not to be discovered; on the other hand, it's in the interests of science and an accurate description of the language that the earlier incorrect analysis be righted. Another case of unethical behaviour would be where you know that a particular analysis is incorrect, but you give it anyway because it's already been worked out.

11.6.5   Anticipating harm

Asking someone about their language is a benign form of research compared to many other things people do, but there are still cases where linguistic research could have negative consequences for a linguistic community. One is if salaries distort the local economy – that could have a bad effect. The fact that someone is working on the language at all may have negative implications for the community, for example it might attract unwanted government attention. The researcher's results might have legal implications – for example a historical linguist might provide evidence in land claims.

In other cases the 'harm' might relate to the behaviour of the researcher rather than the research itself. Try to see how others might see your actions and if they will have any unintended consequences. For example, there was a situation where a non-Indigenous visitor to an Aboriginal community in Australia offered language classes to their non-Indigenous teachers at the local school. The motives were great and the participants were very keen – they wanted to learn something of the language but did not know where to start or who to ask. However, Indigenous community members were insulted that they had not been asked about who should teach their language. This is also an issue discussed by Amery (2000) in relation to the teachers of language revitalization programmes. It may be that the linguist is the most 'qualified' (in language terms) to teach a revitalization class. However, there might be political consequences of an outsider teaching the programme; such as, for example, it losing support amongst the local community. A further potential harm, that of psychological trauma in oral history, is discussed in §11.8.7 below.

Finally, you might do harm by using scarce resources in the community. There might be a food or water shortage and even one extra person might put a strain on community resources. Your working in the area might be taking valuable time away from harvest work. These could also be considered harmful actions.

11.6.6   Local experts

A further potential source of tension is between a short-term fieldworker and long-term researchers or others in the community. There might be missionaries, schoolteachers or other people who have an interest in what you are doing. Such people are potentially wonderful collaborators and sources of help. However, there might be resentment about 'interlopers' among long-term residents (cf. Hyman 2001).

The Canadian Institutes of Health Research and their collborators (rev. 2005:§6.3) encourage the inclusion of Indigenous people with relevant expertise in social science research projects (including linguistic fieldwork). This conflicts, for example, with Vaux and Cooper's (1999) suggestion that it's better to work with 'naïve informants' because they are less likely to offer misleading information or try to second-guess the purpose of the linguist's questions. Abbi (2001) also offers guidance and suggests that village schoolteachers are good contacts, but teachers of the language under study are not good initial consultants because of tendencies to prescription.

It's important in fieldwork to make the most of the natural talents and training of your consultants; this includes making the most of any previous linguistic training that they have. Of course a linguistically trained consultant is going to second-guess the hypotheses behind your questions. The solution is not to avoid fellow linguists, but to collaborate, if they are willing, and to work with more than one person.

11.6.7 Restricted material

In some cultures, information is a managed commodity. That is, some parts of the culture are restricted to particular groups within the community. Some stories may be gender-restricted (i.e., they may be for men only or women only). Others may be 'public', but not for everyday discussion. Other aspects of knowledge might be revealed only at certain times (e.g., Navajo string games are a winter activity (Mitchell 1999; Toelken 1996; and some stories may only be told during particular seasons; see Toelken 1996).

These restrictions on knowledge are part of the culture and abiding by them is both a matter of cultural competence and cultural respect, whether or not you believe in the principle of restricted information or are worried about the consequences of breaking the taboos. Read the available anthropological literature on the culture to get an idea of the subject areas you should avoid. Don't be offended if you ask a question that can't be answered. Do not go digging for such information; wait for speakers to volunteer it. If you are aiming to produce a description of the language, seeking information that you cannot use in your research or distribute will not aid your project. If your consultants give you restricted knowledge, find out if they are telling you this as part of the documentation or because they trust you and want you to know about it as a person, not as a researcher.

Himmelmann (1996:16) argues that any documentation of such knowledge destroys it and renders it non-secret. That is not necessarily true, but it is a very problematic issue. If your consultants want the restricted information to form part of the documentation, have a plan for how to process and archive it so that the restrictions can be respected. Discuss the restrictions, such as why your consultants want to make a record of the materials, and what they want you to do with it. Record such information on separate media, and clearly mark it RESTRICTED. Do the same with fieldnotes. Archive the materials with an archive that has provisions for dealing with restricted information. Discuss what they believe will happen if the wrong people find out about the information.

You will probably learn more than you should about some things, particularly if you are going through old materials and the older researchers did not respect the restrictions. Be careful who you show such materials to, and be careful who knows how much you know.

11.6.8   Linguistic activism

A final issue which has received little attention (although cf. Argenter and McKenna Brown 2004) is 'linguistic activism'; that is, the role of the linguist in linguistic political activities. For example, Stephen Wurm (1998) has commented that the linguist can assist language revitalization projects by encouraging community identity and inciting 'tribal feeling', and tying language to that.

Be careful about inciting anything. It is not your job to recruit speakers for the language. That's the job of your consultants and people within the community. As long as you are a researcher and a temporary guest in the community, you are in no position to dabble in social engineering. You could make things difficult for others and cause more damage than good. Your motives may be impeccable, but you cannot always control how others will read your motives. Inciting or promoting 'tribal identity' may only add to tensions which are already present.

Another type of activism is where the researcher ceases to become impartial; it is easy to become a blinkered advocate for the community. In the long run this does no one much good; it may harm the community and it diminishes the linguist's credibility, thus decreasing their effectiveness as an advocate.

Finally, there is a tradition of linguistic work being conducted under other rubrics. For example, many grammars and dictionaries of previously undescribed languages have been written by anthropologists, who were also engaged in ethnography; by missionaries, who were also translating the Bible and converting communities; or even by doctors and soldiers stationed in remote areas who learnt the local language and wrote a description of it. There are still missionary organizations involved in linguistic work, there are still linguistic anthropologists, and there are still volunteers and service providers who learn the local language and commit that knowledge to paper to share with others. Our knowledge of many languages would be a great deal poorer if it weren't for their work.

However, it also means that it might be assumed that a professional linguist has reasons for being in a community besides linguistics. Many people find it hard to believe that people get paid solely for learning and describing languages which few people speak. They may assume that you are also a missionary, or perhaps you have been sent by the government as a spy (to learn their language in order to learn about other activities). Linguists have been forced to leave sites in the past because of assumptions that linguistics is a cover for other activities, such as espionage. There might not be a great deal of differentiation between journalists, anthropologists and linguists.

Be honest about why you're in the community. It is not ethical to go for one reason but say you're going for another. There is a fine line between temporarily suppressing personal motivations for travelling to the community and being less than honest about the reason for your presence. If you're going there as a linguist, be a linguist.

11.6.9 Summary

Linguistic research involves intensive social interaction, and that social interaction is complex, particularly when it involves simultaneous personal and professional roles, when perceptions of motivations for behaviour might be quite different from the actual motivations, and when previous history might shape assumptions and interactions in a way that has very little to do with the behaviour of an individual. There's not much you can do about it. In fieldwork there is no clear line between the personal and the professional, and your background, motivations and behaviour shape the record.

I have focused on potential problems in this chapter. I do not imply by that that all communities are strife-torn, hostile to researchers, interfering and unaccommodating. Far from it. Take this list of problems as the aggregate, worst case scenario. These are issues that may arise in some form (not necessarily the form that I have presented them in), and it would probably be helpful if you think about what your position is.

11.7 Payment

You should compensate your consultants in some appropriate way for the time that they spend with you. Pay consultants in scale with the local economy, and tie the rate to the closest equivalent job (e.g., a teacher). It might not be appropriate in all cultures to pay people in money; that may be considered insulting. As Abbi (2001:57) writes, 'it is humiliating for them [the consultants – CB] to be paid for talking to a guest'. It's also useless if there's nowhere to spend the money. If monetary compensation is not appropriate, you should still give something back. For example, people might refuse to be paid for their time, but the local school could use some equipment. You might be able to repay your consultants by helping with manual labour (as Schreier (2003) did).

Appropriate compensation can formalize the relationship between researcher and consultants, which can be a good thing. For example, it is easier to prioritize the work if the meetings are structured. It encourages taking the work seriously, and viewing the work as a job that needs to be done, rather than a hobby that happens only if there's time. Be clear about what work constitutes payable work.

Paying cash after each session (in areas where cash is appropriate) is easy. Unfortunately, many grant institutions won't let you do this, because of the difficulties in accounting for the money. You may also run foul of the country's tax regulations. I have found it best to have someone else administer the money (e.g., a local language centre, the community council, etc.). Keep a record of the hours worked, and at the end of each week or fortnight give the time sheet to the person who can arrange to have the salary drawn. It makes the arrangement official, it doesn't cause problems with taxation legislation, and it means you aren't directly responsible for handing out money. This won't work in all areas and has its own problems, for example if it takes a while for payments to be processed. The community may not have easy cheque-cashing facilities. Having cash may expose your consultants to other pressures in their community.

There are other ethical issues to consider too. Your consultants may wish to be paid in alcohol, or in cigarettes. Paying with cigarettes can be more valuable to the recipient than paying in cash, because cigarettes can be traded or used to 'buy' favours. Few people are worried about lung cancer in a community where most people don't live long enough to get cancer, they die of kidney failure or heart failure or in car accidents first. In many parts of the world cigarettes don't have the stigma that they have in the United States or urban Australia. You'll have to decide for yourself how you want to handle situations like this. Having an external source to blame (such as 'the government') for not being able to do this can be helpful.

Consider when you pay people too. For example, if you are in a poor area money is usually spent as soon as it's acquired. So if the weekly fresh fruit and vegetables are delivered on Tuesday afternoon, first thing Wednesday morning is an excellent time to pay people for their time, and Friday is a bad day (if you pay them then the money will probably be gone before there's the opportunity to buy fresh food with it).

Get advice from others who have worked in the area you are going to before you leave, so that you will know your alternatives.

11.8   Minority areas and endangered languages

In many ways, working on endangered languages is just like working on any other language. In other ways, however, there are differences. There are other issues involved in working – particularly in fourth world[10] communities – that it's well to have thought about a bit and be aware of.

11.8.1   Community perceptions of you

In some places people don't have a lot of interaction with the dominant culture and past experiences may not have been positive. In Australia, for example, there were government policies of child removal and governance which controlled Aboriginal people's daily lives.

Previous history will have consequences for your research, even if it's nothing to do with you personally. You are moving into a type of community interaction that is quite different from the type of cross-cultural interaction they might be familiar with from doctors, nurses and teachers. Reactions to you might be formed by previous bad experiences with researchers, or with interactions with the dominant culture in general (and you might be identified as a member of that culture as an outsider and academic, even if you do not identify with it yourself).

There may be resentment of stereotypes and the dominant culture which the dominant culture may not reciprocate or even be aware of. We know a lot of dominant cultures' stereotypes of minority groups, but researchers are sometimes surprised to see that minority groups can have stereotypical views of the majority culture too. One time I found out quite by accident that my consultants were worried about what food I was going to eat while we were camping, as they thought that White people didn't eat bush tucker (such as raw oysters). They didn't want me to starve but they were worried I wouldn't want to eat oysters off the rocks, or damper cooked on the coals, or *noṉḏa* (a type of shellfish). It was a relief to them when I did! (See also Crowley 2007: ch. 6.)

11.8.2   Community problems

In cultural anthropology there is a term 'exhausted community' (see, e.g., Gingrich 1997). These are communities which have undergone severe stress and continue to face problems. They typically have high levels of alcoholism (and drug use) and violence, there may be little in the way of support structures, severely skewed demographics and missing generations (with many children and old people but few people in their forties). There is also a perception, both within the community and of the community, that there is no hope for an improvement.

Perhaps your fieldwork will be in a community like this. If so, there may be tensions over the situation of language loss. This may take the form of resentment that no one is speaking the language nowadays, and converse resentment from younger community members that you are learning the language (and may be able to speak it better than they can). Added to this may be resentment at universally negative perceptions of their community, such as continual reporting of the latest statistics showing that they are more likely to die, are poorer and less educated than the mainstream, or that their chosen way of life is just a problem to be solved. These tensions have little to do with you, and you won't be able to solve them.

Another potential stress is your own feelings about living in a community where you suddenly become one of the richest people in town. That can take a lot of adjustment. Graduate students often live pretty close to (if not below) the poverty line but in their fieldwork community they may well have not only a comparatively large disposable income, but also the opportunity for wealth acquisition beyond any of their consultants' families.

There is a strong desire (as a well-educated outsider) to 'fix' exhausted communities. Looking on from a position of privilege brings up many exceedingly complex feelings. One is what commitment you can make (and indeed, what you feel you could do versus what you should do as a matter of natural justice). Given that you are in the community as a linguist, how far beyond your work do your obligations extend? Would your plans for improving your consultants' lives actually solve any of their 'problems'[11]? Would a half-attempted solution in fact make things worse, both for the community and for you?

11.8.3   Your records of the language

Your fieldnotes and recordings may be the primary representation of the language in the future, or indeed the only representation. That's a responsibility. Do the best you can, record as much as possible, but recognize ultimately that there will always be more to ask and record. You can't do everything.

You might be held up as a model to younger speakers, especially if you learn to speak the language well (but even, in some cases, if you just know a few words); you've come from the other side of the back of beyond to learn this language, so why can't they? This will not earn you friends if you pander to it.

Don't underestimate the degree to which you will be bound up in your fieldwork community (as discussed in the previous section). Consider your own feelings about working on an endangered or moribund language. It's depressing to building up strong and extremely close relationships with elderly people who then pass away. You have complicated links to your consultants, who will become your friends as well as your collaborators and teachers. You may feel guilty that you might have done a better job or recorded more of the language, and it's too late now. This is a very commonly reported feeling amongst linguists who work on highly endangered languages.

11.8.4   Perceptions of linguistics

A common charge in working on endangered languages is that it's a waste of time and money, that the language is not worth recording and it's better if 'these people' speak a 'better' language (like English). You may be accused of 'butterfly collecting', or of profiteering. How will you justify what you do to people who do not believe that all languages are equal and that multilingualism is a good thing? More generally, how will you talk to other locals (e.g., non-Indigenous people) about what you're doing? How will you explain the project and the value of your research? Do you have a moral obligation to produce basic learner's materials and 'useful' materials before you work on a more comprehensive documentation? (See further §14.9 for one possible answer.)

11.8.5   Your position in the community

Your own position in the community might be precarious. If you're an outsider to the community, you'll probably also get to interact with other 'outsiders'. How will you address negative stereotypes directed towards your consultants and their community by outsiders? (e.g., 'why are you studying their language, they don't have a real language!') It is difficult to be in a situation which you are powerless to do anything about. You'll want to defend your consultants, but you won't be able to change bigoted opinions and you may worsen the position for your consultants with such people.

As a sample of the contradictory views that people might have of you, I present some of the negative things that have been said to or about me by non-Indigenous people while I've been working in Aboriginal communities. 'I guess you're living well off government slush money then, part of the Aboriginal industry.' 'Don't worry, I'll hear you scream if they come for you and my shotgun's always loaded.' 'You must be so lonely with no one to talk to.' (This as I was walking home at dusk after spending the day fishing with my 'grannies'.) 'It won't take you long to write down the language, it's pretty simple. I learnt it in about a week.' 'I bet you don't know this word: *gambaj*[12] – are you going to put that in the dictionary?' 'You can't write it down using English letters, it's not English!' 'Race traitor.' 'Racist.'

11.8.6   Some of the positives

After all that, you'd be forgiven for thinking it's not worth the trouble. I have focused on the negatives because you should not ignore the fact that many of these issues exist in endangered language communities. Such fieldwork can be dangerous, frustrating and extremely stressful.[13]

There are positives, too. There's nothing like being told about the relief expressed by an elder that someone else now knows some of what they know, or seeing someone so happy that someone else is interested in the language and wants to talk about it, and the fun of having someone to talk to in a language that hasn't been used for conversation in 20 years.

It's also extremely satisfying to be part of changing expectations, for example to give someone the pleasant surprise that not all outsiders are out to break promises and rip everyone off. Community pride that goes with seeing a language put on paper for the first time, and looking like a 'real language', is indescribable and has to be experienced.

Unfortunately, the negatives of working in endangered language communities are all rather tangible, while the positives are all rather intangible. There are potential practical positive outcomes. Some are listed in Bowern and James (2005). It might include increased literacy, which brings with it increased confidence in rights and dealing with outsiders.

11.8.7   More on fieldworker stress

Many postcolonial Indigenous communities have a long history of persecution, deprivation and oppression, and continue to be disadvantaged. Eliciting personal narratives and community histories in some communities will stir up painful memories and sad events. Your consultants might welcome the opportunity to record their experiences. Recording and transcribing traumatic events isn't confined to work on endangered languages. Forensic linguists deal with this often. For example, they might have to transcribe the last conversation between a pilot and air traffic control before the pilot fails to avoid a fatal crash, or the radioing of fire fighters who are misdirected in a burning building and are trying to get out before they burn to death. Or, perhaps more prosaically, death threats, hate crime threats and the like.

In my fieldwork I've never transcribed language like that, but I have recorded stories on massacres, genocide, forced population removal and resettlement, and child abductions (the 'Stolen Generations').[14] I never directly intended to. When I went to One Arm Point in 2001, I originally intended to work on a reference grammar and learner's guide. However, community priorities were 'stories about the old days'. That was fine with me, I wanted texts, and could ask grammar questions as we were transcribing. So I thought we would be talking about traditional medicines, hunting, and other similar benign topics. We did, for a few weeks. I got better at Bardi and could understand more, and before long I was recording stories about the stolen generation and massacres of Bardi people in the late nineteenth and early twentieth centuries.

I knew about the Stolen Generations. I'd read the report summaries in the news in 1997 and seen the leader of the opposition break down in parliament while discussing it, and I'd read the introduction to various grammars of Australian languages which gave brief stories of massacres and dispossession. I knew a little about the history of European settlement in the Western Kimberley and had read through Bardi stories which involved revenge police raids (see Hercus and Sutton 1986). Somehow, though, I'd never consciously connected these events with the lives of my consultants. It's one thing to read about it in a book, but it's quite a different matter when an old lady describes her feeling when she came home to find that her sister had been taken away by the government, and when she hid in a boat listening to her father and the mission superintendent argue about whether she's light-skinned enough to be removed to an orphanage. In many parts of rural Australia just about everyone middle-aged and older has direct experience of these policies. It's upsetting to listen to these stories, as well as to talk about them.

Remember too that we aren't just talking about listening to the story once. If you're transcribing it, you will hear it again and again. You will have to think about the meaning of every word. You will probably have to discuss good translations with people, which will mean going into details about the semantics of the words and what happened, and it will get to you and upset you. This does not mean that you should not record and transcribe such topics. Having the opportunity to tell their side of the story may be very important to the community, or to individual speakers. They may feel that this aspect of their country's history is not appreciated.

11.9 Further reading

- **Ethics:** Agar (1996), Ellen (1984), Larmouth (1992), McKinney (2000:9–20), Murray and Murray (1992), Rice (2006a), Rieschild (2003), Singleton and Straits (2005: ch. 16). *American Ethnologist*, e.g., issue 33/3 has a feature on IRBs.
- **Endangered language communities:** Caffery (2006), Grenoble and Whaley (2006), Musgrave and Thieberger (2006), Stebbins (2003), Wilkins (1992).
- **Payment:** McLaughlin and Sall (2001:196–7).
- **Researchers:** Cyr (1999), Gabriel (2000), Nagy (2000), Schreier (2003: ch. 4).

12
Grant Application Writing

Doing fieldwork costs money. It's cheap in comparison to some types of research, but there are still expenses to consider. This chapter describes the process of applying for fieldwork research grants, including what applications usually contain, the chronology of an application and budgets.

12.1 Steps to grant writing

The first thing to do is to work out where you want to do fieldwork. Decide on the language, or at least the general geographical area. Next, identify funding agencies to apply to. This often needs to be done at least a year before you want to start your trip to the field, so start looking as soon as you think you might want to do fieldwork.

Make contact with the community you want to work with if possible, get letters of permission, and start the preliminary negotiations about what you'll be doing. Make sure that they know that you haven't yet received funding, and that it is not definite that you will be coming to work with them. If it's not possible to contact the relevant people in advance, make sure that you have reason to believe that they won't mind having someone working on their language.

Next, write the preliminary application for the funding body. There is more on what an application usually includes in the following section. This is a good time to ask for letters of reference in support of your application. If you are a PhD student, your advisor should be one of the writers. Make sure to ask in good time; it's much harder to write a good letter at very short notice. Your letter writers will also be in a good position to give you feedback on your proposal.

Most grants are not awarded to individuals; rather, they require an organization to administer the grant, so you will need to name an administrative body. Usually this will be your university, but sometimes a body local to the community you are going to work in would be more appropriate. Work out the budget.[1] Apply for human subjects approval, if applicable. Even if you do not require ethics approval from your university, you should create a research plan with discussion of ethics and show it to someone. See §12.4.

Make sure you submit your application before the deadline. You may need to submit the application through your university or administrative body, so allow plenty of time for this. You should aim to have the application ready for submission about two weeks in advance of the actual due date, to allow time for the administrative body to approve it and for your university's grants office to submit it.

Finally, start the process again. Apply to several places simultaneously, you can always refuse funds if you get too much. Refuse funds quickly if you are awarded more than one grant, though. All agencies get many more applications than they can fund, and the money can always be used by someone else to do a project just as worthy of funding as your own. Note also that some grant bodies do not let you apply to more than one agency for the same project.

12.2   What to include in a grant application

Almost all grant applications (whatever the country or agency) involve three main components. One is the project summary. The project summary is a statement of what you want to achieve, how you will go about it, and why it's important that someone should pay for it (i.e., what the completion of this project will contribute to society). The best applications will be explicit about all these topics. The second component of grant application writing is the human subjects approval and the ethics statement (see §12.4). The third main component is the budget (see §12.3). Make sure you read the application instructions! Every application will have slightly different sections and formatting requirements. Be specific, and be realistic! Many applications are rejected because the applicant is unclear about what they hope to achieve, or because their promises are unrealistic.

12.2.1   Project summary and description

This is the plan for what you want to do, and how and why you want to do it. A project summary might include answers to the following questions:

1. Give some information about the language and its speakers. Where is it spoken? How many fluent speakers are there? Is it endangered? What genetic family does it belong to?

2. Where will you be working? Have you already made contact with speakers?
3. What do you propose to study? Will you be doing research for a dissertation? Will you be aiming for a full description/documentation of the language? Include a summary of your dissertation proposal.
4. Will your dissertation be the only outcome of the research? For example, will you also be producing materials for community language programmes? Be specific about what you hope to achieve.
5. What is your time frame? How much time will you be spending in the field? You will usually need to provide an explicit timeline.
6. What are the details you propose for conducting your fieldwork? For example, how many hours per day/week do you expect to be working with speakers of the language? How do you plan to make recordings? What software will you be using?
7. How will you be disseminating the results of your research? How will your materials be archived?

12.2.2   Contribution to the discipline

Grant organizations receive many more proposals than they can fund. Therefore, your application should make it clear why your research is necessary and what the benefits of it are likely to be. It is worth stressing the urgency of endangered language description to funding organizations that are not directly involved with linguistics (such as your university's graduate fellowships competition and Social Science boards). Do you know if the language has any features which are particularly rare? Is the language highly endangered?

Grant bodies also vary about how important they consider community contributions (i.e., how useful your work will be to the community you are studying). Some will value that type of research, but others won't. Grant organizations publish the award winners each year and a summary of their projects. Look through these listings to get an idea of the types of research they tend to fund, and tailor your application appropriately.

12.2.3   Your qualifications

Many grant agencies will ask about your qualifications for the project. For example, are you competent in the contact language you will be using? Have you taken enough linguistics courses and done enough to know the basics of data gathering and analysis? Do you know how to use the software tools that you mention in the application? Do you have experience in data elicitation? Have you done any fieldwork before? Are you adequately prepared to make the most of the data?

12.2.4   Permissions

Ethical issues in permissions were covered in §11.5. You may need letters of permission/authorization from the consultants you will be working with, their local community organization (community/tribal/village council), and perhaps also the regional or federal government of the country in which the research is taking place.

Letters of permission may be hard to organize. You might need to obtain translations of them too. Talk to linguists who have worked in the region to find out the best way of making contact and obtaining the relevant letters. Grant agencies vary in how accommodating they are about documentation of permissions.

You may also need visas or other travel documents. Sometimes research visas are conditional on funding, so make sure you understand the relative chronology of all the application materials.

12.3   Budgets

Budgeting requires research and thought. If your budget looks unrealistic to the reviewers of your proposal, they are unlikely to award you the grant. If you don't ask for enough funds, you will either need to apply again to finish the research or make up the short-fall yourself. On the other hand, if you over-budget and end up with a lot of extra funds, you've unnecessarily deprived someone else of funding for their project.

There are core elements of field budgets (such as money to pay consultants, report production, travel to and from the site, and recording media), and there are many grey areas. Most funding bodies have a guide as to what counts as a legitimate expense. Generally, anything that is not directly related to the field trip, or any expenses that you would have incurred anyway, are not legitimate grant items. There are many more projects worthy of funding than will get funded every year. Linguistic fieldwork research is cheap in comparison to most clinical research, but there are also fewer funding sources. Don't pad your budget with things you don't need. Furthermore, it goes without saying that embezzling grant monies or trying to defraud grant bodies are unlikely to win you friends or future grants.

The following categories are taken from NSF (National Science Foundation) applications, however most grant bodies break down budgets into similar categories.

12.3.1 Personnel

We can break down the category of personnel expenses into the following items:

- Your consultants
- Casual help (e.g., with data entry and processing)
- Your stipend, if allowed
- Overheads for employment (e.g., insurance, payroll tax)

To estimate how much you will need to pay your consultants, find out what the usual rate for language work is in the area. Rates vary significantly between countries, and sometimes between regions of the same country. Work out how you will get the money to your consultants. (See §11.7 for discussion on payments.)

You also need to estimate how much time you will spend working with consultants. That will depend on how long you intend to be in the field, how many people you want to work with, and how much time your consultants will probably have available. If you spend much more than two hours a day in working with speakers on new material, you will probably not have time to process all the data. On the other hand, if you need a speaker's help with transcription and translation (and almost everyone working on textual materials will), it would be better to budget more time with consultants. Group work can add considerably to the budget.

Find out if you will need to take into account overheads such as payroll tax, superannuation (i.e., retirement benefits) and insurance, and who this will apply to. In general, you can only claim a salary for yourself if you are not a student or receiving money from another source. Some doctoral grants include a stipend; others do not. Grants to students are sometimes exempt from overheads, and some grant bodies refuse to pay them.

12.3.2 Travel

Make a list of the places you will need to travel to during your trip. Minimally you will need to budget for travel to and from the field site and travel to neighbouring areas, if you need to visit speakers who live away from your main field site. You may also wish to include a few of your consultants in visits to other settlements.

Lodging costs while in the field are also usually included in the 'travel' component of a budget. Not all grants will let you claim this, and some will only let you claim extra expenses over your regular costs. A *per diem* while travelling to the sites may also be allowable.

The cost of insurance for vehicles or health insurance may be an allowable travel expense. Rental vehicle insurance is usually compulsory under the terms of the grant (i.e., you cannot use grant money to hire a vehicle unless you are also fully insured), while health insurance may or may not be covered; it is unlikely to be covered if you already have it.

Travel can be very expensive; vehicle hire, for example, can comprise a large part of the budget. There are some areas where you can save money, and others where you can't. Trying to save money on recording equipment is a false economy, but travel is one area where money can often be saved. If you are thinking of renting a car for the duration of your trip, consider whether you actually need it. Investigate alternative ways of getting to your field site. If you are going for a long period and need a vehicle, it may well be cheaper to buy one and sell it again at the end of the trip, if this is permissible within the terms of the grant.

12.3.3 Equipment

Equipment was discussed extensively in Chapter 2. Work out what new equipment you will need to buy as part of the grant and obtain a price quote for it. The easiest way to do this is to use an online shopping site and print out the information (or compile a 'shopping cart' of all the items and print it). Minimally, you will need a primary recording device and microphone, backup equipment, and a way of duplicating recordings for backup (such as your computer). While it is possible to do all tasks associated with fieldwork using free software (or software bundled with operating systems), you could include any needed non-free software in your budget. For a list of equipment, see Appendix F.

12.3.4 Consumables

The 'consumables' category includes blank media (e.g., DVDs, CDs, Minidiscs, Compactflash cards), paper and notebooks, pens, batteries, and other 'disposable' items which are used/consumed in the process of the project.

Don't be stingy with media. Assume at least one–two hours of recording per day, and round up generously. Make sure you have enough batteries of each type and have at least one spare battery for your video and computer. Make sure you know approximately how long your recorder can record from a fresh battery (or set of fresh batteries, if it takes more than one) and plan accordingly. Don't forget to include enough media for copies for archives and speakers.

12.3.5   Other costs

There are other expenses involved in fieldwork. Postage of items, phone and internet charges are common costs to include. If you are providing copies of learner's materials, don't forget to budget for the cost of posting them from your university or the printer. For the learner's materials I have produced for Bardi and Yan-nhaŋu, I emailed a pdf to a printer in Canberra, and my long-suffering parents picked up the copies and posted them to the right places. That saved many hundred of dollars over printing in the United States and posting the copies overseas.

Other costs might include the buying of any supporting materials, such as copies of previous publications on the language, photocopying of others' unpublished field notes; maps of the area; the purchase of elicitation/stimulus prompts such as picture books and flora and fauna guides. Finally, there is the category of semi-personal items which represent costs you would not have incurred if you had not been going to the field, but are not necessarily directly related to your research. These include vaccinations, medicines (e.g., malaria prophylactics), mosquito net, visa fees, and other equipment. Funding agencies differ on whether these count as legitimate expenses.

12.3.6   Report production

Make sure to budget for the costs of producing and disseminating your final report. This would normally include provision for copies of original materials, such as recordings, photos and field notes for the grant body, the community and other interested parties; paper copies of analysed materials, such as a dictionary, story books, articles and your dissertation, and archival copies of all materials.

12.3.7   Miscellaneous

If you are applying outside the country in which the majority of the funds will be spent, make sure that your calculations of exchange rates are correct. Do the estimates in the currency in which the funds will be spent, and then convert the numbers using a published exchange rate.

Exchange rates change over time, and can effect the amount of money available to you. Here's a concrete example. Assume your award is paid in US dollars but your field site costs will be paid in Estonian kroons. On 12 March 2007, the exchange rate was approximately 12 kroons to the US dollar (i.e., each kroon costs just under 9 cents). If you budget using this exchange rate and the US dollar falls in the meantime, your purchasing power in kroons will fall (and if it rises, you will get extra funds!). It is always wise to have a few items in the grant that you could do without if you had to, so that your core areas of research will still be able to be done if you have unforeseen expenses or exchange-rate fluctuations. Some budgets allow provision for inflation.

Make sure that your costings reflect what you actually intend to do. It is quite easy, especially in multi-year grants, to make errors. For example, if you are planning two field trips, you will need two sets of travel funding (one for each trip), but you will only need one item of final report funding. Make sure that the items occur in the correct year; while it is often possible to roll over funds, funds are usually released only once a year.

12.4   Human subjects applications

Many universities and grant institutions require field research to be cleared by an ethics committee.[2] IRBs exist to make sure that research projects are formulated ethically and are carried out in a way that will not cause undue harm to the research participants. However, what constitutes 'ethical' practice in research is not necessarily the same in linguistics and (for example) medicine.

Ethics boards monitor human experimentation in the medical and social sciences, and as such, it can be difficult to answer their questions in a way relevant to linguistic research. The situation is further complicated by the fact there seems to be no standard across universities, states and countries. Not all boards have social scientists on them; some automatically grant waivers to linguistic field research, while others require full or expedited reviews. Some boards are sympathetic to primarily collaborative fieldwork, while others treat linguistic fieldwork the same way as medical experiments, and review them by the same criteria. Other countries have no legislation in this area at all.

Some care needs to be taken in writing human subjects applications, simply because of the likelihood that the application will be read by someone who is not familiar with the protocols of linguistic research. Therefore you may need to outline some of the differences between medical and linguistic research. Talk to faculty in your department about their experiences with your institution's ethics board.

In the United States, proposals involving human research participants are subject to one of three categories: exemption from further review, expedited review, and full review. Linguistics applications usually fall under one of the first two categories. Somewhat confusingly perhaps, the category 'exempt' does not mean that the proposal is not reviewed. It means that your research has been deemed to be likely to cause minimal potential risk to your research participants and that as long as you keep to the research protocol you outline in the proposal, your project is exempt from further review. Once your protocol is reviewed and approved, you will receive a number. Keep a copy of all documentation, you'll need to give this number to most grant bodies and to reference it in any future proposals for the same project.

12.4.1   The application form

While all forms are different, most IRBs want to know the same type of information. There will be a section on project personnel, and who is in charge. This will usually be you, under the supervision of your advisor. They will need to know who is funding the project (or if funding is pending, who you have applied to) and the project's expected duration. This will include how much time you will spend in the field and associated data processing.

The next section is usually a non-technical summary of the project, including aims and methodology. You will have written something very similar to this for your grant application and it's fine to cut and paste (and edit as appropriate). This summary includes whether you will be just using elicitation techniques, or a mixture of elicitation and participant observation, or other experimental techniques. It is worth stressing the collaborative nature of linguistic research (if that is the way you will be working) and the role that 'consultants' or 'participants' (and NOT 'subjects') have in shaping your research. This is relevant for issues of anonymity below. Your IRB may ask for a copy of all materials shown to consultants. This is usually infeasible for linguistic work, since the questions we ask are highly dependent on the progress of the project and local conditions. Explain this and give a sample of the types of questions you will ask. You will need to include details of whether participants will be deceived or distracted from the actual object of research.

Procedures for the recruitment of participants should be outlined. Mention if you have already arranged consultants to work with, or if you have contacts within the community. If you will be recruiting 'vulnerable' participants (e.g., children, the mentally ill or others in a dependent relationship), you will need to show how you will be protecting their interests (and how you will gain consent from them or their carers). The use of data sources with identifiable personal information (e.g., interviews, medical records) also needs clearance. In general, unpublished data sources are not subject to review but this is a grey area, especially if they contain potentially sensitive information which the original participant may not have wanted to be made public. Payment information is often detailed here.

The next set of questions cover informed consent. Usually informed consent will be required from your consultants, and you might also need to document permission from the community. If you are working with vulnerable people (e.g., the very elderly), their family may also need to give permission. You will need to document your procedures for obtaining informed consent. You will need to include a copy of the consent form you will be giving your consultants. If you are working in an area where written consent is not appropriate, explain why not (e.g., that your consultants do not read or write and a written record of their consent would not be meaningful; that the community/culture has a mistrust of official forms, or that the consultants will trust you and sign the form without reading it – or maybe more than one of these provisions!). If you will be seeking oral consent, include a copy of the script you will be using. See §11.5 and §12.4.3 for more information.

Risks and potential benefits should be documented. See §11.6.5 for some issues. If the language is endangered and the community is in favour of the descriptive work, the potential benefits of the research are very great and are worth stressing. This might be the last chance for documentation, and for the community to make good use of a linguist in making a permanent record of their language. In that case, preventing the linguist from working on the language could be argued to be highly unethical.

Finally, you will need to document what will happen to the research data at the end of the study. That is, will any identifying data and the raw data be destroyed at the end of the project? The answer to this is clearly NO for linguistic research. The raw data should be archived, since it is useful beyond the immediate project.

12.4.2 Anonymity

Ethics boards need to know what provisions have been made to keep the identity of research participants confidential. This is a problem for many types of linguistic research, where we want to be able to identify which data came from which speaker, and where there is an expectation that the consultants' input will be acknowledged. In cultures where particular people 'own' certain stories, not to give them credit would be rude. It may be a particular problem if you want to video your consultants, since then anonymity is almost impossible to provide. Furthermore, if the field site (or the number of speakers of the language) is small, your speakers may be identifiable even if their names are not published.[3]

Ladefoged (2003:15–16) notes that in most places that he has worked, people were proud to be identified with helping to describe their language. That has also been my experience. After all, why should language consultants not be given public acknowledgement for their work on the project when colleagues and co-researchers within academia always would? There may be situations, however, where speakers do not want to be publicly identified. Vaux and Cooper (1999) describe several cases, for example where speaking the language is illegal (as speaking Kurdish was in Turkey).

The best way to address these questions is simply to ask your consultants if they want their name on the book or materials (e.g., 'is it ok/do you want you name to appear on this language work?' 'Is it ok that others know that you're working on this project and that you told me about your language?'). Be careful not to frame these sorts of questions as leading questions. If you aren't sure whether your consultants are just being polite, make up a few different mock-ups of title pages (with names and without) and ask them to choose which one they like the best.

It is impossible to guarantee absolute anonymity in all circumstances. This is particularly true in the case of endangered languages with small numbers of speakers, or remote areas where the community membership is small. So, it is important that you do not promise to guarantee anonymity absolutely.

Another issue with regard to anonymity is the publication of names of people who have passed away. In many cultures this is no problem, but in areas where it is forbidden to speak the name of a person who has died you should make discrete inquiries about the best way to proceed. In some cases it might be all right to write the name down but not say it aloud. Others may want tapes, videos or stories embargoed for a time.

If your consultants wish to remain anonymous, acknowledgement anonymously is still good to do. Respect other's attempts at preserving the anonymity of their consultants.

12.4.3   Informed consent

Informed consent is speakers' consent to your working on the language, their acknowledgment that they understand what you are going to do, how you are going to do it and what the results will be. 'Informed consent' is meaningless if the person does not know what they are agreeing to. For example, a person agreeing to put materials on the internet has not given informed consent if they don't have access to a computer and have never used the internet.

As discussed in §11.2, informed consent is not informed if it is not obtained before the research begins. However, asking many questions about protocol with a consultant who has never been involved with linguists before is hardly likely to produce 'informed' consent. There are some ways to avoid these problems. One is not to come to a decision about all aspects of the project before the first recording session. While it's important to gain permission before starting anything, that does not mean that you have to ask permission for everything at once. For example, you could postpone discussion of web distribution of materials until you have a better idea about what has been collected. You might want to do static palatography, but since it is an invasive procedure you probably wouldn't want to do palatography experiments before you get to know your consultants, and you might want to delay discussing the procedure until the consultants have more of an idea about what linguists do.

Consent is usually 'documented'. That is, there is a record that the consultant has given consent. This is partly to protect the researcher in case of allegations of coercion. The requirement for 'documentation' is often interpreted by ethics boards as 'documented in writing'. There is little provision for informed consent by non-literate community members, or those willing to participate in research but not willing to document their consent. In this case one would have to argue that fieldwork presents minimal potential for harm to the consultants, or that documentation of consent in writing would not be meaningful. In some cases, the consent form itself may cause potential harm.

The Canadian Institutes of Health Research and their collaborators (rev. 2005:§2Ad) say that consent must be documented in writing except in extenuating circumstances. The Helsinki Declaration[4] (1964), which is the first protocol for informed consent and which forms the basis for much legislation on the use of human subjects in research, does not specify how informed consent must be documented (only that it must be obtained before any research can begin).

A consent document (either a read script or a written form) should contain:

- An explanation of your project
- What the data will be used for
- Terms of payment

- Arrangements for recording
- Whether participants wish to be identified, and arrangements for anonymizing results if not
- A statement of the intellectual property rights of the consultant and the linguist
- Arrangements for return of copies of materials, and for archiving

Consent forms should be clearly worded in a way that the average person on the street can understand. You should also make it very clear that potential participants are under no obligation to participate. There should be no coercion. How you approach asking for consent is important. The fact that you are an outsider and a researcher may put implicit pressure on people to participate (it takes courage to refuse someone who is in a position of power). Education brings knowledge of options which increases power; educated people tend to forget that they often have considerably more awareness of their options than most and that automatically makes them better off.

12.4.4   If you are refused ethics clearance

The proposal might be given an exemption, or you might receive conditional approval, absolute approval or rejection. Conditional approval will be accompanied by one or more questions; you might be asked to alter some component of your research protocol, or you might be asked for clarification before the waiver or approval is granted.

If you receive a rejection, do not ignore it and go to the field anyway. Make sure you find out precisely why the refusal was given. Anecdotal evidence from an informal survey suggests that the most common causes of rejection for ethical approval of linguistic projects involve 'inadequate' informed consent (such as not having signed consent forms) and 'inadequate' protection of anonymity. Find out the procedure for appeals.

12.5   Grant management and record keeping

Keep all documents and receipts. You will need receipts in order to be reimbursed for expenses. You will probably need to submit the originals to the organization administering the grant. Keep a record of your spending so that you can monitor how the money is lasting. Note the hours worked with your consultants. Having documentation about what you did at each session is also useful. If in doubt about a piece of paper, keep it.

You will need to submit a final report (and usually interim reports too) to the grant organization, detailing what you did, how the money was spent, and providing them with copies of the outcomes of the research. Ethics boards often require yearly reports on the progress of the project and details of any ethical problems that came up.

In short, expect grant management to take up a large part of your time.

12.6 What if you can't get a grant?

If your research is not funded, there are other options. One is to fund your research yourself. The research is still done, and it can still be done ethically, but you may not have the funds to pay people for their time, and you lay yourself open to allegations of amateurism. Another possibility is to go to the area as part of another organization. For example, there are many volunteer organizations where college/university students can spend a year teaching in a remote area. That gives you the means to get to the field location and the opportunity to learn the local language in your spare time. This may be a great way to scout out possibilities for future field locations.

However, this can also be problematic, particularly because of dual expectations and the difficulty of serving two conflicting jobs. For example, the school might be set up to teach a national language or English, and you would be undercutting that expectation by focusing on the local language. It might be quite difficult to get people to teach you. Furthermore, local people might feel short-changed, if they were expecting someone who is going to the school to teach a particular set of subjects, and that person wants to spend all their time learning something else rather than teaching. It's important to be honest about your reasons for being in the community. Alternatively, it may be possible to work on someone else's project as an assistant.

Apply again, and don't give up. Work through the reviewers' comments and incorporate them into a revised proposal, and get suggestions from others about how to improve your application.

13
Working with Existing Materials

These days, there are few areas of the world where there is no previous work at all on the languages spoken there. There have been many anthropologists, missionaries, linguists and others searching out 'uncontacted' peoples for a hundred years or more. However, much of this material is unpublished and there is great variation in both quality and quantity.

You might feel that it is a waste of time to go looking for old materials when they are unlikely to shed much light on your main interest in the language. A wordlist from 80 years ago is unlikely to be accurately transcribed enough to be useful to a study of phonetics, and item by item wordlists are no help at all for work on syntax. Such materials, however, can help you. The community themselves may also be interested in them. You can use previously recorded materials to identify potential areas of interest. Materials recorded by another person may show differences from your own which are not due to mistakes in transcription or misunderstandings. You will want to make the most of your time in the community, and the most of the community's resources. That includes not repeating the work that others have done. It wastes everybody's time.

13.1 Published resources

The obvious place to start is by searching library catalogues and the internet for the language name (and variant spellings), noting down and reading what you find. Don't forget inter-library loan or friends at other universities for the items that aren't available at your own university.

Don't confine yourself to linguistics books alone. Sometimes you will find linguistic information in non-linguistic publications, for example, in ethnographies you might find the word for a cultural item along with a description of its use, which will help you with definitions. Reo Fortune's (1935) *Manus Religion*, for example, contains a considerable amount of specialized vocabulary in the 'Manus' language of Peri village. Traditional ethnographic literature is often a good place to look for vocabulary. Furthermore, a lot of early twentieth-century linguistic work is published in anthropological journals, such as *Man* and *Anthropos*.

Some areas have linguistic bibliographies or source lists. For Australia there is *Ozbib* (Carrington and Triffit 1999). Other good survey publications to get you started on sources include Mithun (1999) and Campbell (1997) for North America, and Carrington (1996) for Papua New Guinea. Suggestions for online archives (which include other parts of the world) are given on the web site.

13.2 Other people's fieldnotes

Linguists seldom publish (or make freely accessible) the raw data they have collected, and it may be more useful to you to have access to primary fieldnote data than to work entirely from secondary sources. After all, linguists usually collect much more data than they publish. It might be possible to arrange to have a look at such materials, either through the researcher or through an archive if the materials have been deposited somewhere.

Try to find out who previous researchers have worked with, how they found the person, and what they were like to work with. This will give you an idea of who to work with and what the community structures for language work are. It may also give you an idea of who to avoid. It may be easier to work with someone who has already got some experience of linguistic research before; on the other hand it may mean that they have expectations about how you will work on the basis of your predecessor, and it may be more difficult to make progress if you don't live up to those expectations. Everyone has different experiences so do not rely on others' judgements alone.

Appropriate attribution of previous resources is very important. Do not ever place yourself in a position of being accused of plagiarism or stealing someone else's materials. Always keep careful track of where your examples come from, especially if you are combining someone else's work into your own database. If you know that you will be using a lot of resources from other people when you start your fieldwork, you should build this into your reference system. For example, part of the unique identifier may include the linguist's name (or collection ID) as well as the date recorded or other pieces of information. If in doubt, think how you would feel if someone did to your work what you are doing at this point. You have put a great deal of time into your fieldwork and your data collection and analysis, and you would want to make sure that you got the appropriate attribution. Treat others the same way.

Be sure to find out whether there are any access restrictions on any of the documents, and obey any restrictions absolutely, just as you would expect someone else to respect your own access restrictions. Breaking them could place you and your colleague in serious trouble (it's also unethical). Likewise, if someone can't pass on fieldnotes because of access restrictions, respect that. Material obtained from an archive will probably have a note about the access restrictions. Typical classes of access restrictions include 'permission to quote but not to copy' (i.e., you can make notes from the originals and quote from them, but you cannot make copies of the originals), 'copying permitted for private study only' (i.e., you can make a copy to work on yourself but you would need to get permission to make a copy for any other reason), and 'no quotation allowed without the permission of the author'. For some older materials, there may be no access restrictions specified.

Restrictions could exist both on the linguistic materials involved and on the actual fieldnotes. For example, the fieldnotes could be designated 'permission to quote' and would require the permission of the author, but nothing in the materials is restricted knowledge in any way. On the other hand, the fieldnotes could be designated 'open', and you may be free to quote from anything in them, but the person may have recorded material which is secret or otherwise restricted by the language community. Therefore it is very important to consider both aspects of access restrictions, both in your own work and when using the work of others.

13.3   Recordings

You may also find that someone who's worked on the language before you has recordings and may be able to give you copies. If they give you the originals, make copies of them immediately and either return them or put them in a very safe place. Next, check any access restrictions. Access restrictions to recordings can be even more complicated than to fieldnotes. The speaker may have placed restrictions on the recordings. Negotiate any permissions that are required before you start to work on the materials.

Furthermore, talk to the community and make sure that it is acceptable to them that you work on them, and clarify with both the community and the collector (or archive) the extent to which you are able to duplicate materials for others. It's not your job to be the gatekeeper over who gets access to various materials and who doesn't. That is something for the community to decide. This may sound draconian and irrelevant, but it comes up frequently in some places. For example, I have been in the situation where my consultants have had permission to listen to recordings recorded by others, but I have not. That is, the researcher working on the language before has said that they will not withhold any materials from community members, but they do not wish any linguist to have any access to the materials. What happens when my consultants decide that that restriction is silly, because there are things that they want to tell me about the recordings? Who has the final say in such matters? Is it the community member who is deciding on recordings made by their late father, or is it the access restrictions given to the archive by the linguist?[1] Furthermore, it may not be possible to renegotiate restrictions while you are in the community, since it may be difficult to reach the relevant people for permission (or permission may take a long time to arrive, and may not reach you before the end of the field trip!).

Recordings may have been accompanied by transcriptions, or you may need to transcribe the recordings yourself. This is your chance to see first hand the importance of adequate labelling. You may be presented with a large pile of transcripts and a large pile of recordings, with no idea about which goes with which. If you go through all of the descriptions on tapes and sort things out, and provide appropriate metadata for the recordings associated documentation, deposit that information with the archive so that someone doesn't later duplicate your efforts.

It is up to you if you want to share your primary data with others. It's perfectly acceptable to feel that you want to have first shot at the analysis (i.e., that you don't want to have spent all your time producing transcriptions and an annotated corpus so that someone else can publish an important theoretical point). Equally, though, don't sit on your data forever.

13.4   Some further comments about old records

13.4.1   Using old records in fieldwork

Old recordings are excellent conversation starters. You can talk about who the person is in the recording, whether anyone recognizes them, or about what they're talking about (especially if you don't know), you can ask to help with transcription, or they can be general starting points for your own elicitation and discussion of oral history.

Recordings of parents and grandparents, or indeed any all the recordings, can be some of the most highly prized materials that you can return to a community. Therefore, you need to make sure that you have permission to do so. Sometimes archives will grant permission for community repatriation even when they would not otherwise grant permission for duplication of recordings. Make sure that you budget enough funds for copies of media if you plan to do this.

There might be example sentences that would be deemed rather inappropriate today. There might also be ways of referring to Indigenous people which would never be said aloud these days but which appear in print. The materials may contain information of value, on the other hand the language in which such information is couched could be very off-putting and offensive to the people you're working with.

13.4.2   Circumstances of collection

The recordings were probably made under a different research paradigm from what you work in. For example, in 1950 there were few women in academia, the Civil Rights Movement hadn't happened, technology was much less portable and much less information about the world's languages was readily available. It is easy to make judgments about previous materials without taking into consideration the different situation under which they were recorded. For example, the researcher may have had no good access to a recording device. Tape was very expensive and therefore there was a strong incentive to record as little as possible, to record at slow tape speeds, and to start the tape only just before the speaker was going to say something (without 'wasting' tape on recording the prompts). It is easy to be frustrated at recordings where the first syllable of every item is missing because the linguist took the pause button off as soon as the consultant began to speak, and it is easy to swear at a recording where you only have a list of words in the target language with no clue as to what the words mean. However, it's unfair to criticize someone who was working under very different (and much more difficult) conditions.

13.4.3   Restricted materials and access conditions

In general, one assumes that if something is published one can quote it, as long the source is appropriately acknowledged. However, materials have been published which the community regard as restricted. Opinions differ a great deal as to what the responsibilities of the linguist are in such a case. Some take the view that since the materials have been published and are thus in the public domain, there is nothing that anyone can do about it now. Others take the view that even though the material has been published, it may be quite difficult to get access to and there is no need to make such materials more widely available than they already are. In republishing materials that are restricted in some way, you implicitly associate yourself with the idea that it's all right to publish restricted materials (whether that it what you believe or not). You may offend the people you are working with, and you may make things difficult for other researchers who may get the fall-out of community anger that such information has been republished.

There may be no guidance in the materials as to what could constitute restricted knowledge. There might be any number of reasons for this. Perhaps the research did not respect the cultural beliefs that women knowing about men's ceremonies would make them sick.[2] They may have been published as part of a wish to disabuse Aboriginal people of such beliefs and to align them with Christian and Western ideologies (i.e., to show that it is possible to break such taboos and not become ill). Perhaps the researcher did not ask specifically about these issues at any point. It might not have occurred to them that there would be female academics looking at the materials. That is, by publishing men's business in academic journals they may have assumed that only men would see it. The researcher might not have been told that women can't know about the topics under discussion, or the community might not have understood what 'publication' entails at the time they told the researcher the information. The information might not have been restricted at the time, or it might not have been restricted by that group. You should be aware of these potential problems.

13.4.4 Deciphering non-phonemic orthographies

It is not unusual to find in earlier sources that the person writing down the materials has not used a consistent or phonemic orthography. Rather, they have written down words as they heard them using whatever English orthographic convention is closest. This has a couple of implications. First is that any phonemes in the language which can't be represented by English orthography are usually either missing or rendered in a strange and inconsistent fashion. Secondly, you need to know something about the dialect that the person spoke in order to work out which phonemes they are most likely to have meant. Thirdly, it means that the same phoneme might be represented in many different ways, or there might be some allophonic variation which is recorded because it's phonemic in English. Such records cannot be deciphered with any certainty without checking pronunciation with speakers. Thieberger (1995) has a lot of detailed information about how to work with records like this; it was written for an Australian audience but the techniques are more generally applicable.

13.5   Preparing using others' research

In many ways, preparing for the field is just the same as doing any other sort of research. You need to find out as much as you can about the topic, identify any gaps in the existing research, and find out the areas that most interest you.

Once you have looked through the archives and other publications and found previous data on the language you are going to work on, the first stage is to read through everything and work out what's there. Has the previous work on the language concentrated on any particular topics? Does anything strike you as peculiar about the analysis? You may find that the title of a work is not indicative of what the work actually contains. One of my graduate students found an article with a title directly relevant to a topic she was trying to investigate, but when she read the article it turned out only two paragraphs were actually about the subject in the title of the paper! Most of the article was actually about a different language.

Make a bibliography of your sources early on so that you can keep track of materials you already have and know what you still need to find. There are many bibliographic software programs (both free and commercial). You could also just use a word processing document, or make your own database. It is very easy to lose track of which references you already have copies of, so include in your database a field for whether you own a copy of the item or not.

Once you have access to the notes, you need to decide what you want to do with them. Work out what types of materials you have. For example, do you have any primary sources? Or is everything secondary? If all your sources are secondary sources, can you get copies of the materials on which those secondary sources are based? Do you have data on phonetics, morphology, discourse and syntax? How much on each?

You may want to type them into your own database, so that, for example, when you are interlinearizing, you will have access to that material is well as to your own. However, it may not be the best use of your time to process these materials fully. It may be enough to read through them and make notes of any information that you did not know, or where there are things that you may want to come back to later on.

Once you have an idea of the scope of the materials in a language, it is time to work out how your own research is going to relate to them and how you are going to use these materials. If you are aiming to write a full description of the language, the best way to prepare is to type up the materials (assuming that you do not already have digital copies of them) and incorporate them into your own database. That way, before you go to the field, you will already have some data that you can use to refine your database model, and you will already be able to make some hypotheses about how you expect the language to work.

As you work through all the previous materials, you should be on the lookout for various things. Firstly, look for inconsistencies in the data, or unresolved questions. Work out how you would decide between various hypotheses and make a note of what you will be asking in the field in relation to this. It is very easy to make very cryptic notes that you will not be able to understand later! Make sure that you can retrace your thought process when the time comes. If you are just taking notes from the data, make sure that you note the source (e.g., the page number) of examples so that you can find the relevant piece of information again. You want to be able to go back to the originals if necessary without a heap of work.

You should be able to extract your own data from that recorded by others. You might need to do this when you are archiving your materials – you may not have permission to archive that which other people have recorded (you cannot deposit material to which you do not own the copyright, or for which you do not have permission from the copyright owner).

Consider how you will deal with the issue of multiple orthographies in your data. If your language has a standardized orthography and previous linguists working on the language have used it, the issue will probably not arise. You can also use the standard orthography for descriptive purposes. But more often, everyone working on the language has their own system. Perhaps they heard different contrasts or made different decisions about what was phonemic and what was allophonic. It may be useful to record this information in your own database. However, dealing with multiple orthographies in the one field makes finding lexical items very difficult, and can very easily lead to duplicate items in your database.

Look for inherently implausible analyses: for example, there is nowhere in the world to my knowledge where ergative case marking is conditioned by which direction the consultant was facing when they uttered the sentence. Such analyses are always an indication that there is more to investigate. Make a note of any subject areas where authors have written that something is a topic for further research.

Do not expect your own data to necessarily correspond absolutely to what you find in the published sources. There are all sorts of reasons why this might not be the case. One is typographical errors in publications. These days, it is increasingly rare for publications to be professionally copy edited before they are published: most of the work is done by the linguist themselves. Even if a book is copy edited professionally, that person will not have expertise in the language in question. Note also that apparent inconsistencies may not be actual mistakes: it may just be that there is a third factor involved which will reconcile the apparent conflict. The researcher may have been working with speakers of a different dialect, or the speakers may have had different idiosyncratic features.

Finally, you need to be careful to keep analyses distinct. That is, you want to be sure that you can tell which are your own ideas and which are those from previous sources. This is especially important if you disagree! It will also save time later when you're writing up your analyses and you want to write a summary of the previous work on the language and alternative ideas. It will also avoid unintentional plagiarism.

13.6   Further reading

• **Research methods:** Macaulay (2006), Singleton and Straits (2005).

14
Fieldwork Results

In §1.2.6 I gave a definition of successful fieldwork as one that produced results that both the linguist and the community were satisfied with. I have also stressed the importance of making an appropriate contribution to the community you are working in. This chapter addresses issues of 'returning' materials to the community you have been working in and research outcomes.

14.1 General issues

14.1.1 Why return materials?

It is obvious that 'returning materials' is a subject where the appropriate action depends to a great extent on the community. In some places, the only expectation (if any) might be that the work you are doing will contribute in some way to scientific knowledge. It might be inappropriate to 'give back' to the community by means of a learners' guide to the language or dictionary. For example, if you were doing fieldwork on the dialect of English spoken by white teenagers in Houston, it would be bizarre to present speakers with a learners' guide to their language at the end of it!

In other communities, the appeal to scientific knowledge and the 'general good' is less appropriate and constitutes neither a sufficient reason for a consultant to be involved in linguistic research nor adequate payment. In communities with few language materials, making a contribution in that direction is one obvious way in which your skills as a linguist can be put to practical use. Put simply, paying people for their time does not absolve you from a responsibility to contribute to the community in other ways, such as providing literacy materials in the language, or school worksheets, or a dictionary or book of stories. You're getting a lot out of the data they give you – not just the data itself, but the follow-on effects of it, such as a PhD, which will (hopefully!) get you a job; if you do a lot of fieldwork, you could be working from the data you collect well towards tenure!

14.1.2   Who should get the materials?

It may not be obvious who represents the 'community' and who should receive the materials. There may not be one central area (like a cultural centre) to give copies of materials to. Your consultants should have copies of what they gave you. That is, they should be given copies of the final report and any materials that come out of the project, such as recordings. This is important even in areas of low literacy (see further Terrill 2002).

Providing copies of materials like this also avoids charges that you are 'stealing' materials or the language to make a profit. I hear this accusation more and more in endangered language communities in the United States and Australia. Even if your motives are fine, remember that not everyone will have your view of language research.

14.1.3   Documentation and description

As mentioned in §1.2.1 and throughout this book, fieldwork can be undertaken with the intention of producing many different types of materials. One distinction which has become important in recent years is Himmelmann's (1996) division into documentation activities and description activities. Documentary materials might include corpora, annotated audio and video recordings, and dictionaries, whereas primarily descriptive materials would include anything written *about* the language.

Field outcomes can take many forms. Perhaps you want to do fieldwork so you can answer some specific questions about the language. Perhaps you are going to work on a previously undescribed/undocumented language, so you will be aiming to produce as many materials as possible. We can group potential outcomes into several different types. There are the broadly descriptive materials, such as article about a phenomenon in the language, reference grammar, data which are incorporated into larger surveys and typological/theoretical work. You could be producing language learning materials (e.g., alphabet books, learners' guides, talking dictionaries, readers and so on). There are specifically documentary materials, like corpora, text collections and audio/video recordings. We could also consider linguistically oriented community activities, such as training and orthography development.

A question that often arises is 'how do we know when a language is documented?' That is, what is the minimum amount of documentation that is satisfactory? This is impossible to answer. There are many factors that dictate the extent to which materials can be recorded, how many speakers participate, the range of genres included, and the balance of spoken and written materials. The quality of the documentation, the analysis and the associated metadata are equally important. A 'comprehensive' documentation of a language with no metadata is much less useful than a tagged corpus a quarter its size. A documentary team of four people will not be able to produce the materials that a team of 15 could, but a team of four highly dedicated and well-trained people may produce a set of materials which are much more appropriate and more useful to the community.

The following sections cover some of the things you might be called on to do as a 'community' linguist. It is not an exhaustive list, but it does provide some suggestions for appropriate community-based materials and other outcomes of fieldwork.

14.2   Orthography design

Orthographies are not just ways of writing a language. They are also political objects and are powerful symbols. Many community language projects come unstuck at the orthography design stage because of arguments over the right way to write the language. This is probably because orthographic conventions are very salient – they are easy to learn, and easy to have an opinion on. They may come to represent a symbol of other tensions within a community. It is possible to know something about a writing system without knowing very much about the language, and the writing system is often the first thing that new learners are exposed to. Furthermore, there is a tendency to equate the orthography with the language itself.[1]

14.2.1   Community involvement

Even writing the language down might be controversial. Speakers might not want their language to be written, or they might not want writing to be widely available.

Secondly, you should give people a say in how the orthography is developed, especially since they will be the ones using it. How you do this will depend on how familiar writing is, and what writing system (if any) is in use. Don't give choices in isolation, though. Asking someone who doesn't read to make a choice between *ŋ* and *ng* for the velar nasal phoneme is hardly allowing them to make an informed decision. Community decisions on these issues will need to be arrived at after consultation and workshops. Teach a few people first and get their feedback.

14.2.2   Glyph choice

Glyph choice may be a political statement in itself. For example, Uzbek has undergone several script reforms over the last hundred years, both to create distance and as expressions of solidarity (Fierman 1991). As a general rule, however, it's best to use characters that speakers of the language are already familiar with. For example, don't use Burmese if speakers know roman letters. However, the choice of Burmese would be logical if that is what speakers are already familiar with.

Speakers may want to base a practical orthography on the spelling conventions of a language they already know how to write. For example, people familiar with English orthography may wish to write [ə] with <u> and IPA [u] with <oo>. They may not write phonemes in their language which don't appear in English orthography. But there are reasons not to do this. It might make the initial learning easier but anyone trying to learn the language through the orthography will have a great deal of difficulty compared with a writing system that is phonemic.

Avoid lots of diacritics. They can be hard to read, they can disappear on light photocopies and people will probably leave them off when writing anyway. However, under-differentiating contrasts can also be undesirable, since it causes problems in reading. It is possible to have different degrees of information represented in the orthography. For example, tone markings could be present or absent. Arabic and Hebrew writing systems can be written with or without vowels, depending on the target readership.

It's tempting to create orthographies which use only those characters on standard QWERTY keyboards and which use digraphs for any phonemes not covered by the roman alphabet. Many digraphs can make the writing system cumbersome, though. Some of the Kimberley language orthographies have more than half their phonemes represented by digraphs (cf. Kimberley Language Resource Centre 1999). This adds considerably to the length of words and makes reading daunting and difficult for people with limited literacy. Example (22) shows a fairly standard Bardi verb in the community-approved orthography, and the same word with the digraphs replaced with single characters.

(22)   ingoorroongoorringorribinirr   'They were chasing them'
       iŋuruŋuriŋuribinir

On the other hand, using entirely roman characters (or the equivalent if you're not using a roman-based writing system) makes documents considerably more portable and avoids font problems, which may otherwise be extremely time-consuming, and require less computer knowledge on the part of users; they don't have to use keyboard mapping software, for example.

Some writing systems reassign roman letters to other values. For example, *v* represents a schwa-like vowel in Choctaw (Haag and Willis 2001). Q is used for /ŋ/ in many languages of the Pacific (Lynch 1998), and for languages with a contrast between (voiced) prenasalized and voiceless stops, the voiced series is usually written without prenasalization.

(23) <p> <t> <k> represent   /p/ /t/ /k/
      <b> <d> <g> represent   /mb/ /nd/ /ŋg/

14.2.3 Alphabetical order

Think about the alphabetical order for your new orthography. Consider having digraphs listed separately. For example, (24) gives the order for the alphabet in Yolŋu Matha (used for a number of languages in Arnhem Land, northern Australia; cf. Zorc 1986):

(24) a ä b d ḏ dh dj e g i k l ḻ m n ṉ nh ny o p r rr t ṯ th tj u w y

In this orthography, digraphs and non-English characters are listed separately. Compare English alphabetical order, where digraphs don't get any special treatment (e.g., words beginning with *th* occur between words beginning with *te* and those beginning with *ti*). An alternative alphabetical order groups together sounds by place and manner of articulation.

Sometimes dictionaries are organized not by initial letter, but by initial CV combination. Learners' dictionaries are often organized like this and it's a common strategy in reading pedagogy.

14.2.4 Phonemic or phonetic? How phonemic?

A further issue is how abstract the orthography is. It is possible to represent many different degrees of detail in a writing system. A wholly phonemic system may be very abstract and may not correspond well with what speakers actually say. For example, a language like Kabardian has only two underlying vowels, but many surface realizations of those vowels (Colarusso 1992:16ff.). If we were to write Kabardian with a purely phonemic system, we would have to know the conditioning environments in order to read the words correctly. (From the learner's point of view, we would already have to know quite a bit about the language in order to read anything in it.) On the other hand, making too many distinctions adds another complication to the system and may make reading harder for people who already know the language.

A related question is whether to show morphophonemic alternations in the system. One example: if a language has a rule of simplifying clusters at morpheme boundaries, do you still write the cluster, even if it is not pronounced? Not writing it obscures the morphology; writing it distances the system from what people say. There are many different opinions about this issue. Furthermore, you'll need to decide where the word boundaries go. Should clitics be written with their host, marked by a −, + or =, or written as a separate word?

14.2.5 Standardization

Standardization is useful. It helps if everyone writes a language the same way. It aids searching materials and it makes it much easier for language learners. Therefore consistency in transcription is something to aim for, not only in your own work but also in an orthography design project.

However, I don't believe a consistent orthography is the most important aspect of literacy (although this is a minority view). As long as people are writing and reading what others have written, it doesn't really matter what spelling system they use and how consistent they are. It's much worse to turn away or turn off potential writers who feel that they aren't going to spell things correctly. There'll be plenty of time later to fight about standardization, and spending a lot of time early on to establish a standard prescriptive orthography won't guarantee that people will use it, and it can set up factions and turn people off. In fact, it can ruin the whole project. This doesn't stop you being consistent, and from teaching people consistently (and if you do a dictionary you'll want to be consistent in that), but don't let your zeal for a 'standard' prevent people from using the orthography, even if it's not used consistently.

14.3 Learners' guides and sketch grammars

There are two common results of community-friendly language projects – learners' guides and sketch grammars. The main difference is audience: learners' guides are designed to teach the language to someone with no previous knowledge. Sketch grammars, on the other hand, are a brief description of the language. They are closer to reference grammars, or smaller versions thereof, rather than being overtly pedagogical. It is usually easier for a linguist to write a sketch grammar then it is to write a good learners guide. We are trained in grammatical description, but we are not trained in pedagogy and language teaching. The two may contain quite similar pieces of information: the differences are more in presentation than in content (although it would be much more appropriate to use statements about minimal pairs and allophony conditions in a sketch grammar than it would be in a learners guide, even though an implicit comprehension of allophony is important for attaining fluency). A learners' guide or sketch may be a good place to start if there is little or no published information on your fieldwork language. They can be used as a basis for elicitation of the basic structures of the language. Use the table of contents of a sketch of a related language as a set of suggestions for the contents of your guide, and work through the topics with speakers. A set of suggestions are given on the web site.

Learners' guides come in several shapes and sizes. On the one hand, there are learners' guides which are organized by linguistic topic, and cover basic sentence types. They are rather similar to reference grammars in layout and could more appropriately be grouped with sketch grammars. They may contain a wordlist at the end of the book, but they seldom contain exercises and they're not very learner-friendly. At the other end of the spectrum are learners' guides which are closely based around a set of exercises. Such learners' guides lead the students through various grammatical topics, gradually introducing different aspects of the language. They use little (if any) grammatical terminology and tend to present vocabulary in dialogues rather than in individual wordlists. While such guides are considerably less daunting to new learners and might be more appropriate for children, they are very difficult to use as reference guides. Adult learners may therefore find them frustrating to use since it can be hard to look up information. More recently, there have been a number of learners' guides which combine these two approaches (e.g., Simpson 2004).[2]

Expectations can be very high with a learners' guide. Some people may be disappointed that they can't speak the language fluently by the end of the book. Others might feel that the language presented in the book is very simple. It is important to make sure that expectations are realistic without putting a dampener on enthusiasm.

14.4   Reference grammars

A reference grammar is a comprehensive presentation of the author's analysis of the language; it traditionally includes detailed information about phonetics, phonology, morphology and syntax. Increasingly reference grammars also describe information structure, intonation and discourse principles too. The book may include (or be accompanied by) sample texts and a dictionary or wordlist. Reference grammars have a fairly standard content. They always begin with some information about the language and its speakers – where it is spoken, dialectal variation, how many speakers there are, the history of the community, and the sources of the data for the grammar. You should also describe your field situation.

The phonology chapter(s) will minimally include the information listed in Appendix C of this book. You should also explain transcription and orthographic conventions. The bulk of the reference grammar usually describes morphophonology and morphosyntax (for topics, see Appendix D). How all of this information is set out in the book varies. A good index or detailed table of contents will make your grammar much more useful.

Many students write reference grammars of previously undescribed languages for PhD dissertations. In recent years there has been further encouragement to make reference grammars community-friendly too. I am, however, sceptical about the utility of these grammars. They still require a great deal of background to understand the contents, and avoiding linguistic terminology does not necessarily make the concepts easier to understand. It implies that a reference grammar, less the terminology, is a tool that will be helpful to communities (which is not necessarily true). It also puts off linguists, who are used to reading and looking to information which is labelled in specific ways. They may lead to frustrated expectations within the community as well, when something billed as 'friendly to the community' is still inaccessible. The retail cost may make them unaffordable to community members. Therefore, I do not see reference grammars as part of the same movement of returning materials to the community.

14.5   Training community members

Part of giving back to the community might involve training community members. Perhaps the most useful type of training that a linguist can provide is help in trying to use the materials that the linguist has been involved in developing. For example, a community which has never had a dictionary before would get more out of the book after some guidance in how to use it.

As we have seen in the previous sections, data collection involves many different techniques. Some techniques involve more technical expertise than others. For example, static palatography requires training, both in the methods and in the wordlist design. Recording oral history requires interview skills and a willingness to listen, along with some training in recording. Therefore, text collection is something that community members can do without a technical knowledge of linguistics. Moreover, your consultants will probably get better data than you will. They could conduct interviews with their friends, parents, grandparents or other community members. If your consultants have already been working with you for a while, they will probably be familiar with the types of questions that you ask. Letting someone else take your recorder will almost certainly produce a large amount of surprising data. More recently, it has become popular to create language videos and this is a useful way of getting younger people involved in language work. You could make videos of people acting out traditional stories for example, or you could turn the video camera over to your consultants for the day and get them to make the video and choose the content.

You may be able to employ speakers in the community to help with transcription. The first thing you need to do is to make it clear that what you want transcribed is what is exactly on the tape. When most people transcribe, they do not try to write down exactly what is on the recording. They will automatically correct any hesitations, or they may try to 'improve' the text. They may feel that the person was speaking very colloquially and it is more appropriate to speak in a more formal register when writing. Secondly, you should provide guidance about the format of the transcription. Do you want full sentences and standard punctuation and capitalization? Thirdly, will your consultants be interlinearizing the text or will you be doing it yourself? Interlinearizing requires considerably more linguistic knowledge than transcription does. Native speakers many intuitively know what words mean without being able to gloss them.

14.6 Web materials

The Web allows you to give a great many people access to the materials that you and your consultants create. Bear in mind that the community you work with may not want their language to be widely available to outsiders. In many cultures access to information is a privilege, not a right. It may be that one only learns certain things when one reaches a certain age. In some other areas, knowledge might be a commodity to be traded and ordered and bartered for an appropriate price. Do not automatically assume that everyone will be happy for you to put the results of your fieldwork on the web. This is something that needs to be negotiated as part of informed consent.

Assuming that you've been given permission to develop a web site, you now need to think about what the content and site design will be. It's quite common to see work sites that are little more than print books (or catalogues) based on the web. It may be the best option if your web site is primarily for people who are going to download materials and print them themselves (such as the papers section of an academic's web page). Another possible model for publishing language materials is the wiki model. In this model, content is organized by articles which are linked to one another. The best known example is Wikipedia, but there are also variations on this model. There are free versions of wiki software available from numerous sources; examples are linked from the book's web site.

14.7   Talking books

It is now very easy to link audio to text in digital files, and it is another reason why recording digitally in the first place is a good thing to do. Therefore a set of materials where audio, images and text are linked is now much easier to produce. Such materials may also be more useful than print books, since print may be a barrier to language learning for young kids, or in areas where literacy and writing is identified as an imposition from outside rather than a tool that anyone can use.

Talking books could take several different forms, depending on what would be most useful. They could be as simple as edited field recordings with a selection of stories. Such recordings are easy to produce and are often appreciated. A variation on this would be a 'slide show' on computer where the audio and text are aligned (and illustrated with pictures). For a language with only written records where literacy is not high and written materials are not accessible, the best way to make the materials accessible might be for you to read them aloud and record it for others to listen to. This will only work if you know the language well enough to read comprehensibly.[3]

Talking dictionaries are also good learners' materials and can be made while compiling a print dictionary (that is, it's possible to use the same underlying database to generate both print and computer versions). There is software which will let you link audio clips to lexical entries and include graphics. Leave the recorder running while you record the wordlist (with some markers in the recording for what word occurs where). Then mark the beginnings and ends of the items you want to extract. Allow about half a second before the beginning of the word, otherwise the recording will sound cut off. The book's web site has more information.

14.8   Dictionaries and wordlists

If you are using an interlinearization program such as Toolbox you will be producing a wordlist anyway. It is relatively easy to make your lexical database exportable into a dictionary or wordlist for use in the community. You do not have to produce a full multi-volume dictionary; that is a major undertaking. A good dictionary will take many years of full-time work. But if there are no materials for the language, anything you do will be useful. It could be a simple wordlist, organized by semantic fields (or alphabetically), for example.

14.8.1   Readership

The first point in the writing of the dictionary is to consider your target readership. Different types of readers will be using the dictionary for different purposes. For example, a linguist who uses a dictionary is after different types of information from an ethnobotanist. On the other hand, a school learner is probably not very interested in the scientific names of various plants and animals, but they might be more interested in common vocabulary. A syntactician would primarily use a dictionary to look for example sentences exhibiting particular grammatical constructions. Such sentences might also be useful to learners of the language.

Most commonly, a dictionary is designed with several different users in mind. This makes it extremely important that the information in the dictionary is presented in a very clear format so that those who need extra information are able to find it, but those who would be distracted by such information are not turned off using the dictionary because of it. An electronic dictionary can be a good way of filtering information for various audiences.

Another important consideration is the literacy level of the target audience. Will most of your audience have a high school education? Or will it be aimed primarily at younger users or people who have not spent much time at school? Whatever your audience, keep clarity of presentation in mind when deciding on the layout – lots of different fonts and fiddly layout will just interfere with readers' ability to find the information they need.

There are further ways of making dictionaries more user-friendly for those with limited literacy. Putting a banner with the alphabetical order across the top or bottom of each page is a good reference guide for those for whom alphabetical order is not automatic. A larger font and a little more space on the page make a dictionary a little less daunting. Consider including pictures. You can include other community members by recruiting them to draw the pictures.

14.8.2 Dictionary format

When we think of dictionaries, we tend to think of the monolingual English dictionary model, that is, a dictionary organized by head word in alphabetical order, which provides information about the definition of a word, associated morphology and other information (such as etymology and pronunciation). However, there are many other models. For example, dictionaries do not have to be organized in alphabetical order: they could be grouped by semantic field. An example of this can be seen in the series of handbooks of Australian languages, edited by Dixon and Blake (e.g., 2000). There are also bilingual dictionaries, and multilingual dictionaries. These formats are especially useful if the community has schooling in one particular language, but uses another language in day-to-day conversation.

If you are creating a bilingual dictionary, you have a couple of options for formats. A very popular model is a field language to English (or contact language) dictionary with the reverse finderlist of English words at the back of the book. Such a dictionary is very easy to create in Toolbox. However, it has one large disadvantage if you're working with endangered language. In such a set up, most of the information is contained in the language to English section. The finderlist is just a list of English and language words with very little detail. Therefore, if non-fluent language learners are trying to translate into the target language, they need to look up words twice – first in the finderlist, then in the main dictionary. The utility of the dictionary is therefore strongly tied to how detailed the finderlist is. Having to look at each word in multiple places adds considerably to the amount of time needed to use the dictionary effectively. That can be a big turnoff for learners of the language.

An alternative is to organize the dictionary by English words and have a Language to English finderlist (i.e., create something which is the reverse of the usual Toolbox dictionary). However, it's much easier to create a Language to English dictionary when learning the language for the first time. Furthermore, a language to English dictionary is more useful for interlinearization.

14.8.3 Dictionary contents

As mentioned above, the dictionary's target readership is one factor dictating the scope of the contents. Whatever the scope, don't forget to include basic vocabulary. There is a temptation to concentrate on vocabulary that is rare and difficult to remember and it is easy to leave out high frequency words (this is because you look up rare words but might not notice if high-frequency items are missing, unless your dictionary is built from an interlinearized corpus).

People may have different opinions regarding the suitability of various words in a dictionary. Some people may not want to see tabooed body parts in their dictionary. There might be secret/sacred words which might not be appropriate to give detailed definitions of in a general access dictionary. There may be a strong feeling that only the best language goes in a dictionary; after all, it's a book that will have a great deal of time spent on its preparation, and it is therefore natural to want to show the language in its best light. Think carefully about this question. It is good to have as complete a record as possible, but it might not be appropriate to print all of these words in the final dictionary and if their presence would discourage potential users, completeness would only be achieved at the expense of use.[4]

English dictionaries tend not to contain proper names such as place names and people's names. Likewise, there is a strong feeling that some information is appropriate to an encyclopaedia, while other information belongs in a dictionary. For example, a dictionary might define a word such as *adze*, but not give any information about what it is used for. That type of information would be more appropriate for an encyclopaedia. Such a division of labour is all very well if there is time, money and personnel to create both books, but few documentation projects have such resources. Therefore it would make more sense for you to have a less strict division of dictionary versus encyclopaedia contents.

No matter what you decide to put in the dictionary, being consistent in data entry is very important. It is very tempting to think that you will always be able to go back later and make any corrections. While that is true, it is far less time consuming to get things right the first time.

14.8.4 Citation forms

The next consideration in your dictionary work will be the citation form of lexical items. The choice is very important in languages with complex morphology. Will you include bound forms? Will your citation forms be inflected forms, such as third-person singulars? In either case, you will be requiring some morphological knowledge of the users of your dictionary. By listing roots without inflection, the reader must strip off any morphology in order to know what to look up. In the case of using a citation form with morphology, the learner will need to know how to generate such forms in order to come up with the citation form and to find out what the word means. An uninflected root may have no independent status in the language, and therefore may require a degree of abstraction and understanding which is unrealistic to expect in new learners. If your dictionary is for fluent speakers, choosing a relevant citation form is still relevant. It is important to discuss the implications of such decisions with the target group.

14.8.5   The dictionary creation process

Making a fully fledged dictionary requires an extensive time commitment. Frawley, Hill and Munroe (2002) discuss common complaints about the dictionary-making process. Close to the top of the list is that it always took much more time and money than anyone expected. Expect it to do so. However, it is possible to make a dictionary without investing 10 or 15 years of your professional career in the process. The first stage is to think about the format of your dictionary and what you would like to include in the long run. The second stage is to see how feasible that will be in the time available. Is there some way that you can break down the task so that the community will be able to see the work in progress? Thirdly, have a defined endpoint. Dictionaries have a tendency to expand to fill the time available, so if there is no clearly defined goal, the project continues. A dictionary is never truly 'finished' – there are always new words to record and further exploration of semantics. An endpoint might be a certain number of headwords, or it might be a time period.

Compiling a dictionary from field materials can take many forms. You could start with a wordlist for phonetic research, or the contents of the texts and elicitation that you have already done. You could build up your dictionary from the interlinearization list. Extensive drafting is especially important with dictionary materials. There is so much information in such a concise form that there are bound to be large numbers of errors, omissions and other ways that the book may be generally made better. This is one of the reasons that dictionaries take so long to produce.

14.8.6   Dictionary publishing

Over the last few years there has been an explosion in small publication. Dictionaries are usually not commercially viable books, and you may have difficulty finding an appropriate publisher. Publication on the internet may be an option – it is certainly likely to be cheaper. You will also probably reach a much larger audience than you would if you had published in print alone. However, web publication brings its own set of issues, as we have discussed elsewhere in this book. For example, if the book is not refereed before it is published, it will not count in your publications list for job applications and tenure. The community may not be happy that potentially many people have access to their language. Finally, the community themselves may not have good internet access, and therefore publishing the book online would deprive access to the very people who have the most interest in it.

14.9 Language revitalization

Language revitalization is a cover-term for a set of activities designed to increase the profile of a language in a community, or to assist in its reintroduction in areas where it has ceased to be spoken. The model revitalization project is that where a language goes from having no native speakers to being a useful means of communication.

In some cases, it will be expected of the linguist that they will be involved in a revitalization project as part of working on the language. In others, there will be no such expectation. In some quarters there is a profound depth of feeling that it is the duty of the linguist to be involved if at all possible. Elsewhere, there might be active resistance to such involvement. In such cases it seems bizarre for a linguist to press the community to speak a language which they have voluntarily given up. We are, after all, not in the business of telling people what language they should speak.

There are some very high profile cases of language revitalization. Probably the most well-known is that of Hebrew (cf. Fellman 1973), where the language went from one used almost entirely in religious contexts to a national language of an important state and the first language of several million people. Although Hebrew may be the most well known case of successful revitalization, nowhere else has a programme had such success. There are also cases of programmes that could be said to have failed in various ways, or at least have not succeeded yet. Many of these projects have become mired in political concerns, and that has either alienated the target of the revitalization programme or has prevented any progress in the actual linguistic aspects of the project. For example, one project is currently stalled because no one can agree on which of the four different orthographies should be used. I do not mean to belittle these efforts, since if one is planning for the long-term, it is worth getting the orthography right. However a programme with a standard orthography but no increase in language use could not be considered 'successful'.

The impetus for a revitalization programme **must** come from the community itself. The linguist is an outsider and can learn (and work on) the language or not, as they please. A linguist cannot tell a community what language they should speak. The linguist can't revitalize the language for the community – that is guaranteed to result in failure. It's the same idea as having schools teach languages for a few hours a week with the expectation that such a programme will produce fluent speakers. It's simply implausible.

What, then, is the role of the linguist in a revitalization project? I suspect that the best role of the linguist is to do what linguists are most qualified to do. That is, they should take an active role in the *linguistic* aspects of language revitalization. I have stressed the consultant model throughout this book, and while I have also stressed the importance of community bonds and producing results that the community are happy with, I am not at all convinced that having the linguist take a starring role in a revitalization programme is a good way to succeed. After all, the linguist is already learning the language as part of their job. It's up to others to decide whether they want to learn it to speak it and to promote it, and there is nothing that the linguist can do to play an active role in that decision.

The linguist can probably be most useful to a project by applying their professional skills. For example, it is quite possible that only the linguist will have access to university libraries or to the knowledge of how to acquire out of the way sources. If you're the only person with a university library card, it's quite possible that you are the only person on the team with access to online journal back issues. Therefore you might be the only person on the team with easy access to the old materials on language.

Next, the old materials are probably not written in an off-the-shelf orthography. That is, it is likely that only someone with training in IPA or other orthographies will be able to make sense of the materials once they're found. The materials might not have been written in any regular orthography at all, but in an *ad hoc* English-based spelling system. Therefore there will be a lot of work needed in order to decode what the researcher intended by the transcription.

If the language is not well attested, you may need to plan vocabulary expansion. Some revitalization programmes have made use of vocabulary from surrounding languages in order to increase the vocabulary of the target language (see Amery 2000 for an example). In such programmes, the linguist compiles lexical lists of related languages, identifies the sound correspondences and works out what words missing from the target language are likely to have been (if they had descended without replacement from the proto-language). This requires a knowledge of historical linguistics. Depending on the family and the number of sound changes involved, this could be rather complex. In other cases, words are borrowed or calques are created using known elements in the language.

A successful language revitalization programme is truly a long-term commitment. It will be chronically underfunded and understaffed, and there will be times when motivation is scarce and progress appears to be slow. Do concentrate on the success stories, but remember that they were achieved after many years of very hard work. Unlike a learners' guide, a revitalization programme is not something that takes a few weeks or months of elicitation, editing and typing.

14.10   Summary and further reading

14.10.1   Summary

I suggest, perhaps in opposition to some of my colleagues, that in an endangered language community the linguist's priority should be on documentation and description as much as – if not more than – revitalization. It is in the best interests of the community for the linguist to produce materials that will be immediately useful. Given that the linguist's time is limited and activities will be prioritized, that will lead to revitalization activities occurring at the expense of detailed documentary work. However, if the language is highly endangered, concentrating on basic materials (rather than detailed documentation) simply guarantees that any future revitalization efforts will be all the more difficult. It is surely not a coincidence that successful revitalization programmes have been achieved by communities whose languages are extensively attested. Moreover, the production of good quality language learning materials is not something that the linguist is necessarily trained to do. Working on a highly endangered language will always involve picking and choosing priorities. It will not be possible to do everything before the language dies. That makes it all the more important that what is done is done for the right reasons.

14.10.2   Further reading

- **Dictionaries:** Corris, Manning et al. (2004), Frawley, Hill and Munro (2002), Landau (2001).
- **Language teaching:** Richards (2001).
- **Literacy and orthography:** Siefart (2006), Waters (1998).
- **Multimedia:** Bowden and Hejek (2006), Nathan (2004, 2006).
- **Reference grammars:** Ameka, Dench and Evans (2006), Mithun (2006), Payne and Weber (2006), Rice (2006b).
- **Sketch grammars:** Mosel (2006), Pacific linguistics shorter grammars series (Australia and the Pacific).
- **Other:** Fife (2005) lists useful anthrolinguistics materials (such as evaluative reports). Austin (2004) contains many papers on capacity building (i.e., increasing language community participation in documentation thereby increasing the scope and results of the enterprise).
- **Revitalization:** Grenoble and Whaley (2006), Harkin (2004), Hinton (2002).

Appendix A: Metadata Sheets

Applying to the recording as a whole

Session Number:	Media Type: Audio/Video
Recorded by:	Date: Place:
Language:	(Variety:)
Speaker(s):	
Other languages spoken on tape:	
Rights:	
Quality:	Transcription Cross-reference:
Sampling rate:	

Individual tracks

Track	Duration	Speaker	Data type	Contents	Notes	Transcribed?	Checked?
1	3'	AA	Elicitation	body parts		Yes	No
2	5'	AA	Narrative	'What I did yesterday'	Excellent source of past tense marked verbs	Yes	Yes

Computer file

Folder	File name	Format	Created by	Contents	Cross-reference

Appendix B: Suggested Fieldwork Programme for an Undescribed Language

Everyone has their own interests, priorities, pace of working. The tasks are roughly in order of increasing complexity. Feel free not to follow this set of guidelines!

1. A wordlist of basic vocabulary, including some nouns, verbs and adjectives. At least 100 items, for use on making a preliminary analysis of the phonology.
2. A few phrases – how to say 'How are you?' 'Please say it again', 'My name is X' or other culturally appropriate phrases.
3. Basic sentences with one or two participants, pronouns and full nouns, and simple noun phrases, in present and past tense. Use a mixture of new and familiar vocabulary.
4. Commands, questions, some brief exploration of more complex structures. (See the checklist in Appendix D.)
5. A short text, e.g., a children's story. Transcription of that text and elicitation based around new structures.
6. Consolidation – compile a summary of what is known so far and list important unsolved problems.
7. Intensive vocabulary expansion.
8. A short break on eliciting new material, to consolidate what is already known. Checking questions arising from previous materials (this done throughout the trip, but a specific consolidation phase is useful).
9. Complex structure elicitation, e.g., embedded clauses
10. More recording, transcription and elicitation on the basis of new items.
11. Primarily discussion, interviewing in the language, more participant observation, as well as gap-filling by questions based on materials.

Appendix C: A Basic Phonetics/ Phonology Checklist

The following list could be taken as a guide for what to include in a sketch phonology:

1. Distinctive segments, described in terms of:
   a. Active articulator
   b. Passive articulator
   c. Airstream
   d. Voicing
2. Allophones of the above
3. Syllabic segments
4. Canonical syllable structure
5. Phonotactics
   a. Distribution of segments (initially, finally, etc)
   b. Clusters (including any restrictions), both vocalic and consonants
   c. Within roots vs across morpheme boundaries;
   d. Phonology of roots versus affixes, if boundary effects are evident
6. Vowel and consonant harmony
7. Suprasegmentals
   a. Length
   b. Pitch
8. Tone
   a. Melodies
   b. Allotony
   c. Downdrift, downstep
9. Morphophonology
   a. Prefixes versus suffixes
   b. Hiatus resolution for each
10. Stress
    a. Primary
    b. Secondary
    c. Manifestation and correlates

Appendix D: A Basic Morphology/Syntax Checklist

This list will give you some ideas about topics for elicitation. The following checklist is loosely based on the *Lingua* Questionnaire of Comrie and Smith 1977. The items listed below are in approximately a useful order for elicitation (i.e., it is useful to start with simple verbal clauses before doing subordination, etc.), but I do not recommend adhering rigidly to the order. For example, it is quite useful to know something about basic negation early in your fieldwork, especially if it affects tense or aspect. For definitions of terms used in this list, see Trask (1993).

1. **Verbs**
   a. TAM marking
      • Tense: past, present, future, degrees of remoteness, interaction with other categories
      • Aspect: Perfect(ive), aorist, imperfect(ive), continuous, inchoative, semelfactive, etc.
      • Mood: subjunctive, realis, irrealis, optative; uses
   b. Argument structure
   c. Marking of agreement (extent)
2. **Noun phrases**
   a. Articles
   b. Demonstratives
   c. Relative ordering of constituents (and possible constituents)
   d. Multiple appearance of constituents (e.g., adjective chaining)
   e. Gender or class marking
   f. Classifiers
   g. Marking of definiteness, specificity and referentiality
3. **Case marking**
   a. Core cases
   b. Oblique cases
   c. Variable and optional marking
   d. Affixation versus cliticisation
   e. Expression of particular semantic roles
   f. Multiple case marking (i.e., more than one case affix on a single item)
4. **Adverbial phrases**
   a. Temporal adverbs and other types of temporal marking (e.g. 'at 4 o'clock')
   b. Spatial marking
   c. Manner adverbs
   d. Adpositional phrases

5. **Adpositional phrases**
   a. Possibilities of complements of adpositions
   b. Case marking of complements
   c. Coordination of adpositional phrases
   d. Multiple adpositions
   e. Derivational possibilities for adpositional phrases
   f. Adpositional subjects?
6. **Pronouns**
   a. Free versus bound pronouns
   b. Circumstances under which pronouns are used
   c. Inclusive/exclusive distinctions
   d. Number marking
   e. Case marking as compared with nominals
   f. Position in clause (as compared with nominals)
   g. Emphatic pronouns
   h. Possibilities for modifying pronouns (e.g. with adjectives)
7. **Imperatives**
   a. Positive imperatives
   b. Negative imperatives
   c. Second person imperatives versus first or third person
   d. Degrees of politeness
8. **Valency**
   a. Reflexives (direct and indirect – that is, the syntacticrole of the relative pronoun/affix)
   b. Other functions of reflexives; reflexive marking on intransitive verbs
   c. Reciprocals
   d. Causatives
      • Of intransitive verbs
      • Of transitive verbs
      • Direct and indirect
      • Omission of causer or causee
   e. Passives
      • Personal versus impersonal
      • And argument structure (e.g. of intransitive verbs, with various case frames)
      • Omission of arguments
      • Marking of the instrument/actor
   f. Antipassives
   g. Interactions in valency marking
9. **Subordination**
   a. Marking
   b. Finiteness
   c. Finite subordination
   d. Sequence of tense marking
   e. Purpose clauses
   f. Manner clauses
   g. Conditional clauses
   h. Result clauses

10. **Interrogatives**
    a. Yes/no (polar) interrogatives
    b. Wh- (content) questions in different grammatical relations
    c. Questioning elements of main clauses and subordinate clauses
    d. Interrogative verbs
    e. Direct and Indirect questions
    f. Leading questions (expecting the answer *yes*, expecting the answer *no*)
    g. Multiple interrogatives
    h. Clefted interrogatives
    i. Echo questions
    j. How are answers to questions given?
11. **Relative clauses**
    a. Headed relative clauses
    b. Placement of relative pronoun (if present) and relative clause in relation to the head noun
    c. Headless relative clauses
12. **Direct versus indirect speech**
13. **Adjectives**
    a. Word class status
    b. Argument-taking adjectives
    c. Modification of adjectives
    d. Comparatives and superlatives, and associated syntax
14. **Numerals**
    a. Ordinal
    b. Cardinal
    c. Classifiers
    d. Interaction with number marking
15. **Possession**
    a. Alienable versus inalienable
    b. Current versus former
    c. Location of marking of possession
    d. Possessive pronouns
16. **Focus and topic**
    a. Marking: affixation, intonation, etc
    b. Clefting, pseudo-clefting, dislocation
    c. What items in the clause can be focused?
17. **Copular clauses**
    a. With nominal predicates
    b. With adjectival predicates
    c. With other predicates (adverbial, pronominal, locational)
    d. Order of items
    e. And tense marking
18. **Coordination**
    a. *And*-coordination
    b. *But*-coordination
    c. *Or*-coordination
    d. Position of conjunction
    e. Lists

19. **Negation**
    a. Sentential/clausal
    b. Phrasal
    c. Negative polarity items
20. **Anaphora and related issues**
    a. Means of marking
    b. Kataphora
21. **Deixis**
    a. Distance categories
    b. Visible/non-visible
    c. Known/unknown
    d. Neutral
    e. In texts versus in conversation
    f. Temporal versus spatial deixis
22. **Formal and distributional criteria for the word class status**
23. **Constituent order**
    a. Phrasal
    b. Clausal
    c. Effects of animacy of constituents, definiteness of the NP, topic status, etc
    d. (Non)configurationality
24. **Quantification**
    a. *some*
    b. *any*
    c. *all*
    d. *each/every*
    e. Mass/count distinction
25. **Evidentiality**
26. **Derivational morphology**
    a. Changing word class
    b. Within the word class
27. **Compounding**
    a. With items of same/different word class
    b. Relations between elements
28. **Omission (gapping) of constituents**
29. **Number marking**
    a. On nouns
    b. On verbs
    c. On other word classes
30. **Complex predicates**
    a. Serial verbs
    b. Light verbs
    c. Associated motion
    d. Other types
31. **Incorporation**
    a. Noun
    b. Verb
    c. 'Preposition'

32. **Proper nouns**
    a. Place names
    b. Personal names
    c. Other categories, e.g., pets' names
33. **Clitics**
34. **Auxiliary verbs**
    a. Tense
    b. Mood
    c. Other
35. **Sentence particles**
36. **Ideophones**

Appendix E: Sample Consent Form

The following consent form was prepared by the author for field-methods classes, based on questions discussed in relation to establishing informed consent.

I, ..., agree to participate in elicitation conducted by .... at .... for the period ....

I will be paid $..... per hour.

I understand that sessions will be recorded, and that I may request that the recorder be turned off at any time, for any reason.

I understand that the recordings may be duplicated for members of the class to listen to, but that they will not be further distributed without my permission.

I do / do not give permission for video recordings to be made.

I do / do not wish to remain anonymous in all materials produced as the result of this fieldwork. I understand that if I choose to be anonymous, all effort will be made to respect this wish but complete anonymity cannot be guaranteed.

I do / do not give permission for primary materials (fieldnotes, audio and video recordings) to be made available to others.

I do / do not give permission for secondary materials (such as academic papers giving analyses of the language) to be made available to others, or published on the internet or in print.

I do / do not wish to be informed before language materials collected in this class are used for a purpose other than that for which they were originally intended.

Any other restrictions or specifications are listed below:

Signed by consultant:

Date:

Signed by class members and instructor:

Date:

(Signed by witness:)

Date:

In areas where it is not possible or meaningful to use a signed consent form, the following checklist of points is discussed, with the discussion recorded.

Informal script for verbal consent

It is part of the conditions of this project that I obtain 'informed consent' from everyone working with me. That is, we need to have it recorded that you want us to do this work, and we need to be clear about any restrictions that you want to put on the work (for example, things that we shouldn't talk about). I need to know about it so that your wishes can be respected. I'm going to ask you some questions about our language work. Please interrupt me at any time if you have any questions.

Project logistics
- You may stop working with me at any time and you don't need to tell me why you want to stop.
- You'll get paid $__ per hour while we're working.
- You can work as much as you'd like, when you like.

Recording
- Is it all right if the sessions are recorded? (They are recorded so that I can make sure that I have written down the words correctly, and so that people can listen to the words and stories later on.)
- If you are uncomfortable with being recorded, we can turn off the tape at any time. You do not need to give a reason.
- Is it all right for other people to listen to this tape? (Your family? Other people from this area? Anyone?)

Identification of participants
- Is it all right if I tell other people that you are working with me on Language (for example, is it all right if your name goes on the list of storytellers)?
- If not, should I use a nickname? (ask for nickname)
- (Make sure person understands that I will do my best to respect these wishes but it can't be absolutely guaranteed.)

Permission to disseminate materials
- Who can have access to this work when we finish? Do they need to ask permission first? Who should they ask? Can I show my students and colleagues the work we've done so far?
- Can they listen to the recordings and look at the written transcriptions?
- How about stories?
- Is there anything that should be kept secret?
- Can I put copies of everything in an archive (*explain archive*) in case anything happens to my copies?

Permission to use the raw materials in other linguistic projects
- Is it all right for me to write articles and books about your language? (for example, to use words and phrases in writing about language in Australia?)

- Do you want to see a copy before it is published, and should I send you a copy afterwards?
- Can I use language work for more than one purpose? For example, if we write a dictionary of your language, is it all right if I use that information to study the sounds in your language?

Appendix F: Equipment Checklist

- Primary recorder
- Primary microphone
- Backup of each (and make sure equipment can be mixed and matched)
- Video camera
- Stills camera (or video with stills capability)
- Popshields for all microphones
- Blank media
- Headphones
- External speakers
- Tripod for video and stills camera
- Spare batteries, power cables, chargers
- Equipment for analysis – computer, pens and paper and associated software
- Means of backing up data regularly
- Specialised equipment (e.g., palatography kits)
- Protective bags for all equipment
- Modem cable
- (Receipts of expensive equipment to prove to customs that it's yours)
- Head/lens cleaners

Other

- Stapler
- Rubber bands
- Sticky tape
- Paper clips
- Glasses repair kit (for the small screwdriver), swiss army knife and/or screwdriver set.

Suggested packing list

- Personal items
- Health items (e.g., sunscreen)
- Water-proof bags of different sizes for tapes, fieldnotes
- Daypack for carrying equipment around
- Motion sickness tablets (some have the same active ingredient as cough medicine!)
- Pain reliever
- Tweezers
- Bandaids
- Oral rehydration salts
- Snakebite/pressure bandage
- Antiseptic and antifungal cream
- Space blanket

Appendix G: Basic Wordlist

The following basic vocabulary list was taken from Comrie and Smith (1977):

1. all
2. and
3. animal
4. ashes
5. at
6. ack
7. bad
8. bark
9. because
10. belly
11. big
12. bird
13. bite
14. black
15. blood
16. blow
17. bone
18. breast
19. breathe
20. burn
21. child
22. claw
23. cloud
24. cold
25. come
26. count
27. cut
28. day
29. die
20. dig
31. dirty
32. dog
33. drink

34. dry
35. dull
36. dust
37. ear
38. earth
39. eat
40. egg
41. eye
42. fall
43. far
44. fat/grease
45. father
46. fear
47. feather
48. few
49. fight
50. fire
51. fish
52. five
53. float
54. flow
55. flower
56. fly
57. fog
58. foot
59. four
60. freeze
61. fruit
62. full
63. give
64. good
65. grass
66. green

67. guts
68. hair
69. hand
70. he
71. head
72. hear
73. heart
74. heavy
75. here
76. hit
77. hold/take
78. horn
79. how
80. hunt
81. husband
82. I
83. ice
84. if
85. in
86. kill
87. knee
88. know
89. lake
90. laugh
91. leaf
92. leftside
93. leg
94. lie (be in lying position)
95. live
96. liver
97. long
98. louse

99. man/male	140. sharp	181. tree
100. many	141. short	182. turn
101. meat/flesh	142. sing	183. two
102. moon	143. sit	184. vomit
103. mother	144. skin	185. walk
104. mountain	145. sky	186. warm
105. mouth	146. sleep	187. wash
106. name	147. small	188. water
107. narrow	148. smell	189. we
108. near	149. smoke	190. wet
109. neck	150. smooth	191. what
110. new	151. snake	192. when
111. night	152. snow	193. where
112. nose	153. some	194. white
113. not	154. spit	195. who
114. old	155. split	196. wide
115. one	156. squeeze	197. wife
116. other	157. stab/pierce	198. wind
117. person	158. stand	199. wing
118. play	159. star	200. wipe
119. pull	160. stick	201. with
120. push	161. stone	202. woman
121. rain	162. straight	203. woods
122. red	163. suck	204. worm
123. right/correct	164. sun	205. ye
124. rightside	165. swell	206. year
125. river	166. swim	207. yellow
126. road	167. tail	
127. root	168. that	
128. rope	169. there	
129. rotten	170. they	
130. round	171. thick	
131. rub	172. thin	
132. salt	173. think	
133. sand	174. this	
134. say	175. thou	
135. scratch	176. three	
136. sea	177. throw	
137. see	178. tie	
138. seed	179. tongue	
139. sew	180. tooth	

Notes

1 Introduction

1. Kibrik (1977) and Cameron et al. (1992) discuss these questions in detail.
2. A parallel comes from a physician friend of mine who watches TV medical dramas in order to understand how his patients are likely to think about genetic diseases and the (mis)information they are likely to have. His diagnosis and treatment are not informed by TV, but it does form part of how to make his diagnosis comprehensible to his patients.
3. Of course, there are some types of linguistic experimentation that are very difficult to explain to someone without linguistic training. Perhaps you are interested in studying vowel harmony; you could say (as Maddieson (2001) recommends) that you are studying the sounds of the language and how people speak. You might not want people to know exactly what you are studying until later in the process, because that knowledge may bias the outcome of the research.
4. Both the people mentioned here have now passed away.
5. Let's be honest, Indiana Jones was a terrible linguist.

2 Technology in the Field

1. I've given a suggested list of equipment in Appendix F.
2. Some machines have automatic level control which prevents clipping; however, it is in general not recommended (especially for recording music).
3. This book's web site has specific information about recording devices.
4. Both my field microphones are condenser microphones, however, and I have never had them malfunction despite humidity.
5. Sitting side by side works much better. In field methods classes it may be possible to use a laptop with a data projector so everyone can see the transcriptions. Be aware of projector noise on the recording, though!
6. Another possibility is to use good quality bud earphones and just use a bud in one ear.
7. I am grateful to the Max Planck Institute for Psycholinguistics' Language and Cognition Group for permission to quote from their recording tips.
8. Don't forget to turn it back on again at the end of the session!

3 Starting to Work on a Language

1. While listening to your recordings later, you can work out how you might have phrased questions more clearly.
2. You may need to make it clear that the reason for the repetition is because your ears aren't used to the sound of the language, not because you think the consultant is saying it incorrectly.

4   Data Organization and Archiving

1. You can also make scans of your notes in colour and convert the scans to PDF files. It's best to create TIFF images for archival purposes, and convert these to PDF.
2. When you are making copies of analogue cassettes, it is best to make the copies from the original; each stage removed from the original has slightly poorer quality. However, you do not want to damage the original in case you need to make more copies later on, so all the editing and transcription work should be done from a copy.
3. Don't forget to budget for backup media in your grant application. Sometimes universities provide backup facilities, but many don't.
4. Audition sheets document the contents of a recording. See further §4.4.
5. In 2005 an archivist friend of mine was presented with six tapes from the 1960s with no covers or information. At the time she told me this story she had spent an entire day listening to the tapes for clues as to who might have made the recordings and what language they were!
6. http://www.linguistics.berkeley.edu/Survey/index.html
7. http://hrelp.org/
8. http://www.aiatsis.gov.au/

5   Fieldwork on Phonetics and Phonology

1. Appendix C gives a basic checklist of items to be included in a phonological sketch of a language. Many of these items could be investigated from the point of view of both phonetics and phonology.

6   Eliciting: Basic Morphology and Syntax

1. Back-translation is where you obtain a translation of the translated sentence, either by the same consultant who gave you the sentence in the first place or by someone else.
2. The sentence means *I'm reading a book.*
3. It's ungrammatical; *-m* on *durdum* marks first-person singular.
4. I sometimes receive requests to fill out questionnaires for languages I've done fieldwork on. Some have been so long that I would not have had time to complete them in a week of fieldwork!
5. The titles are *Frog, where are you? A boy, a dog and a frog; One frog too many; Frog on his own;* and *Frog goes to dinner.* A few of these books are quite culturally specific (as in they require a lot of vocabulary for first world items – the worst from this point of view is *Frog goes to dinner*) but the first four mentioned can be used in areas without an extensive material culture, or where the need to invent or borrow new vocabulary might distract from the storytelling.
6. See http://www.pearstories.org/.
7. These are stimulus materials on different verbs of placement published by the Max Planck Institute for Psycholinguistics, Nijmegen.
8. I'm not vouching for it being grammatical Yan-nhaŋu. Ideally I would have got help translating my stimulus materials, or I would have explained the

procedure in English, but I had to decide quickly what to work on with someone who didn't speak English.

9. Bardi reactions were different when there were lots of items with no Bardi word. My consultants did not want to make up a new word, and in this case, elicitation based entirely on local objects was more successful.

10. This known as the *Gavagai* problem; see Quine (1969).

7 Further Morphology and Syntax

1. This can be done using a concordance program.

2. I'm using the term 'construction' informally here, not necessarily in the sense of construction grammar (e.g., Goldberg 1995), but in the sense of any collocation of structures.

8 Lexical and Semantic Data

1. Antonymy is culturally specific and not everyone will know what you mean by 'opposite' here.

2. Mosel (2004:50) argues that this is a bad idea because it takes time away from other dictionary tasks; however, it can be useful to do some research in this area if you work in a multilingual community.

3. However, it's useful to know if there's a necronym taboo (i.e., a prohibition on saying the names of people who have passed away) before trying to tie kinship terms to real people. If there is, don't do this type of elicitation until you are on good terms with your consultants, and start off with living people only.

9 Discourse, Pragmatics and Narrative Data

1. Note 'text' includes not only narratives and traditional stories, but any piece of language which has been produced by a native speaker.

2. Milroy (1987) has a discussion of how interviews and elicitation encourage formal dialects and registers.

3. One way to do this is to point out how weird you sound speaking the formal language to your friends, and that you need to know how to speak the right way to them too.

10 Consultants and Field Locations

1. In this chapter I have concentrated on fieldwork in rural locations, particularly in hot climates. I do this for two reasons. First, I assume that most readers of this book have experience in living in cities, whereas most probably have never spent much time in remote areas. Secondly, a great deal of the world's linguistic diversity is concentrated in equatorial regions.

2. Things become more tricky when the community is split, and some are strongly in favour and some against. That is not the best place for a first field site. There may also be very strong academic reasons why a description of the language is desirable.

3. This may sound counterintuitive – after all, shouldn't fluency in the language be more important? I have found that even non-fluent speakers are potential allies and collaborators and make invaluable contributions to a project.
4. I am not really thinking of the monetary cost of going to school, but more of the cultural and emotional cost of spending a large amount of time away from the community and culture.
5. It's useful to make a distinction between partial speakers, who have some speaking ability, and 'passive' speakers who can understand what is said to them but cannot or do not speak the language themselves. Another term is 'rememberers', who can recall snippets of the language but who might not know what they mean.
6. Take a broad spectrum sports sunscreen – it's better if it's hot and you are sweating a lot – and sunglasses.
7. Consider Eva Lindström's point (pers. comm.) that you might not want to be obvious about treating your water as it might make people feel bad. Some may say some hurt feelings aren't worth getting sick over. Getting sick will have an impact on your ability to work, but hurt feelings can also have a big effect on your ability to do your work. There is a fine line between death and ostracism. Explaining that you get sick easily might help.
8. Mouthwash can be used as a general antiseptic in an emergency.
9. On a fieldtrip to Northern Australia I was working mostly with women who weave pandanus into baskets and mats. The leaves need preparation before they can be dyed and woven, and it's quite time consuming. I started hanging around while the leaves were peeled and split and eventually learnt how to do it. The work is fiddly but not difficult and was a great way to turn off my brain and hang out. It also gave me licence to be present but silent during conversations!
10. Non-prescription reading glasses with various magnification strengths can be bought from chemists quite cheaply.
11. Pictures of your consultants may also be good gifts in areas where film and cameras are hard to come by. Photos of your own family and friends are good to bring to the field too.

11 Ethical Field Research

1. I am quoting from anthropological fieldwork guidelines because most of those guidelines also apply to fieldwork more generally, and because there is a larger body of literature on ethics in anthropology; linguistic ethics has received comparatively little attention (although cf. Rice 2006a).
2. See http://www.mapuche.info/index.html
3. Co-authorship may seem like a good way to acknowledge your consultants, but there is anecdotal information that too many co-authored publications can hurt your tenure case.
4. If your ethics board is insisting on protocols which are not appropriate to linguistic research, such as full anonymization of results or destruction of primary materials, it could be helpful to refer the board to books such as this one, which provides guidelines for current best practice. Further linguistic ethics best practice guides are referenced on the web site. It may also

be worth mentioning the ethical consequences of *not* working on a severely endangered language, particularly when the speech community is willing.

5. One way to discuss this is to point out that the great majority of 'Westerners' don't actually know very much about Linnaean classification, and that English does not correspond to the Linnaean system either. For example, Koala 'bears' are not actually bears (and neither are panda 'bears'), flying 'foxes' are not foxes, and English robins and American robins are different species.

6. It should be noted that these ideas are not at all confined to Indigenous groups; see Niedzielski and Preston (2000) for relevant discussion.

7. For a set of criticisms, see Deloria (1995), for example.

8. Such feelings are not confined to Indigenous and colonialized groups; see also Schreier (2003: ch. 4) for a similar discussion relating to speakers of Tristan da Cunha English.

9. http://itre.cis.upenn.edu/~myl/languagelog/archives/002444.html

10. That is, 'third world' areas within first world countries.

11. Here is one example of how even simple situations usually turn out to be much more complex. Imagine you are working in a community with a high incidence of goitre, such as rural India, China or Central Asia. Most goitre is readily prevented and cured by iodine supplements (e.g., in table salt). In some areas, however, fortified salt is not obtainable, or its introduction has been prevented by suspicions of genocide: i.e., that the introduction of iodized salt is actually an attempt at mass sterilization. (A web search for *iodine*, *salt* and *genocide* will produce examples, including claims that link the introduction of iodized salt with the spread of HIV in India.) What do you do? On the one hand, you have the opportunity to help drastically improve public health in your field site. On the other, you risk being associated with attempts to wipe out the community.

12. The word in question is roughly equivalent to *motherfucker*. It's usually the only word that white men in this community know.

13. See also Crowley's (2007:161ff.) section on 'going troppo'. Fieldwork stress isn't confined to endangered languages, but it's often worse for linguists working in such communities because of the other features of 'exhausted communities' mentioned above.

14. I provide this reminiscence as an example of the way that it's possible to fall into these topics without intending to.

12 Grant Application Writing

1. Something to note is that most research grants operate on a reimbursement system. Universities are not always very quick about processing reimbursements, and this can cause cash flow problems for students.

2. Whether US field-methods classes need approval is unclear. While classroom activities are not subject to review, activities that result in publications are, whether or not they occurred as a classroom activity. Therefore if students are intending to write papers for submission to conferences, working papers or journals based on their research (and that is an excellent thing to do!) the class should have IRB approval.

3. In the sociolinguistic literature, such communities are usually not explicitly identified, but this is infeasible if the language is only spoken by a very small number of people.
4. The Declaration can be read at http://www.cirp.org/library/ethics/helsinki/. A version with slightly different wording is available at: http://onlineethics. org/reseth/helsinki.html. The second version has 'the doctor should then obtain...the subject's consent, preferably in writing'.

13   Working with Existing Materials

1. In this case, I did listen to the tapes and we discussed them, but the results of the discussions are 'restricted' in my database and I haven't used any of the information in my published work on Bardi unless it appeared in other sources.
2. In many traditional Aboriginal communities improper discussion of sacred materials is said to be dangerous to people who might not be aware of the taboos.

14   Fieldwork Results

1. In this section I present a selection of solutions that have been successful in various language programmes. See Waters (1998) for more guidance. It is my impression that there is considerable variation in orthography design and the single most important criterion for success is what the community would like to use.
2. Note that Mosel (2006) appears to conflate the two completely.
3. Some of the most popular materials that I made for the Bardi community were where I read some texts from the 1920s. Even though my accent was not very good and I stumbled over some sentences, older community members said it reminded them of the stories from their childhood. It was infeasible for anyone except me to read these stories because I was the only person who could decipher the transcription.
4. Define a 'status' field in your database and then release all records except the ones marked as 'not for final printing'.

References

Abbi, Anvita (2001). *A Manual of Linguistic Field Work and Structures of Indian Languages*. München: Lincom Europa.

Agar, Michael (1996). *The Professional Stranger: An Informal Introduction to Ethnography*. California: Academic Press, 2nd edn.

Aikhenvald, A. Y. (2000). *Classifiers: A Typology of Noun Categorization Devices*. Oxford: Oxford University Press.

Aikhenvald, A. Y. (2004). *Evidentiality*. Oxford: Oxford University Press.

Aikhenvald, A. Y., R. M. W. Dixon and M. Onishi (eds) (2001). *Non-Canonical Marking of Subjects and Objects*. Philadelphia: John Benjamins.

Aklif, Gedda (1999). *Ardiyooloon Bardi Ngaanka: One Arm Point Bardi Dictionary*. Halls Creek, Western Australia: Kimberley Language Resource Centre.

Ameka, Felix, Alan Dench and Nicholas Evans (eds) (2006). *Catching Language*. Berlin: Mouton de Gruyter.

American Anthropological Association (1998). *Code of Ethics of the American Anthropological Association*. http://www.aaanet.org/committees/ethics/ethics code.pdf.

Amery, Rob (2000). *Warrabarna Kaurna! Reclaiming an Australian language*. Lisse, Netherlands: Swets & Zeitlinger.

Anderson, Gregory (2005). *Auxiliary Verb Constructions*. Oxford: Oxford University Press.

Antworth, E. L. and J. R. Valentine (1998). Software for doing field linguistics. In J Lawler and Helen Dry (eds), *Using Computers in Linguistics: A Practical Guide*. London, New York: Routledge, pp. 170–98.

Argenter, Joan and R McKenna Brown (eds) (2004). *Endangered Languages and Linguistic Rights: Foundation for Endangered Languages Barcelona (Catalonia), Spain 1–3 October 2004*. Foundation for Endangered Languages.

Austin, Peter (1981). *A Grammar of Diyari, South Australia*. Cambridge: Cambridge University Press.

Austin, Peter and Joan Bresnan (1996). Non-configurationality in Australian languages. *Natural Language and Linguistic Theory* 14: 215–68.

Austin, Peter K. (ed.) (2003). *Language Documentation and Description*, volume 1. SOAS, The Hans Rausing Endangered Languages Project.

Austin, Peter K. (ed.) (2004). *Language Documentation and Description*, volume 2. SOAS, The Hans Rausing Endangered Languages Project.

Austin, Peter K. (ed.) (2005). *Language Documentation and Description*, volume 3. SOAS, The Hans Rausing Endangered Languages Project.

Azra, J. L. and V. Cheneau (1994). Language games and phonological theory: Verlan and the syllabic structure of French. *Journal of French Language Studies* 4: 2.

Bagemihl, Bruce (1995). Language games and related areas. In *Handbook of phonological theory*. Oxford: Blackwell, pp. 697–712.

Bailey, Guy, Jan Tillery and Claire Andres (2005). Some effects of transcribers on data in dialectology. *American Speech* 80: 3–22.

Baker, Mark (1996). *The Polysynthesis Parameter*. Oxford: Oxford University Press.

Baker, Mona (1992). *In Other Words: A Coursebook on Translation*. London: Routledge.

Barnard, Alan (2000). *History and Theory in Anthropology*. Cambridge: Cambridge University Press.

Barwick, Linda (2005). A musicologist's wish list: Some issues, practices and practicalities in musical aspects of language documentation. In *Language Documentation and Description* (3), SOAS, pp. 53–62.

Barz, G. F. and T. J. Cooley (1997). *Shadows in the Field: New perspectives for Fieldwork in Ethnomusicology*. Oxford: Oxford University Press.

Bauer, Laurie (2003). *Introducing Linguistic Morphology*. Washington, DC: Georgetown University Press.

Berlin, B. (1992). *Ethnobiological Classification: Principles of Categorization of Plants and Animals in Traditional Societies*. New Jersey: Princeton University Press.

Bernard, H. Russell (2006). *Research Methods in Anthropology: Qualitative and Quantitative Approaches*. Walnut Creek, CA: Altamira, 4th edn.

Bicker, Alan, Paul Sillitoe and Johan Pottier (eds) (2004). *Investigating Local Knowledge: New directions, New Approaches*. Burlington: Ashgate.

Bird, Steven and Gary Simons (2003). Seven dimensions of portability for language documentation and description. *Language* 79(3): 557–82.

Blake, Barry (1979). *A Kalkatungu Grammar*, vol. B57. Canberra: Pacific Linguistics.

Bouquiaux, Luc and Jacqueline Thomas (1992). *Studying and Describing Unwritten Languages*. Dallas: SIL.

Bowden, John and John Hajek (2006). When best practice isn't necessarily the best thing to do: dealing with capacity limits in a developing country. In L. Barwick and N. Thieberger (eds), *Sustainable Data from Digital Fieldwork. Proceedings of the Conference Held at the University of Sydney, 4–6 December 2006*.

Bowern, Claire (2004). *Bardi Verb Morphology in Historical Perspective*. PhD dissertation, Harvard University, Cambridge, Massachusetts.

Bowern, Claire (2006). The syntax of Turkic complex predication. MS, Rice University.

Bowern, Claire (2008). History of Research on Bardi and Jawi. In William McGregor (ed.), *History of Research on Australian Languages*, Canberra: Pacific Linguistics, p. 30.

Bowern, Claire and Bentley James (2005). Yan-nhaŋu documentation: Aims and accomplishments. CLS 41 special session documentation and revitalization of endangered languages. Chicago, April 7–9.

Breen, Gavan and Rob Pensalfini (1999). Arrernte, a language with no syllable onsets. *Linguistic Inquiry* 30(1): 1–25.

Brown, Keith (ed.) (2005). *Encyclopedia of Language and Linguistics*. New York: Elsevier.

Caffery, Jo (2006). Issues to think about before and after working on indigenous language projects in remote areas. In Keith Allan (ed.), *Selected Papers from the 2005 Conference of the Australian Linguistic Society*, 8pp.

Cameron, Deborah, Elizabeth Frazer, Penelope Harvey, Ben Rampton and Kay Richardson (1992). *Researching Language. Issues of Power and Method*. London: Routledge.

Campbell, L. (1997). *American Indian Languages: The Historical Linguistics of Native America*. Oxford: Oxford University Press.

Canadian Institutes of Health, Natural Sciences and Engineering Research Council of Canada and Social Sciences and Humanities Research Council of Canada (2005). *Tri-council Policy Statement: Ethical Conduct for Research Involving Humans, 1998* (with 2000, 2002, 2005 amendments).

Carrington, L. (1996). *A Linguistic Bibliography of the New Guinea Area.* Canberra: Australian National University.

Carrington, L. and G. Triffitt (1999). *OZBIB: A Linguistic Bibliography of Aboriginal Australia and the Torres Strait Islands.* Canberra: Pacific Linguistics, Research School of Pacific and Asian Studies, The Australian National University.

Casagrande, Joesph B. and Kenneth L. Hale (1964). Semantic relationship in Papago folk-definitions. In *Studies in Southwestern Linguistics*: The Hague, Paris: Mouton, pp. 165–93.

Chafe, W. L. and J. Nichols (1986). *Evidentiality: The linguistic coding of epistemology.* Norwood, NJ: Ablex.

Clark, J. E. and Colin Yallop (1995). *An Introduction to Phonetics and Phonology.* Oxford: Blackwell.

Clifford, J. (1980). Fieldwork reciprocity and the making of ethnographic texts. *Man* 15: 518–32.

Clifford, J. (1983). On ethnographic authority. *Representations* 1: 118–46.

Clifford, J. and G. E. Marcus (1986). *Writing Culture: The Poetics and Politics of Ethnography.* Berkeley: University of California Press.

Colarusso, J. (1992). *A Grammar of the Kabardian Language.* Calgary: University of Calgary Press.

Comrie, B. (1976). *Aspect.* New York: Cambridge University Press.

Comrie, B. (1985). *Tense.* Cambridge: Cambridge University Press.

Comrie, B. and N. Smith (1977). Lingua Descriptive Series: Questionnaire. *Lingua* 42: 1–72.

Comrie, B. (1989). *Language Universals and Linguistic Typology.* Oxford: Blackwell, 2nd edn.

Corbett, G. G. (1991). *Gender.* Cambridge: Cambridge University Press.

Corbett, G. G. (2000). *Number.* Cambridge: Cambridge University Press.

Corbett, G. G. (2006). *Agreement.* Cambridge: Cambridge University Press.

Corris, Mariam, Christopher Manning, Susan Poetsch and Jane Simpson (2004). How useful and usable are dictionaries for speakers of Australian Indigenous languages? *International Journal of Lexicography* 17(1): 33–68.

Cotton, C. M. (1996). *Ethnobotany: Principles and Applications.* London: John Wiley & Sons.

Coupland, Nikolas and Adam Jaworski (eds) (1997). *Sociolinguistics: A Reader and Coursebook.* Basingstoke: Palgrave Macmillan.

Craig, Collette Grinevald (1979). Jacaltec: Field work in Guatemala. In Timothy Shopen (ed.), *Languages and their Speakers*, Cambridge, MA: Winthrop Publishers, ch. 1, pp. 3–58.

Crain, S. and R. Thornton (1998). *Investigations in Universal Grammar: A guide to Experiments on the Acquisition of Syntax and Semantics.* Cambridge, MA: MIT Press.

Crowley, Terry (2007). *Fieldwork Linguistics: A Beginner's Guide.* Oxford: Oxford University Press.

Cyr, Danielle (1999). Metalanguage awareness: A matter of scientific ethics. *Journal of Sociolinguistics* 3: 283–6.

Deloria, V. (1995). *Red Earth, White Lies: Native Americans and the Myth of Scientific Fact*. New York: Scribner.

Dickinson, Connie (2007). The Tsafiki text factory. LSA Annual Meeting, Anaheim.

van Dijk, Teun A. (ed.) (1997). *Discourse Studies: A Multidisciplinary Introduction*. 2 vols. London: Sage.

Dimmendaal, Gerrit (2001). Places and people: Field sites and informants. In Newman and Ratliff (2001), pp. 55–75.

Dixon, R. M. W. (1984) *Searching for Aboriginal Languages: Memoirs of a Field Worker*. Chicago: University of Chicago Press.

Dixon, R. M. W. (1994). *Ergativity*. Cambridge: Cambridge University Press.

Dixon, R. M. W. (1997). *The Rise and Fall of Languages*. Cambridge: Cambridge University Press.

Dixon, R. M. W. and A. Y. Aikhenvald (2000). *Changing Valency: Case Studies in Transitivity*. Cambridge: Cambridge University Press.

Dixon, R. M. W. and Barry Blake (eds) (2000). *Handbook of Australian Languages*, vol. 5. Cambridge: Cambridge University Press.

Dorian, Nancy C. (1994). Varieties of variation in a very small place: Social homogeneity, prestige norms, and linguistic variation. *Language* 70(4): 631–96.

Du Bois, John (1980). Introduction – the search for a cultural niche: Showing the pear film in a Mayan community. In *The Pear Stories: Cognitive, Cultural, and Linguistic Aspects of Narrative Production*. Norwood, NJ: Ablex, ch. 1, pp. 1–7.

Duranti, A. (2001). Linguistic anthropology: History, ideas, and issues. In A. Duranti (ed.), *Linguistic Anthropology. A Reader*. Oxford: Blackwell Publishers: 1–38.

Edwards, J. A. and M. D. Lampert (1993). *Talking Data: Transcription and Coding in Discourse Research*. New York: Lawrence Erlbaum Associates.

Edwards, Jane A. (2001). The transcription of discourse. In Deborah Schiffrin, Deborah Tannen and Heidi Hamilton (eds), *The Handbook of Discourse Analysis*, Oxford: Blackwell, pp. 321–48.

Ellen, R. F. (1984). *Ethnographic Research*. London: Academic Press.

Emerson, R. M., R. I. Fretz and L. L. Shaw (1995). *Writing Ethnographic Feldnotes*. Chicago: University of Chicago Press.

Enç, M. (1991). The semantics of specificity. *Linguistic Inquiry* 22(1): 1–25.

Evans, Nicholas (2003). *Bininj Gun-wok: A Pandialectal Grammar of Mayali, Gunwinygu, and Kune*, 2 vols. Canberra: Pacific Linguistics.

Evans, Nick and Hans-Jürgen Sasse. 'Searching for meaning in the Library of Babel: field semantics and problems of digital archiving'. Researchers, Communities, Institutions, Sound Recordings, ed. Linda Barwick, Allan Marett, Jane Simpson and Amanda Harris. Sydney: University of Sydney, 2003. p. 42.

Evans-Pritchard, E. E. (1973). Some reminiscences and reflections on fieldwork. *Journal of the Anthropological Society of Oxford* 4: 1–12.

Everett, Daniel (2001). Monolingual field research. In Paul Newman and Martha Ratlif (eds), *Linguistic Fieldwork*, Cambridge: Cambridge University Press, pp. 166–88.

Everett, Daniel (forthcoming). *Linguistic Fieldwork: A Student's Guide*. Cambridge: Cambridge University Press.

Feagin, Crawford (2004). Entering the community: Fieldwork. In J. K. Chambers, Peter Trudgill and Natalie Schilling-Estes (eds), *Handbook of Language Variation and Change*, Oxford: Blackwell, ch. 1, pp. 20–39.

Fellman, J. (1973). Concerning the revival of the Hebrew language. *Anthropological Linguistics* 15(5): 250–7.

Fierman, W. (1991). *Language Planning and National Development: The Uzbek Experience*. Berlin, New York: Walter de Gruyter.

Fife, Wayne (2005). *Doing Fieldwork*. New York/Basingstoke: Palgrave Macmillan.

Florey, Margaret (2004). Countering purism: Confronting the emergence of new varieties in a training program for community language workers. In Austin (2004), ch. 1, pp. 9–27.

Foley, William A. (2004). Genre, register and language documentation in literate and preliterate communities. In Austin (2004), pp. 85–98.

Fortune, R. F. (1935). *Manus Religion*. New York: The American Philosophical Society.

Frawley, W., K. Hill and P. Munro (2002). *Making Dictionaries: Preserving Indigenous languages of the Americas*. Berkeley: University of California Press.

Fujimura, O. and Donna Erikson (1999). Acoustic phonetics. In W. J. Hardcastle and J. Laver (eds), *The Handbook of Phonetic Sciences*, Blackwell, pp. 65–115.

Gabriel, John (2000). Whiteness: Endangered knowledges, endangered species? In Lee-Treweek and Linkogle (2000), ch. 10, pp. 168–80.

Gerdts, Donna B. and Thomas Hukari (2006). The Halkomelem middle: A complex network of constructions. *Anthropological Linguistics* 48(1): 44–81.

Gibbon, D., C. Bow, S. Bird and B. Hughes (2004). Securing interpretability: The case of Ega language documentation. In *Proceedings of the Fourth International Conference on Language Resources and Evaluation*, Lisbon, Portugal, pp. 1369–72.

Gingrich, Andre (1997). Inside an 'exhausted community': An essay on case-reconstructive research about peripheral and other moralities. In *The Ethnography of Moralities*. London: Routledge, ch. 6, pp. 152–77.

Gippert, J., N. Himmelmann and U. Mosel (2006). *Essentials of Language Documentation*, Trends in Linguistics, Studies and Monographs, vol. 178. New York: Mouton de Gruyter.

Goldberg, Adele (1995). *Construction Grammar*. Illinois: University of Chicago Press.

Gordon, Matthew and Peter Ladefoged (2001). Phonation types: A cross-linguistic overview. *Journal of Phonetics* 29: 383–406.

Green, G. M. and J. L. Morgan (1996). *Practical Guide to Syntactic Analysis*. Stanford, CA: CSLI Publications.

Grenoble, Lenore and Lindsay Whaley (2006). *Saving Languages*. Cambridge: Cambridge University Press.

Haag, M. and H. Willis (2001). *Choctaw Language and Culture: Chahta Anumpa*. Oklahoma: University of Oklahoma Press.

Hale, Kenneth (1965). On the use of informants in fieldwork. *Canadian Journal of Linguistics* 10: 108–19.

Hale, Kenneth (2001). Ulwa (Southern Sumu): The beginnings of a language research project. In Paul Newman and Martha Ratliff (eds), *Linguistic Fieldwork*, Cambridge: Cambridge University Press, ch. 4, pp. 76–101.

Harkin, M. E. (2004). *Reassessing Revitalization Movements: Perspectives from North America and the Pacific Islands*. Nebraska: University of Nebraska Press.

Harris, Alice C. (2000). Where in the Word is the Udi Clitic? *Language* 76(3): 593–616.

Harrison, K. D. (2007). *When Languages Die: The Extinction of the World's Languages and the Erosion of Human Knowledge*. Oxford: Oxford University Press.

Haspelmath, Martin (2002). *Understanding Morphology*. London: Arnold.

Haspelmath, Martin, Matthew Dryer, David Gil and Bernard Comrie (2005). *The World Atlas of Linguistic Structures*. Oxford: Oxford University Press.

Hayward, Richard (2001). Qafar. In *Handbook of Morphology*, Oxford: Blackwell, ch. 29, pp. 624–47.

Hellwig, Birgit (2006). Field semantics and grammar-writing: Stimuli-based techniques and the study of locative verbs. In Felix K. Ameka, Alan Dench and Nicholas Evans (eds), *Catching Language*, Berlin: De Gruyter, pp. 321–58.

Hercus, Luise A. and Peter Sutton (eds) (1986). *This is What Happened: Historical Narratives of Aborigines*. Canberra: Australian Institute of Aboriginal Studies Publications.

Hill, Jane (2006). The ethnography of language and language documentation. In Gippert et al. (2006), pp. 113–28.

Himmelmann, N. (1996). Documentary and descriptive linguistics, full version of article published in 1998, available from: http://www.hrelp.org/events/workshops/eldp2005/reading/himmelmann.pdf.

Himmelmann, N. (1998). Documentary and descriptive linguistics. *Linguistics* 36: 161–195.

Hinton, Leanne (2002). *How to Keep Your Language Alive*. Berkeley, California: Heyday books.

Holy, L. (1996). *Anthropological Perspectives on Kinship*. Chicago: Pluto Press.

Honeyman, T. (2004). Powerless in the field: A cautionary tale of digital dependencies. In L Barwick and N Thieberger (eds), *Sustainable Data from Digital Fieldwork*, Sydney: Sydney University Press, pp. 17–22.

Hyman, Larry (2001). Fieldwork as a state of mind. In Paul Newman and Martha Ratliff (eds), *Linguistic Fieldwork*, Cambridge University Press, ch. 1, pp. 15–33.

Hyman, Larry (2006). Word-prosodic typology. *Phonology* 23: 225–57.

Jelinek, Eloise (1984). Empty categories, case and configurationality. *Natural Language and Linguistic Theory* 2: 39–76.

Johnson, Heidi (2004). Language documentation and archiving, or how to build a better corpus. In Austin (2004), pp. 140–53.

Johnson, Keith (2003). *Acoustic and Auditory Phonetics*. Oxford: Blackwell.

Johnstone, Barbara (2000). *Qualitative Methods in Sociolinguistics*. Oxford: Oxford University Press.

Kennedy, Graeme (1998). *An Introduction to Corpus Linguistics*. London: Longman.

Kibrik, Alexander (1977). *The Methodology of Field Investigations in Linguistics: Setting up the Problem*. Ianua Linguarum, The Hague: Mouton.

Kim, Yuni and Mischa Park-Doob (2005). Fieldwork strategies for endangered dialects of Huave. LSA Annual Meeting.

Kimberley Language Resource Centre (1999). *Guide to Writing Languages of the Kimberley*. Halls Creek, Western Australia: Kimberley Language Resource Centre.

Kiss, K. É. (1998). Identificational focus versus information focus. *Language* 74(2): 245–73.

Kroeger, Paul (2004). *Analyzing Syntax*. New York: Cambridge University Press.

Kulic, Don and Margaret Wilson (eds) (1995). *Taboo: Sex, Identity and Erotic Subjectivity in Anthropological Fieldwork*. London: Routledge.

Ladefoged, Peter (1996). *Elements of Acoustic Phonetics*. Chicago: University of Chicago Press.

Ladefoged, Peter (1997). *Instrumental Techniques for Linguistic Phonetic Fieldwork*. Oxford: Blackwell.

Ladefoged, Peter (2003). *Phonetic Data Analysis: An Introduction to Fieldwork and Instrumental Techniques*. Oxford: Blackwell.

Ladefoged, Peter and Ian Maddieson (1996). *The Sounds of the World's Languages*. Oxford: Blackwell.

Landau, S. I. (2001). *Dictionaries: The Art and Craft of Lexicography*. Cambridge: Cambridge University Press.

Larmouth, D. W. (1992). The legal and ethical status of surreptitious recording in dialect research: Do human subjects guidelines apply? *Legal and Ethical Issues in Surreptitious Recording*, Publication of the American Dialect Society no. 76: 1–14.

Lee-Treweek, G. and S. Linkogle (2000). *Danger in the Field: Risk and Ethics in Social Research*. London: Routledge.

Levinson, Stephen and David Wilkins (eds) (2006). *Grammars of Space: Explorations in Cognitive Diversity*. Cambridge: Cambridge University Press.

Lynch, J. (1998). *Pacific Languages: An Introduction*. Hawai'i: University of Hawai'i Press.

Lyons, C. (1999). *Definiteness*. Cambridge: Cambridge University Press.

Macaulay, Monica (2005). Training linguists for the realities of fieldwork. *Anthropological Linguistics* 46: 184–209.

Macaulay, Monica (2006). *Surviving Linguistics: A Guide for Graduate Students*. Somerville, MA: Cascadilla Press.

Maddieson, Ian (2001). Phonetic fieldwork. In Paul Newman and Martha Ratliff (eds), *Linguistic Fieldwork*, Oxford: Oxford University Press, pp. 211–29.

Maiden, Martin (2004). Into the past: Morphological change in the dying years of Dalmatian. *Diachronica* 21(1): 85–111

Matthewson, Lisa (2004). On the methodology of semantic fieldwork. *International Journal of American Linguistics* 70(4): 369–415.

Matthewson, Lisa (2005). Presuppositions and cross-linguistic variation. In *Proceedings of NELS 36* .

McConvell, P. and F. Meakins (2004). Gurindji Kriol: A mixed language emerges from code-switching. *Australian Journal of Linguistics* 25(1): 9–30.

McDonald, M. A. and S. A. Wurm (1979). *Basic Materials in Wangkumara (Galali)*, vol. B-65. Canberra: Pacific Linguistics.

McEnery, Tony and Andrew Wilson (1996). *Corpus Linguistics*. Edinburgh: Edinburgh University Press.

McKinney, C.V. (2000). *Globe Trotting in Sandals: A Field Guide to Cultural Research*. Dallas, TX: SIL International.

McLaughlin, Fiona and Thierno Seydou Sall (2001). The give and take of fieldwork: Noun classes and other concerns in Fatick, Senegal. In Newman and Ratliff (2001), chap. 9, pp. 189–210.

Milroy, Lesley (1980). *Language and Social Networks*. Oxford: Blackwell.

Milroy, Lesley (1987). *Observing and Analysing Natural Languages: A Critical Account of Sociolinguistic Method*. Oxford: Blackwell.

Mitchell, Mike (1999). *Navajo String Games*. Rough Rock: Navajo Studies Press.

Mithun, Marianne (1992). Is basic word order universal? In N. Pyne (ed.), *Pragmatics of Word Order Fexibility*, John Benjamins Publishing Company, pp. 15–61.

Mithun, Marianne (1999). *The Languages of Native North America*. Cambridge Language Surveys, New York: Cambridge University Press.

Mithun, Marianne (2001). Who shapes the record: The speaker and the linguist. In Newman and Ratliff (2001), pp. 34–54.

Mithun, Marianne (2003). Pronouns and agreement: The information status of pronominal affixes. *Transactions of the Philological Society* 101(2): 235–78.

Mithun, Marianne (2006). Grammars and the community. *Perspectives on Grammar Writing: Special issue of Studies in Language* 30(2): 281–306.

Moreno, Eva (1995). Rape in the field: Reflections from a survivor. In Don Kulic and Margaret Wilson (eds), *Taboo: Sex, Identity and Erotic Subjectivity in Anthropological Fieldwork*. London: Routledge, pp. 219–50.

Mosel, Ulrike (2004). Dictionary making in endangered speech communities. In Austin (2004), pp. 39–54.

Mosel, Ulrike (2006). Sketch grammar. In Gippert et al. (2006), ch. 12, pp. 301–10.

Murray, L. J. and Keren Rice (eds) (1996). *Talking on the Page: Editing Aboriginal Oral Texts*. Toronto: University of Toronto Press.

Murray, T. E. and C. R. Murray (1992). On the legality and ethics of surreptitious recording. *Legal and Ethical Issues in Surreptitious Recording*, Publication of the American Dialect Society 76: 1–14.

Musgrave, Simon (2006). Archiving and sharing data using xml. In *Sustainable Data from Digital Fieldwork. Proceedings of the Conference Held at the University of Sydney, 4–6 December 2006*, Sydney University Press.

Musgrave, Simon and Nick Thieberger (2006). Ethical challenges in documentary linguistics. In Keith Allan (ed.), *Selected Papers from the 2005 Conference of the Australian Linguistic Society*.

Nagy, N. (2000) What I didn't know about working in an endangered language community: Some fieldwork issues. *International Journal of the Sociology of Language* 144:143–160.

Nathan, David (2006). Thick interfaces: Mobilizing language documentation with multimedia. In Gippert et al. (2006), pp. 363–80.

Nettle, D. and S. Romaine (2000). *Vanishing Voices: The Extinction of the World's Languages*. Oxford: Oxford University Press.

Newman, Paul and Martha Ratliff (eds) (2001). *Linguistic Fieldwork*. Cambridge: Cambridge University Press.

Nichols, J. and A. C. Woodbury (1985). *Grammar Inside and Outside the Clause: Some Approaches to Theory from the Field*. Cambridge: Cambridge University Press.

Nichols, Johanna and Ronald L. Sprouse (2004). Documenting lexicons: Chechen and Ingush. In Austin (2003), pp. 99–121.

Nida, Eugene (1947). Field techniques in descriptive linguistics. *International Journal of American Linguistics* 13: 138–46.

Niedzielski, Nancy A. and Dennis R. Preston (2000). *Folk Linguistics*. New York: Walter De Gruyter.

Page, John Wiliam. (1938). *Primitive Races of To-day*. Harrap: London.

Palmer, F. R. (1986). *Mood and Modality*. New York: Cambridge University Press.

Patton, Michael Quinn (2002). *Qualitative Research & Evaluation Methods*. Thousand Oaks, CA: Sage Publications.

Patz, Elizabeth (2002). *Kuku Yalanji*. Canberra: Pacific Linguistics.

Payne, Thomas E. (1997). *Describing Morphosyntax: A Guide for Field Linguists*. Cambridge: Cambridge University Press.

Payne, Tom and David Weber (eds) (2006). *Perspectives on Grammar Writing: Special Issue of Studies in Language*, vol. 30. Amsterdam: John Benjamins.

Pensalfini, R. (1999). The rise of case suffixes as discourse markers in Jingulu: A case study of innovation in an obsolescent language. *Australian Journal of Linguistics* 19(2): 225–40.

Post, Jennifer C. (2004). *Ethnomusicology: A Research and Information Guide*. London: Routledge.

Quine, Willard (1969). *Word and Object*. Cambridge, MA: MIT Press.

Rice, Keren (2001). Learning as one goes. In Newman and Ratliff (2001), pp. 230–49.

Rice, Keren (2006a). Ethical issues in linguistic fieldwork: An overview. *Ethics in Academia* 4(1–4): 123–55.

Rice, Keren (2006b). A typology of good grammars. *Perspectives on Grammar Writing: Special Issue of Studies in Language* 30(2): 385–415.

Richards, J. C. (2001). *Curriculum Development in Language Teaching*. Cambridge: Cambridge University Press.

Rieschild, Verna (2003). Origami in a Hurricane: Current challenges to linguistic research. *Australian Journal of Linguistics* 23(1): 71–98.

Robinson, Laura (2006). Archiving directly from the field. In Linda Barwick and Nicholas Thieberger (2006), pp. 23–32.

Samarin, W. J. (1967). *Field Linguistics*. New York: Rinehart & Winston.

Schachter, Paul (1985). Parts-of-speech systems. In Timothy Shopen (ed.), *Language Typology and Syntactic Description*. Bath: The Pitman Press, vol. 1, ch. 1, pp. 3–61.

Scherer, William M. (1997). *Experiment Design and Techniques in Speech Science*. Oxford: Blackwell.

Schreier, Daniel (2003). *Isolation and Language Change: Sociohistorical and Contemporary Evidence from Tristan da Cunha English*. Basingstoke, New York: Palgrave Macmillan.

Seifart, Frank (2006). Orthography development. In Gippert et al. (2006), ch. 11, pp. 275–300.

Shopen, Timothy (ed.) (1985). *Language Typology and Syntactic Description*. Cambridge: Cambridge University Press, 3 volumes.

Sillitoe, Paul, Peter Dixon and Julian Barr (2005). *Indigenous Knowledge Inquiries: A Methodologies Manual for Development*. Rugby: ITDG Publishing.

Simpson, Jane (2002). *A Learner's Guide to Warumungu*. Alice Springs: IAD Press.

Singleton, R. and Bruce C. Straits (2005). *Approaches to Social Research*. New York: Oxford University Press.

Spencer, A. and A. M. Zwicky (2001). *The Handbook of Morphology*. Oxford: Blackwell.

Stebbins, Tonya (2003). *Fighting Language Endangerment: Community Directed Research on Sm'algyax (Coast Tsimshian)*. Osaka Faculty of Informatics.

Stevens, K. N. (2000). *Acoustic Phonetics*. Cambridge, MA: MIT Press.

Strömqvist, S. and L. Verhoeven (eds) (2004). *Relating Events in Narrative: Vol. 2. Typological and Contextual Perspectives*. Mahwah, NJ: Lawrence Erlbaum Associates.

Sutton, P. and M. Walsh (1987). *Wordlist for Australian Languages*. Canberra: Australian Institute of Aboriginal Studies.

Terrill, Angela (2002). Why make books for people who don't read? A perspective on documentation of an endangered language from Solomon Islands. *International Journal of the Society of Language* 155/156: 205–19.

Thieberger, Nicholas (1995). *Paper and Talk: A Manual for Reconstituting Materials in Australian Indigenous Languages from Historical Sources*. Canberra: Aboriginal Studies Press.

Thieberger, Nicholas (2004). Documentation in practice: Developing a linked media corpus of South Efate. In *Language Documentation and Description, Vol. 2*, London: SOAS, pp. 169–78.

Thomas, David (1975). *Notes and Queries on Language Analysis*. Asian-Pacific Series no. 10, California: SIL.

Thurgood, G. (2003). The causatives in Sun Hongkais Anong: Language death and rapid restructuring. *Proceedings of the Twenty-Eighth Annual Meeting of the Berkeley Linguistics Society*. Berkeley, California.

Toelken, B. (1996). *The Dynamics of Folklore*. Utah: Utah State University Press.

Trask, R. L. (1993). *A Dictionary of Grammatical Terms in Linguistics*. New York: Routledge.

Trilsbeek, Paul and Peter Wittenburg (2006). Archiving challenges. In Gippert et al. (2006), ch. 13, pp. 311–36.

Tsunoda, T. (2004). *Language Endangerment and Language Revitalization*. Trends in Linguistics. Studies and Monographs, The Hague: Mouton de Gruyter.

van Maanen, John (1988). *Tales of the Field*. Chicago and London: University of Chicago Press.

Vaux, Bert and Justin Cooper (1999). *Introduction to Linguistic Field Methods*. Munich: Lincom Europa.

Waters, G. (1998). *Local Literacies: Theory and Practice*. Summer Institute of Linguistics, Academic Publications.

Werner, David (1993). *Where There is No Doctor: A Village Health Care Handbook*. Basingstoke: Macmillan.

Whaley, Lindsay (1997). *Introduction to Typology: The Unity and Diversity of Language*. London: Sage Publications.

Whitehead, T. L. and M. E. Conaway (1986). *Self, Sex, and Gender in Cross-Cultural Fieldwork*. Urbana: University of Illinois Press.

Wilkins, David P (1992). Linguistic research under Aboriginal control: A personal account of fieldwork in Central Australia. *Australian Journal of Linguistics* 12: 171–200.

Woodbury, T. (2003). Defining documentary linguistics. Peter K. Austin (ed.), *Language Documentation and Description* 1: 35–51.

Wray, A., A. Bloomer, K. Trott, C. Butler, S. Reay and C. Butler (1998). *Projects in Linguistics: A Practical Guide to Researching Language*. London: Hodder Arnold.

Wurm, Stefan (1998). Methods of language maintenance and revival, with selected cases of language endangerment in the world. In K. Matsumura (ed.), *Studies in Endangered Languages: Papers from the International Symposium on Endangered Languages, Tokyo, November 18–20, 1995*, Tokyo: Hituzi Syobo, pp. 191–211.

Wynne, M. (2005). *Developing Linguistic Corpora: A Guide to Good Practice.* [Distributed by] New York: David Brown Book Company.

Yip, Moira (2002). *Tone.* Cambridge: Cambridge University Press.

Zorc, David (1986). *Yolŋu-Matha Dictionary.* Darwin: School of Australian Linguistics, Darwin Institute of Technology.

Index